b24589226

DESERTION
AND THE
AMERICAN SOLDIER
1776 - 2006

DESERTION
AND THE
AMERICAN SOLDIER
1776 - 2006

Robert Fantina

Algora Publishing
New York

Library of Congress Cataloging-in-Publication Data —

Fantina, Robert.
  Desertion and the American soldier, 1776-2006 / by Robert Fantina.
    p. cm.
  ISBN 0-87586-452-X (trade paper: alk. paper) — ISBN 0-87586-453-8
(hard cover: alk. paper) — ISBN 0-87586-454-6 (ebook) 1. Sociology, Military—
United States—History. 2. Desertion, Military—United States—History. 3.
Military deserters—United States—Interviews. 4. Peace movements—Unied
States—History. I. Title.

  UA23.F348 2006
  355.1'334—dc22

                    2006005023

Cover Image: © Patrick Robert/Corbis

For Edwina and Travis

and in memory of
William H. Howe, executed August 26, 1864
Eddie P. Slovik, executed January 31, 1945

TABLE OF CONTENTS

ACKNOWLEDGEMENTS

This book could not have been written without the assistance of several people. My sincere thanks to Carl Rising-Moore for helping me contact former soldiers who were very open in sharing their stories for this book; to Gary Condon for his story and referrals; to Jeff Paterson, Camilo Meijo and Monica Benderman for sharing their stories with me. In addition to being grateful for the information shared by these generous individuals, I'm in awe of their courage and commitment, and am honored to have become acquainted with each of them.

Also, I'm grateful for the assistance of Michael Monahan and others at the US Military Institute at Carlisle, PA, who promptly provided a variety of records that my research required.

FOREWORD
by Becky Oberg

In 2004 I accompanied Brandon Hughey, a suicidal young Army private, and human rights activist Carl Rising-Moore across the US-Canada border, where Hughey would seek political asylum on the grounds of his opposition to the war in Iraq. In doing so, he would desert the military. I did not know then that desertion is an action as old as the military itself, and that throughout history, many of the reasons for doing so have remained the same. Bob Fantina masterfully tells the "why" behind the "what," in this book.

For example, two reasons Fantina gives for desertion are disagreement with the cause of the war and inability to accept military life. Hughey's decision was made with both of these factors in mind. Shortly before resisting the war in Iraq, Hughey wrote, "I do not want to be a pawn in the government's war for oil, and have told my superiors I want out of the military. They are not willing to chapter me out and tell me that I have no choice but to pack my bags and get ready to go to Iraq."

Disagreement with the cause of the war is increasingly becoming a reason to desert. We live in a time of abundant, easily accessible information. While the public can still be deceived — for example, many believed that Saddam Hussein did indeed have weapons of mass destruction hidden in Iraq — the capacity now exists to rectify a deception. While at times it may seem that the majority of people are in agreement — for example, George W. Bush had an approval rating over 90 percent on the eve of the invasion of Iraq — conflicting opinions are also available. Even in a restrictive setting such as the military, this wealth and diversity of information is easily accessible. It is easier to form and come to one's

3

own conclusions than ever before. Should we be surprised that some come to conclusions contrary to 'I will follow orders without question'? Should we be surprised when people disagree with a cause that is vague at best and a lie at worst?

Inability to accept military life is natural. There is a rhetorical question among some anti-war activists: 'Would you sign up for slavery?' When one enlists, one gives up certain rights available to all US citizens: the right to choose one's own employment (the military is under no obligation to keep a service member in his or her chosen MOS), the right to terminate one's employment (penalties for AWOL and desertion include prison time, forfeiture of all pay and allowances, demotion, a dishonorable discharge, and death), and the right to form one's own opinion and act accordingly. One also surrenders basic human desires: to be adequately compensated for risk, to provide for one's family, to be safe and secure, to be treated with respect. The American military seeks to break the individual so these desires no longer exist. Fantina gives poignant descriptions of the resistance to this brutalization, and shows how this dehumanizing treatment has changed yet remained in every armed conflict in American history.

Fantina also attempts a difficult task: to counter the centuries of government propaganda equating desertion with cowardice or lack of moral character. After reading his book, one wonders how people can believe such a blatant lie. While doubtless there are some who desert for less than noble reasons, many choose to leave the military for perfectly understandable reasons. Fantina tells their stories with compassion and understanding.

Becky Oberg
Co-author, *Freedom Underground*

INTRODUCTION

Desertion, defined here as the willful departure from a military obligation — either conscripted or volunteered — is not new. The ancient Greeks contended with this issue and no nation since then has been exempt from it.

In order to maintain the discipline necessary for any nation to achieve its military goals the government of that nation has traditionally framed desertion in the most negative light possible. Deserters are referred to as cowards and traitors who, if caught, face execution. While this portrayal has had at least some effectiveness in discouraging desertion, it has, as will be shown, not met with more than a modicum of success.

For the United States, the consolidation of its economic and military power base over two centuries has often involved invasions of sovereign nations. "[T]he nation born of the first colonial revolution in modern history had itself become a colonial ruler."[1] During many of those and other military campaigns a policy of conscription has been used to assure the manpower necessary to achieve the nation's goals. Desertion remains an issue whether military personnel have volunteered or been conscripted. Nations sympathetic to the plight of Americans seeking asylum within their borders are generally more tolerant during times of conscription.

During times of any armed conflict, whether the fledgling nation sought its independence from its colonizer, or when interfering in a civil war in Southeast Asia, the populace, at least initially, generally supports the government and its

---

1. Cooper, John Milton. 1990. *Pivotal Decades: The United States, 1900 – 1920*; p. 17.

stated goals, however nebulous or false they may be. Opposition is downplayed; this is particularly simple to do since ownership of much of the country's media is held by corporations generally supportive of conservative political goals. This great body of supportive citizens, nicknamed "the great silent majority"[2] by President Richard M. Nixon, feeds on stories of heroics and thus disdains those with an opposing view. That this contempt is greatly and even dangerously exaggerated in this first decade of the new millennium is beyond the scope of this work, although aspects of it will be obvious during the discussion of the Iraqi occupation and the analysis of trends throughout history.

Although execution for desertion was always an option, early in the nation's history a policy of demeaning those who deserted, often humiliating them in public, was regularly practiced instead. It appears that accusations of cowardice crept in more frequently during the War of 1812, and have increased since that time. Branding deserters as traitors or cowards certainly serves the national purpose as defined by whatever administration happens to be in power at the time. Yet it is a significant deception and one that has been accepted for generations.

If cowardice and betrayal are not, in fact, the motivating factors for the majority of those who illegally depart from the US military, the question must be asked: Why do they desert? Are the issues that cause soldiers to flee to Canada in 2005 the same as those that caused Union soldiers to leave campaigns in Richmond, Virginia and return to their homes in the north? If not, how have the motivations evolved? What, exactly, causes a soldier, sometimes with a history of battle campaigns, to say "enough"?

These are complex questions and it is folly to look for only one or two predominant reasons. But there are significant similarities throughout America's history, along with some differences, in why soldiers leave their assignments, knowing that doing so could result in their execution. Throughout the following chapters, each detailing desertion during a US war or period of peace, many causes are repeatedly seen: lack of pay; disagreement with the cause of the war; incompetent leadership; inadequate food or other supplies, and homesickness, among others.

Along with the differing reasons for desertion the government's response to deserters has also changed. Various forms of what can only be classified as torture have been often been implemented, with either tacit or open approval by

---

2. Speech given November 3, 1969.

the government. Although execution has always been an option, not since the shocking and patently unfair execution of Pvt. Eddie Slovik on January 31, 1945 has any deserter been executed, although many have been tried.

The government's response to desertion must be viewed for what it is: a political tool to not only keep soldiers in the ranks, thus helping to further the country's goals, whether honorable or not, but also to keep the average citizen behind those goals. While the tactics of so doing have advanced through the last two centuries, the purposes have changed little.

The issue of desertion must be viewed in the larger context of military recruitment and conscription. Within this framework, several questions must be considered:

Does the good of the whole take precedence over the good of the individual? That is assumed when conscription is utilized. The answer to this question is not simple.

Should anyone make life or death decisions for another person? When conscription is part of national policy, is it morally acceptable for the government to mandate that young men (and possibly in the future, young women), must disrupt their lives and possibly be put at mortal risk? If the government does not have this right, catastrophic consequences can ensue. However, if the government does have this right, the result can be equally disastrous as an administration can freely wage wars that lead to the destabilization of volatile areas of the world. And the individual consequences to the drafted soldier must not be discounted.

What are the rights and responsibilities of the citizens if they do not believe a war is just? In 2002 President George W. Bush stated that Saddam Hussein's regime presented an 'imminent threat' to the security of the US. Now that that claim has been completely disproved, should soldiers who are called to fight in Iraq have the right to refuse?

Who is to judge what is a "just" war? To again use the example of the US invasion of Iraq, had Mr. Bush's claims been true, one could have argued that this war is just. If a soldier enlisted believing those claims, and then learned the truth, what is his/her obligation?

To what extent should an individual's personal circumstances influence his obligation to be part of the military? Are age, martial status, student status, parenthood, etc. grounds for exclusion, or during times of war should all people within a specific age range (such as 19 – 22) be required to serve? If, for example, married men with children should be exempt from serving, what would be the outcome if a single soldier married and fathered a child while serving in the military?

Since there are people willing to accept high-risk, life-threatening employment (e.g. police officers, fire fighters), is having a highly-paid, professional army an option? This would permit the government to embark on any military initiatives it chooses, without concern about enlistment or the draft, assuming the salary and benefits were sufficient to attract the required number of soldiers. One could also postulate that the desertion rate would decrease, since the military would be seen as a highly-paid career choice. The downside is the expense of maintaining such an army.

No attempt is made to answer these complex questions in this work. However, they help to provide a context for examining the reasons soldiers have deserted, throughout history, and to understand the US government's response to desertion.

The first eleven chapters each describe a separate conflict in which the United States participated. Each includes a brief overview of the generally-accepted causes of the war. One cannot say with any real surety why the country went to war; the reasons given to the public may not be the real reasons, and looking back through the lens of scores of years may further cloud the picture. Today, as always, all the public knows is what the government chooses to tell it. But the causes as listed help provide a view of what information, both official and societal, a potential recruit or draftee had.

Chapter 12 includes information about some of the United States' lesser wars and conflicts, as well as information on desertion during peacetime.

The final chapter, Summary and Analysis, includes some observations and analyses, including similarities and differences between governmental policies and motives for desertion throughout US history. Contemporary examples paralleling historical events are discussed and analyzed.

CHAPTER 1: THE REVOLUTIONARY WAR

Few major historical events are really explained by the easy descriptions found in most history books. The circumstances that lead to war are extremely complex, but a sense of those complexities is frequently sacrificed on the altar of expediency. Only certain facets are emphasized when "selling" the war to the people, and many details are lost with the passage of time. The American Revolution is no exception.

The so-called Boston Tea Party of December 16, 1773, is often seen as the start of the Revolution. This riot occurred in response to the British Tea Act of 1773, which "aimed at insuring a monopoly of tea sold in America by the British East India Tea Company."[3] When a shipment of East India tea arrived in Boston, rebels in disguise boarded ship and threw the tea overboard. The British responded to this event with a series of restrictive and punitive measures that threatened the livelihood of working class people in Boston and the surrounding area.

What the ruling party may have misunderstood was that the Colonists did not see themselves as Britons. They "had forged a society and a culture from multi-ethnic elements (English, Dutch, German, Scots-Irish and other Europeans), affected also by contact with Native Americans and African slaves."[4] Thus, by the time of the Tea Act and the rebellion it caused, Colonists saw themselves as separate and distinct from Britain.

---

3. Ward, Harry M. 2000. *The War for Independence and the Transformation of American Society*, p. 1.
4. Ward, p. 1.

This is not meant to imply that the colonies were a cohesive union of any sort. There was rivalry between individual colonies, and rivalry between groups of north, central and southern colonies. Parliament unwittingly overcame some of that rivalry by creating a common enemy — Britain — for the colonists.

Many revolutionaries in the mid 1770s saw their mission as no different from that of their forebears who had left Europe for the New World centuries earlier.

> [T]hey claimed their predecessors as courageous forerunners in the cause that now called for independence. The enemy in those early times had been the American continent and the Indians. The first settlers, according to their descendants, had left Europe and faced such enemies in order to preserve self-government and liberty of conscience.[5]

The current revolutionaries felt they were only enhancing and strengthening the accomplishments of their forebears.

Added to this most gallant feeling of patriotic fervor was the concept of a godly mission. "Many revolutionaries believed that God had chosen America to preserve and to exemplify self-government for the world."[6] In the New Jersey Journal, a letter to the editor of March 29, 1780, four years into the war, and signed by "a Soldier," shows that this feeling did not abate, at least in some circles: "We ought to rejoice that the Almighty Governor of the universe hath given us a station so honourable, and planted us the guardians of liberty, while the greatest part of mankind rise and fall undistinguished as bubbles on the common stream."[7] This attitude has remained pervasive in American culture, climaxing in extremely dangerous policies in the early years of the new millennium (see Chapter 13, Summary and Analysis).

The optimism of some people early in the war was obvious: an unsigned letter to the editor of the New Hampshire Gazette in November 1776, said the following: "In return for continued exertions, Liberty will soon triumph, wealth flow in through ten thousand channels and America become the glory of all lands."[8] A positive viewpoint of the war was reflected in most of the popular press.

---

5. Royster, Charles. 1979. *A Revolutionary People at War: The Continental Army and American Character, 1775 – 1783*, p. 4.
6. Royster, p. 5.
7. Royster, p. 6
8. Royster, p. 154.

Most American newspapers came to support independence, and increasingly, their pages urged their readers to do the same. By and large, the American press set a positive agenda concerning the war by emphasizing the certainty of American success.[9]

The press also strove to stir up anti-British feelings with stories — real or imagined, and/or real and grossly exaggerated — of the evils of the British.

> All newspaper narratives concerning the "barbarity and insults" of the British in America sought to convince colonials of the cruelty and degeneracy of the British and instill in Americans a hatred for the British. Aimed at destroying any reputation the British may have once held, the Virginia Gazette described the colonials' former countrymen as "royal thieves," "savage brutes," "uncivilized banditti," and "pirates and bloodsuckers." In 1775 [Virginia Gazette publisher John] Pinkney declared that "the repeated insults which this distressed country has suffered call aloud for everything tending to its preservation and protection." All wartime efforts on the part of the Williamsburg printers to picture the British as cruel, depraved, and undeserving of American support aimed at ensuring that Virginians answered Pinkney's call.[10]

As a result of these beliefs, early American patriots had a potent combination of reasons to throw off the yoke of British rule: economic necessity, maintenance and furtherance of ancestral efforts, and perceived divine guidance. The skirmishes at Lexington and Concord triggered all this patriotic zeal.

Once hostilities resulted in war, the abstract virtues so ardently proclaimed translated into more mundane realities. For many men, this transformation was sufficient to cause the same problem that had plagued every nation at war since recorded time: desertion.

Obtaining a precise measure of desertion during the American Revolution is difficult for a variety of reasons, not the least of which is an absence of accurate records. The most likely estimates suggest that of the approximately 250,000 members of the army who served throughout the war — including both the Continental army (the organized military force) and the militia (similar in some regards to today's National Guard) — between 20% and 35% of the army deserted. Even this somewhat conservative estimate is far higher than the 10%–12% desertion rate experienced by European armies at this time in history.[11] Additionally, many soldiers who were listed as " 'sick absent,' 'on furlough' or 'on command' were actually deserters."[12] This was apparently done to lessen the

---

9. Chiasson, Louis Jr. 1995. *The Press in Time of Crisis*, p. 2.
10. Chiasson, p. 10.
11. Edmondson, James Howard. 1971. *Desertion in the American Army during the Revolutionary War*, pp. 12 –13.
12. Ward, p. 135

effect on the remaining soldiers, who certainly would have experienced an over-whelming sense of demoralization had they known in what numbers their compatriots were fleeing the military.

Desertion was a problem throughout the war. "Soon after the fighting broke out at Lexington in 1775, the throng of militiamen that eventually emerged as the American Continental army began defecting."[13] This set the tone for the rest of the war. "William Davies, Virginia's Commissioner of War, in March 1781, complained to Governor Jefferson that 'I have no doubt If every draft in future raises one third soldiers and two thirds deserters, the latter will soon become too formidable to be meddled with.'"[14] Washington himself had no illusions about the problems of desertion. Said he: "unless the people helped in returning the runaways he would 'be obliged to detach one half of the Army to bring back the other.'"[15]

As in any conflict, the reasons for desertion were as varied as the personalities and circumstances of the soldiers themselves, yet some common threads can be found.

> Repulsion at the frequent corporal punishment, the arduous military duty, lack of pay and food, contemptuous attitude of many of the officers, fear of combat, crowded and unsanitary camp life, rampant spread of disease, fear of capture by the British, enticement by the enemy, and opportunity to serve aboard privateers all were factors impelling soldiers to escape military service.[16]

Any one of these reasons may have been sufficient to inspire a soldier to desert, but many soldiers experienced several of them. A brief study of each is instructive.

CORPORAL PUNISHMENT

This usually and officially meant lashes, anywhere from a maximum of thirty-nine during the first year of the war to one hundred for the duration of the conflict. However, officers routinely exceeded this penalty.

The method of administering this punishment was particularly cruel. These 100 lashes could be administered over a period of "four days, with salt rubs

---

13. Edmondson, p. 4.
14. Ward, p. 136. Original spelling, grammar and punctuation retained.
15. Edmondson, p. 5.
16. Ward, p. 135.

between the four floggings. Before 50 lashes the back was 'like jelly, and the cat got clogged with blood. A dry one was substituted to cut more sharply."[17]

Flogging, however, was not the only form of punishment used by officers. Often they hit the enlisted men, either ostensibly as a disciplinary measure or simply to vent their own frustration.

> Most generals approved of calculated blows to correct stubborn men. However, some officers seemed to have succumbed simply to rage. At West Point one writer saw an officer and a subordinate beat a soldier bloody: "many officers gathering round, said lay on, and damning him that dare say otherwise," until one officer stopped them. To this witness, beating a man who dared not resist was the sure sign of a coward. A few officers who inflicted especially cruel beatings were court-martialed. One who was found guilty of "a malevolence of temper scarcely to be equaled" got a severe reprimand.[18]

In either event, "[s]triking a man, especially to gratify anger, undermined the self-respect of both the striker and the victim. It conveyed both the officer's contempt for the soldier and the officer's loss of self discipline, which invited the soldier's contempt for him."[19]

The fact that such behaviors were legal is the result of the military code created by John Adams in 1776. For this "he copied the handiest tyrannical code available — namely that of the British military, which in turn had been shaped from some of the sterner European codes."[20] That Adams believed in adopting the cruel military "justice'" system of the country from which he was attempting to free himself is itself puzzling. "Adams himself was surprised when he got by with these harsh and archaic regulations, which were intended, he said, to produce not justice but discipline."[21] Adams apparently believed that the system of military justice that was inherent in the British system was required to successfully remove the yoke of British imperialism. Unfortunately, the soldiers charged with fighting the British were deprived of the lofty freedoms espoused for all citizens not unfortunate enough to be part of the armed forces.

---

17. Royster, p. 78.
18. Royster, p. 79. Original spelling, punctuation and grammar retained.
19. Royster p. 79.
20. Sherrill. Robert. 1970. *Military Justice is to Justice as Military Music is to Music*, p. 71.
21. Sherrill, p. 71.

ARDUOUS MILITARY DUTY

When Washington was unable to convince Congress to approve of flogging to 500 lashes, "he considered punishing men by confinement at hard labor, but this was not implemented, perhaps because it would have been hard to tell from routine service in the Continental army."[22]

LACK OF FOOD

During the Revolution, food for the soldiers was in short supply; often they went days without eating. Because of this, one General reported: "Our Desertions are astonishingly great; the Love of Freedom, which once animated the Breasts of these born in the country, is controlled by Hunger, the Kennest of Necessities."[23]

A soldier reported in May of 1778 that he and several others were "venting our spleen at our country and government, then at our officers, and then at ourselves for our imbecility in staying there and starving in detail for an ungrateful people who did not care what became of us, so they could enjoy themselves while we were keeping a cruel enemy from them."[24] He describes a situation that was not unusual. That this lack of food impacted the war effort is evidenced by the following:

> In a letter to Congress, Washington stated his mortification to learn that his troops were unable to move out against the enemy who were foraging in the area near Derby, Pennsylvania, because there were no provisions. He feared the men were on the point of mutiny at that time, for there was not a single hoof to slaughter and less than twenty-five barrels of flour for the entire force, nor was any expected to arrive.[25]

With starvation a very real possibility, desertion must have been seen as a reasonable and sensible alternative.

---

22. Royster, p. 78
23. Edmondson, pp. 106-107. Original spelling, grammar and punctuation retained.
24. Royster, p. 300.
25. Edmondson, p. 107.

LACK OF CLOTHING AND RELATED PROVISIONS

Among the necessary commodities that the government had serious problems providing was clothing. Trails of blood from the feet of barefoot soldiers were not uncommon, and soldiers often dressed in clothes so ragged as to border on being naked. Washington himself "expressed astonishment that the army should 'be deficient in any article of Cloating when it is commonly asserted that the Eastern States alone can furnish Materials enough, to cloath 100,000 men.' If this was true, he said, then 'there is a fatal error somewhere, to which may be attributed the death and desertion of thousands.'"[26]

In addition, tents, bedrolls and other basic supplies were rare. Men slept outside in the rain and snow with no protection from the elements. "During the first year of fighting Sergeant Ephraim Squire of the Connecticut Line explained some of the conditions the troops endured:

> This morning early it began to rain and we [had] no shelter, and are obliged to go to carry over our Battoes, and Barrells, the way muddy and slippery, hard for poor soldiers, that have to work hard in the rain and cold, and wade a mile and a half knee deep in water and mud, cold enough and after night, to camp in the rain without any shelter.[27]

While many Americans have heard that harsh conditions plagued the army at Valley Forge, few know that such hardships were typical of the experiences of many soldiers throughout the colonies.

ILLNESS

The causes of illnesses among the soldiers were numerous. "Open latrines for thousands of men were bad enough, but many soldiers would 'set Down and Ease themselves' wherever they felt like it. The remains of slaughtered cattle often rotted unburied."[28] Although conditions improved later in the war, sanitation was never good.

When lack of food, inadequate clothing and provisions combine with harsh weather and unsanitary conditions, illness must be expected. Military hospitals were reputed to be so bad that soldiers ill from exposure or wounded

---

26. Edmondson, p. 114. Original spelling maintained.
27. Edmondson, pp. 100 – 101.
28. Royster, p. 60.

in war often opted to seek medical attention elsewhere. Upon recovering from their illness or wounds, many chose not to return to the military. It was not uncommon for them to go home for medical attention, and once there, the thought of returning to the same horrors they'd so recently left kept many of them at home.

LACK OF PAY

Wages for America's soldiers have never been good; during the Revolution, any common laborer could expect to earn more than military personnel.[29] The families of soldiers often petitioned the government for relief, but it was seldom granted. Even if other conditions had been favorable — and they were far from being so — it is likely that men still would have deserted in order to assist their struggling families.

> An American officer commented on the misery of many wives and children as reported to him by one in his command: "Not a Day Passes by head, but some Soldier with Tears in his Eyes, hands me a letter from his Wife Painting forth the Distresses of his family in such strains as these, 'I am without bread, and Cannot get any, the Committee will not Supply me, my Children will Starve, or if they do not, they will freeze, we have no wood, neither Can we get any, Pray Come Home.'"[30]

This problem was not lost on the common man. A letter to the editor of the Connecticut Courant included the following: "How is it that the poor soldiers wives in any of our towns go from door to door, begging a supply of the necessaries of life at the stipulated prices, and are turned away, notwithstanding the solemn agreement of the towns to supply such?"[31]

The situations in which many families found themselves sometimes caused mutiny in the army.

> In 1779 Sergeant Samuel Glover was executed for leading a mutiny in the North Carolina Line in which he, on behalf of "His Brother Soldiers" — unpaid for fifteen months — "demanded their pay, and refused to obey the Command of his superior Officer, and would not march till they had justice done them." His widow told the General Assembly of North Carolina that "the poor soldiers" were "possessed of the same attachment and affection to their Families as those in command." She further asked: "What must the Feeling of the Man be who fought at Brandywine, at Germantown, and at Stony Point and did his duty, and when on another March in

---

29. Edmondson, p. 123.
30. Edmondson, p. 179. Original spelling, grammar and punctuation retained.
31. Royster, p. 296.

defense of his Country, with Poverty staring him full in the face, he was denied his Pay."[32]

As early as 1776, with the need to raise an army foremost on the minds of the revolutionaries, Congress refused to grant bounties for reenlistments. There seemed to be a general feeling that service for its own sake was sufficient reward. An article in the Connecticut Courant asked the following: "Will it not be criminal, at a crisis like the present, to bury your martial talents because more of your money is not taxed from you and returned as a bounty....The pay of the sol-diery, though not equal to intentions of bribery, is equal to all the purposes of comfortable and manly subsistence."[33] This early in the war, the problems stemming from late pay may not have caused extreme hardship for soldiers and their families, but they did by 1779, as evidenced by the mutiny of Sergeant Glover after his distinguished and dedicated service to his country. Certainly this became a major problem before long, notwithstanding the Connecticut Courant's assurance that a soldier would receive sufficient pay with which to live.

HOMESICKNESS

The draw of home wore many faces. Few Continental or militia soldiers had ever been more than a few miles from home, and never for any significant length of time. Never had they been required to live with thousands of other men, in unfamiliar and uncomfortable circumstances. Their response to these conditions included loss of appetite, restlessness and depression. They may have volunteered to defend their homeland, but once away from home they could not always associate the military's mundane activities with protection of home.

Coupled with this was the gradual dissolution of their individual belief in their personal valor and God's reward for it. "[T]hey could see that they were often failing to achieve the virtuous strength that was a mark of God's favor."[34] This led to further demoralization, which often resulted in a desire for the comfort and familiarity of home.

Although there was a negative public perception of deserters, this seemed to do little to deter them. It was said that "[a] deserter cheated his country, failed

---

32. Royster, pp. 296 – 297. Original spelling, grammar and punctuation retained.
33. Royster, p. 64.
34. Royster, p. 63.

those who depended on him, and showed himself a coward."[35] This may have caused some soldiers to have second thoughts about deserting. No one would feel welcome at home under these circumstances. Yet on a more personal level, the soldier's family usually wanted him home. Newspaper editorials castigating deserters, or advertising rewards for anyone who turned in a deserter notwithstanding, many civilians just wanted to be united with their loved ones. As will be seen in subsequent chapters, the assistance of civilians has often been crucial in a successful desertion.

Washington believed that stern measures needed to be enacted to punish civilians who assisted a soldier in deserting. The states enacted legislation that levied fines and other penalties on persons so guilty. "States offered rewards for the arrest of deserters and threatened to draft, fine, and flog people who sheltered them."[36] Yet there is little evidence that these measures discouraged great numbers of people from aiding friends and family members in leaving the army.

In November of 1777, Washington offered a reward of 10 pounds to anyone, soldier or civilian, who delivered a deserter to the army. Instead of strengthening the army, this had the opposite effect: officers on furlough often remained away from the army for extended periods as they searched for deserters.[37]

ECONOMIC NEED

Feelings of homesickness and the need to help out the family were not the only reasons for deserting. Closely associated with homesickness and lack of pay was the need for many soldiers to plant crops in the spring, and harvest them in the fall. Their families depended on the crops for food and income; their very existence was threatened without the harvest. Desertion rates tended to increase during these times. Some soldiers returned to the army after they completed their farming responsibilities; others simply remained at home.

---

35. Royster, pp. 72-73.
36. Royster, p. 71.
37. Ward, p. 136

BRITISH ENTICEMENT

The British used a variety of measures to encourage revolutionaries to desert. This included the following offers:[38]
- 1776: Full pardon, $16.00 (later raised to $24.00 if the soldier surrendered his musket) and a land grant;
- 1777: Full pardon, purchase of their weapons, and the opportunity to join a newly formed British army corps;
- 1777: 200 acres for non-commissioned officers, and 50 for privates if they enlisted for two years.

The pardons were offered because revolutionary soldiers were seen by the British as traitors.

These methods met with at least some success, causing Washington to comment that these attempts had "an unhappy influence on too many of the Soldiers."[39]

BRITISH PRISONERS OF WAR

Another problem that the fledgling nation created for itself was the enlisting of British prisoners of war into the Continental Army. Often these men used the first opportunity to return to the British lines. In 1778, Congress prohibited the practice of enlisting British prisoners of war.[40]

BOUNTY-JUMPING

Bounty-jumping refers to the practice of enlisting with one unit to collect a financial reward, or bounty, and then deserting that unit and re-enlisting with another in order to collect another financial reward. Since some states offered higher bounties than did others, soldiers sometimes enlisted in their home state, deserted, and then enlisted in the army of a neighboring state.

---

38. Edmondson, pp. 185-186.
39. Edmondson, p. 186.
40. Ward, p. 105.

AMBIVALENCE TO THE CAUSE

Although sanitized versions of American history show a populace completely committed to the lofty goals of independence, the reality as documented casts more than a little doubt on this picture. "Most estimates place one-third of Americans as loyalist, one-third on the fence, to be swayed by whomever was winning, and one-third rebel."[41]

In addition, "large numbers left the ranks of the American army to join the opposition. These defectors had obviously lost confidence in the ability of the Continental forces to win a victory over the better trained British troops."[42] Others seemed to believe as the war dragged on that a revolutionary victory was a remote possibility. Deserting to the British side would prevent them from being hanged as traitors after an American defeat.

The US government during the Revolution largely ignored a major source of manpower: African-Americans. This substantial population was not completely forgotten; as recruitment consistently fell far short of goals there was some hesitant recognition that African-Americans could serve in the military. Legislation was eventually passed allowing freemen to enlist. As early as January 1777, Washington approved the recruitment and enlisting of African-Americans as long as they were free. Many runaway slaves escaped their slavery by telling recruiters they were free and anxious to fight for the nation's independence.

The following year Washington approved Rhode Island's plan to establish an entire regiment composed solely of slaves. By 1781 Massachusetts, Maryland and New York were enlisting African-Americans.

Although accepted only out of desperation, the African-American soldiers distinguished themselves. Additionally, unbeknownst to the revolutionaries, the acceptance of large numbers of African-Americans marked a milestone in military integration in the new nation's history that would not be soon repeated.

> In June 1781, the French and American armies joined forces at White Plains. Baron Closen, a German officer in the French Royal Deux-Ponts, estimated the American army to be about one fourth black, about 1,200–1,500 men out of fewer than 6,000 Continentals! On the eve of its decisive victory over Lord Cornwallis, the Continental Army had reached a degree of integration it would not achieve again for another 200 years. Among the troops at White Plains was the Rhode Island Regiment (the two battalions had been consolidated on 1 January 1781) with its high percentage of African-Americans, which Closen considered the best American unit:

---

41. Ward, p. 35.
42. Edmondson, p. 185.

"the most neatly dressed, the best under arms, and the most precise in its maneuvers."[43]

The recruitment of African-Americans to the Continental army resulted in another reason for desertion. In 1779 British general Sir Henry Clinton promised that " 'every NEGRO who shall desert the Rebel Standard, [is granted] full security to follow within these Lines, any Occupation which he shall think proper.' In response, thousands of slaves fled behind British lines."[44] The fledgling American government was not willing to allow such a reward to slaves risking their lives on its behalf. Departing to obtain for themselves the freedom they were fighting to provide wealthy white landowners can only be seen as reasonable.

Laws regarding desertion during the eight-year Revolutionary War can be placed generally into three categories:[45]

1. Those pertaining to the militia forces;

2. Rewards for capture of deserters and punishment for those assisting deserters, and

3. Laws dealing with treason.[46]

The Articles of War provided for additional penalties for desertion within the Continental army.

In 1775, Congress adapted the Massachusetts laws for the Continental army. Where these new regulations pertained to desertion, punishment was not detailed but was left to the discretion of the court-martial. Execution was only mandated in three cases:

- For abandoning a post or inducing others to do so;
- Revealing the watch-word to any person not authorized to receive it, or
- Compelling a commander of a post to give up to the enemy.

Each of these offenses had the potential of jeopardizing the lives of many soldiers; therefore, the punishment was severe.

State laws establishing and regulating militias included, of course, penalties for violation of those laws. State-imposed penalties for desertion were originally often so mild as to encourage it; paying the fine was less inconvenient than fulfilling the obligation. When the war began, some states enacted tougher

---

43. Selig, Robert A. The Revolution's Black Soldiers. http://americanrevolution.org/ Accessed October 21, 2005.
44. Selig, Robert A.
45. See Table A at the end of the chapter for a summary of state desertion laws during the war.
46. Edmondson, p. 15.

laws, including provisions for the death penalty. However, this was not universal. New Hampshire law, for example, specified "that a court-martial could inflict only 'degrading, Cashiering, drumming out of the camp, whipping not exceeding thirty-nine, fines or imprisonment, not exceeding one month.'"[47]

As desertion became a greater problem over time, it was addressed in a number of ways. In September of 1776, the Congressional Articles of War provided flogging of up to one hundred lashes, or death, as the penalty for desertion. The policies related to desertion were not adhered to with any rigor; of 137 men officially convicted of desertion, 40 were executed and the rest pardoned. In some instances, however, deserters caught during battle were court-martialed and executed on the spot. The number of men victimized in this way is unknown.

Another common abuse was to sentence a man to one hundred lashes for multiple crimes. Two cases will serve as an example.

> Robert Kennedy of the Eighth Pennsylvania Regiment received four hundred lashes: three hundred for repeated desertion and one hundred for theft. A deserter belonging to the Fourth Pennsylvania Regiment was captured on July 21, 1779, along with two others. He was immediately tied up and given five hundred lashes, which was justified as being "back allowance" for a previous desertion for which he had received a reprieve from his colonel.[48]

To his credit, George Washington did not allow this excess whenever he was aware of it. However, as Commander-in-Chief, he felt that the maximum flogging should be increased to five hundred lashes.[49] He apparently felt that there should be some punishment between one hundred lashes and death, but Congress would not agree. Congress kept the maximum at one hundred, and Washington expected that law to be strictly followed.

Floggings, like executions, were generally done in public, with the belief that they would serve as a deterrent to other soldiers.

Throughout the war, the practice of public executions continued, although executions alone did not satisfy all those in authority. In 1779, Major Henry Lee "proposed decapitating deserters and sending their heads on spikes to the troop areas."[50] Washington did not approve. His response seems somewhat ironic, considering his support for and encouragement of execution as a pun-

---

47. Edmondson, p. 16. Original spelling, grammar and punctuation retained.
48. Edmondson, p. 324.
49. Royster, p. 215.
50. Edmondson, p. 307.

ishment and deterrent: "examples however severe ought not to be attended with an appearance of inhumanity otherwise they give disgust, and may excite resentment rather than terror."[51] Despite this, there is at least one recorded decapitation, documented in a letter from Peter Ten Broeck to his parents dated July 9, 1779:

> We hear there is a great Number of Men Deserts Dayly both to and from the enemy; yesterday three men belonging to the Maryland line were found going into the enemy, they were brought to their camp. The one was shot and his head cut off and this morning was brought to the Virginia Camp and was put on top of the gallows.[52]

Assorted other penalties were enacted. Although they were seldom legal, this did not prevent them from occurring. These included running the gauntlet, often with another soldier holding a bayonet at the prisoner's chest to slow his steps. As he ran between two lines of soldiers, he was hit repeatedly with switches held by the soldiers. Another barbaric punishment was "riding the wooden horse," a particularly painful consequence wherein the deserter sat on a sharp ridge with legs tied tightly and hands bound behind the back. This often resulted in mutilation.

Some men had a log chained to their leg for a specific period of time. Others were confined with only bread and water, or whipped with a birch rod. Another particularly cruel punishment was "picketing." "The offender was suspended in mid air by a rope tied to his wrist with a very sharp stake driven into the ground just high enough for him to rest his bare heel. The stake did not break the skin but caused great pain. The only means of relieving the heel was to allow the wrist to bear the weight, which was also intolerably painful."[53] The lack of official sanction for many of these draconian measures did little to lessen their frequency of occurrence.

The effectiveness of punishment was always a question, and how best to make it effective was never determined during the war. "Although the viewpoint of the Marchese di Beccaris's Essays on Crimes and Punishment (1764) was beginning to have influence in America that certainty rather than severity of punishment was most effective, the American military leaders favored severity in sentencing."[54] Possibly because of the severity, pardons were granted inconsis-

---

51. Edmondson, p. 307.
52. Edmondson, p. 341. Original spelling, punctuation and grammar retained.
53. Edmondson, p. 336.
54. Ward, p. 135.

tently, and any deterrent effect that severity might have had was lost or at least greatly diminished as a result.

On four occasions during the war Washington issued general amnesties. On April 6, 1777, the government pardoned all deserters who surrendered before May 15. Six months later a second pardon was issued, covering all deserters who surrendered by January 1, 1778. On March 10, 1779, a third pardon was granted to deserters if they returned by May 1. "This grace period proved too short since few came in, and it was extended to July 1."[55] Finally, in 1782 a pardon was issued that applied only to deserters who had joined the British forces.

These general pardons were issued in addition to those occasionally offered by the states. Few deserters took advantage of them, possibly because they didn't know about them, or simply because they did not want to return to the army.

The pardons actually had a detrimental effect on the army. Soldiers who had not deserted saw the few returning deserters, and were emboldened to desert themselves, believing that a future pardon would be offered. Said Washington:

> I have tried the efficacy of proclamations of pardon to deserters so often....and have found so little good result from them, that I am inclined to think desertion is rather encouraged than remedied by a frequent repetition of them. The Soldier goes off or remains at home after a furlough, and looks for a proclamation as a thing of course.[56]

One might add that there was little reason for Washington to think a pardon would produce a positive benefit; since the reasons the soldiers deserted remained unchanged, there was little to induce them to return.

Within the context of military service, the ideals for which the soldiers were to fight caused difficulties for them. "A soldier could not practice the free autonomy and communal self-determination promised by the revolution."[57] Why, a soldier might ask himself, was he fighting for independence when by the very act of volunteering to fight for it, he was deprived of it? Many men could not tolerate this irony, and simply left.

---

55. Edmondson, p. 353. Original spelling, grammar and punctuation retained.
56. Edmondson, p. 355.
57. Royster, p. 215.

FEAR

Although often portrayed as the only reason for desertion, and coupled with terms such as "traitor" or "coward," fear is sometimes a reason for desertion but often has nothing to do with cowardice. Continental and militia soldiers frequently did not have the physical strength to fight, due to illness and lack of food. If confronted by the enemy under these conditions — as they frequently were — desertion can only be seen as a sensible course of action.

SELF-PRESERVATION

The strongest of human motives — self-preservation — also factored into desertions, as it always has done. The rage militaire — that passion for arms that was so prevalent in 1775 — evaporated almost instantly once the realities of war set in. "[T]he rifle was a fragile weapon, soon fouled, slow to load, and of little use at close quarters against a bayonet, which it lacked."[58] Given such poor odds, desertion proved a reasonable option for some soldiers. Self-preservation may simply be a different, more realistic description of what is sometimes referred to as fear.

As America progressed through two centuries, growing into both a military and industrial imperial power, the government strove to change the situation and reduce men and women to soldiers, first and foremost (see Chapter 13, Summary and Analysis, for further information on this topic).

Although Washington recognized and apparently understood the causes for desertion, he still considered it a cowardly act.

> Men just dragged from the tender Scenes of domestic life; unaccustomed to the din of Arms; totally unacquainted with every kind of Military skill, which being followed by a want of confidence in themselves, when opposed to Troops regularly train'd, disciplined, and appointed, superior in knowledge and superior in Arms, makes them timid, and ready to fly from their own shadows. Besides, the sudden change in their manner of living, (particularly in the lodging) brings on sickness in many; impatience in all, and such an unconquerable desire of returning to their respective homes that it not only produces shameful, and scandalous desertions among themselves, but infuses the like spirit in others.[59]

---

58. Royster, p. 34.
59. Ward pp. 135-136. Original spelling and punctuation maintained.

One can only wonder why Washington, the "Father of the Country," called desertion "shameful" and "scandalous" when he, as commander-in-chief, was unable to secure for the soldiers the food and clothing they needed or to provide them with the money that had been promised to them and which was needed to keep their families alive. From the viewpoint of twenty-first century America, some people may be blinded to all but military considerations, but certainly most citizens can identify with the need for soldiers to be clothed, fed and paid. Desertion may not, in Revolutionary War-era America, have been an act of courage. But when seen in greater detail and when the war and its horrors and hardships are studied, in few cases can it be described as cowardice. In most situations for which any documentation remains, desertion was simply the best option for many soldiers seeking to provide for their families or escape the injustice of a system they couldn't possibly have anticipated before entering it.

Table 1: State Desertion Laws[60]

State	Year	Law
Massachusetts	1742*	"Any soldier who deserted would be seen as a felon and shall suffer the pains of death, or some other grievous Punishment."[a]
	1780	An Act to prevent, punish and apprehend desertions and return them to the army, or jail. Pardons were granted for any deserter who turned himself in within three months.
	Nov. 2, 1781	A law authorizing anyone to apprehend deserters, with the state reimbursing them for expenses. Reward reduced from 30 pounds to 6 pounds. Also provided penalties for those who neglected to apprehend deserters.
Pennsylvania	Feb. 20, 1777	The burden of apprehending deserters was placed on local constables. The deserter would be delivered to the army for prosecution under military law. The Pennsylvania law included fines for anyone harboring or otherwise assisting a deserter. The law specified that a house could not be entered and searched without a warrant. Additional rewards were given to civilians capturing deserters.
	March 12, 1778	A person of draft age who caught a deserter had the choice of exemption from active duty for two months, or being excused from paying the fine if he refused to join when called to do so.
	Sept., 1780	Anyone assisting soldiers who deserted, boarded armed vessels and jumped ship in a foreign port were fined 10,000 pounds or imprisoned for a year.

a.*Edmondson, p. 40.*

---

60. Edmondson, pp. 38 – 62

State	Year	Law
New Hampshire	1777	Anyone is authorized to apprehend a deserter. A fine of 40 shillings was levied against anyone who refused to assist in the apprehension of a deserter. A fine of nine to fifteen pounds was levied against anyone harboring a deserter.
State	Year	Law
Maryland	April 20, 1777	Law providing rewards for capturing deserters. Penalties for harboring deserters: First offense — fine or three months in jail Second offense — heavier fine or thirty-nine lashes.
New Jersey	Feb. 26, 1777	Citizens were required to assist in the capture of deserters. A reward of $5.00 plus expenses was granted. Persons harboring, concealing or encouraging desertion: First offense: Ten pounds Subsequent offenses: Fifteen pounds
Connecticut	1777	Named it a duty of every citizen to assist in the apprehension of deserters. Provided fines for anyone assisting in desertion.
Delaware	Feb. 22, 1777	Provided penalties for deserters and those harboring them
Virginia	May 5, 1777	Provided penalties for deserters and those harboring them
New York	July 1, 1781	Capture of a deserter by anyone of draft age exempted him from duty for one year.

* One of the oldest laws on desertion in the colonies.

Note that some laws changed over time, but other states relied on Federal law to deal with desertion. Also note that most states originally passed desertion laws in 1777. This was in response to a letter sent by George Washington to each state, complaining about desertion and civilian assistance of deserters.

Chapter 2: The War of 1812

Although sometimes referred to as America's second war for independence, the War of 1812 had its origins in continued conflict with Britain over trade-related issues and America's imperial designs related to North American territorial expansion. The reason for the war, ostensibly, was retaliation for the seizure of American ships and seamen by the British. [61]

For some, this war evoked the memories and purposes of the American Revolution. "Nevertheless, the supposed threat to American independence in 1812 was more imagined than real. It existed mainly in the minds of thin-skinned Republicans who were unable to shake the ideological legacy of the Revolution and interpreted all British actions accordingly."[62]

During this period, the British were allied with Spain in a war against Napoleonic France. Britain had established a blockade of Europe and accused the US of violating it. In order to enforce the blockade, Britain seized US ships and took possession of their cargo, and pressed captured US seamen into forced labor on British naval vessels. US companies were doing a brisk business with Europe and, although demanding naval protection, were willing to sacrifice some cargo in order to keep the flow of goods to Europe uninterrupted.

The kidnapping of the seamen, however, while all but ignored by the business community, had a tremendous impact on the American public. They were enraged by the actions of the British, although their anger did not translate to universal enthusiasm for war.

---

61. Hickey, Donald R. 1989. *The War of 1812: A Forgotten Conflict*, p. 300.
62. Ibid.

Support for the war, however, was found in different areas of the country, and for very different reasons. The kidnapping of American seamen may have only been an excuse.

In the northwest area, including Ohio, frontier people were in constant conflict with Indians, and blamed this on the British, with whom the Indians had a comfortable relationship. Many also had a view of expanding the frontier northward by taking possession of Canada.

The southern states — Georgia, Tennessee and the Mississippi territory — envisioned expansion to the south, in the area of Spanish-owned Florida. With Spain embroiled in a war with France, this appeared to be a perfect opportunity to achieve this goal.

With these varied purposes, on June 18, 1812, Congress declared war on England.

In spite of the enthusiasm in some quarters for the war, two major factors plagued it from the start. First was the incompetence of nearly everyone in a leadership capacity.

> The War of 1812 ranks as one of the most ineptly fought and poorly managed efforts in American history. According to Robert Sherman Quimby (1916-98), the "story of the War of 1812 is...a study in how not to conduct a war." American political leaders at the highest levels lacked, in many cases, even the remotest idea of their roles and responsibilities in war.[63]

Added to this serious issue was the problem of finding men willing to fight the war. "Congress had authorized the President to accept volunteer forces and to call upon the states for militia. The difficulty was not planning for an army, but raising one."[64]

In the years leading up to war the country had failed to prepare for it, despite growing tensions with Britain.

> By January 1810 relations with Britain had so deteriorated that President Madison recommended the recruitment of a volunteer force of 20,000. Congress, apparently satisfied with the existing militia system, again refused to vote a volunteer force; not until January 1812 did it increase the Army's strength when it added thirteen additional regiments, totaling about 25,700 men, and authorized the President to call 50,000 militiamen into service.[65]

---

63. Quimby, Robert S. 1997. *The US Army in the War of 1812: An Operational and Command Study.* P. vii.
64. Matloff, Maurice, ed. 1996. *American Military History: 1775 – 1902*, p. 124.
65. Matloff, p 121.

At the start of the war the government decided to rely on state militias as a support to the small Continental army. The war planners seemed to believe that "the militia could be used primarily as an auxiliary force without extensive reform."[66] Acting upon this belief had highly detrimental effects on the war effort. Many soldiers in the militia felt that their obligation was the protection of the state in which they lived; because of this they often were hesitant, and sometimes refused, to cross state lines. Many refused to enter Canada. Once the war started, "volunteers continued to offer their services to the state instead of the national government."[67]

This problem was compounded by the states themselves. In 1813, Vermont Governor Martin Chittenden summoned his militiamen home, saying that they were needed for the defense of their home state. While this move was supported within Vermont, the rest of the country vilified the governor. The New York Columbian called Chittenden's summons the "most scandalous and unwarrantable stain on the political history of America that ever disgraced its annals."[68] The US attorney general was pressured to prosecute Chittenden for encouraging soldiers to desert (he declined to do so).

Once the problems associated with the militia became apparent, it was too late to raise an army while prosecuting the war. The attempt to do so was made with only limited success.

Laws governing conscription had been on the books since the Revolution, and were open to adjustment and interpretation, as any given situation seemed to require.

> [O]n the 10th April, 1812, in anticipation of the war about to take place, Congress passed an act...which authorized the President "to require the different Executives of the States to organize their respective proportions of 100,000 militia, and to call into service the whole, or a part, of these quotas; which detachments were not compelled to serve longer than six months...." This act was an enlargement of the act of 1795, which restricted the service of the militia, when called out by the authority of the United States, to three months.[69]

This extension of time from three to six months caused endless problems for both the army and the individual soldiers; for many soldiers, as will be shown, it proved fatal.

---

66. Skeen, C. Edward. 1999. *Citizen Soldiers in the War of 1812*, p. 17.
67. Hickey, p. 77.
68. Skeen, p. 114.
69. Douthat, James L., ed. 1993. *1814 Court Martial of Tennessee Militiamen*, p. 4.

Many men enlisted in the militia believing it to be a three-month commitment; the government, however, believed it to be six months based on the authorization referenced above. In a lengthy report on court martials of Tennessee militiamen in 1814 is reported the following:

> That these offences, first, consisted in "exciting and causing mutiny"; secondly, in the commission of an actual mutiny, accompanied by circumstances of aggravated robbery and spoliation of the public stores; and, thirdly, in the crime of desertion.

> That some of the mutineers were deluded into a belief that they were about to be wrongfully detained in service, beyond the term for which there were legally drafted, our Committee think not improbable; and those who were thus likely to be deluded, the Court recommended to the clemency of the commanding General, who, it appears, pardoned them; and that all the rest of the mutineers and deserters were condemned to trivial punishments, neither affecting life nor limb, excepting six of the ringleaders....[70]

Dozens of men were tried and convicted, and many of them were executed. For example:

> The Court next proceeded to the trial of Jacob Webb, a private of Captain Strother's Company, charged with desertion, mutiny and robbery.

> To which charge or charges, the prisoner, Jacob Webb, pleaded Not Guilty.

> The Court, after mature consideration on the evidence adduced, find the prisoner guilty of desertion and mutiny, and not of robbery, and sentence him to receive the punishment of death by shooting.[71]

The difference between punishment for enlisted men and for officers should be noted. Captain Strother, Mr. Webb's commanding officer, was convicted of exciting to mutiny, conniving at mutiny and disobedience of orders. His punishment consisted of being dismissed from the service as unworthy of holding a commission in the army of the United States.

These Tennessee court martials and executions were conducted under the supervision of future president Andrew Jackson, who was the commander of the Tennessee troops who were court martialed. The circumstances surrounding these court martials were to haunt Jackson during his electoral campaign against President John Quincy Adams. During that campaign Jackson was accused "of being 'an unfeeling Tyrant' who 'has done this bloody work.'"[72] This accusation

---

70. Douthat, pp. 5 - 6.
71. Douthat, p. 58.
72. *The William C. Cook Collection: The War of 1812 in the South,* The Williams Research Center, The Historic New Orleans Collection.

was laid at Jackson's door because of the men's misunderstanding regarding their committed length of service. Perhaps the most damning aspect of the accusation is that the executions were held after the war ended.

It should be noted that Jackson maintained some semblance of order among his troops "because they feared him more than they feared the enemy.... Twice he leveled his own gun against men threatening to leave."[73] Given that he was known for this type of behavior, it is not surprising that he arranged the court martial and execution of six men formerly under his command.

The extension of service from three to six months, and its accompanying resistance by many soldiers, was just one of many factors leading to desertion during this war. Disease, including dysentery, typhoid fever, pneumonia, malaria and smallpox, among others, killed many men.

The rate of desertion during the War of 1812 increased throughout the duration of the war. "A statistical study has shown that 12.7 percent of American troops deserted during the war, and almost half of these were recruited during 1814."[74] The total army averaged between 40,000 and 45,000 soldiers each year of the war.[75] Within the militia, desertion rates were higher.

In most wars, the issue of desertion becomes apparent quickly. The War of 1812 was no exception. "Desertion was common — so common, in fact, that less than four months into the war President Madison felt obliged to issue a proclamation pardoning all deserters who returned to duty within four months."[76] Desertion continued to cause problems for the administration, and in June of 1814 Madison issued a second pardon, conditional on the deserters surrendering to authorities within three months.[77]

The reasons for desertion during the War of 1812 were not far different from those that caused men to desert during the American Revolution. Some of the conditions that were prevalent during the War of 1812 and that encouraged desertion were:

1. Difficulty receiving pay;
2. Lack of supplies;
3. Poor and/or insufficient food;
4. Illness;

---

73. Hickey, p. 149.
74. Hickey, Donald R. 1989. *The War of 1812*, p. 222.
75. Hickey, Donald R. 1995. *The War of 1812: A Short History*, pp. 53-54.
76. Hickey, p. 76.
77. Hickey, p. 222.

5. Poor leadership, and

6. Inadequate weaponry.

A closer look at each of these factors indicates the young country's inability to learn from and to correct its mistakes, and indicates that the reasons many men had for deserting were generally valid.

PROBLEMS WITH PAY

The system by which the troops were to be paid broke down early in the war. By law, pay to the members of the army could not fall more than two months in arrears, although this guideline was rendered meaningless by the generous caveat: "unless the circumstance of the case should render it unavoidable."[78] It did not take long for such circumstances to occur, but as a result of administrative inefficiency rather than any conditions of the war. As early as October 1812, four months after the war began, soldiers who had enlisted five months previously refused to march until they were paid. The situation did not improve; by 1814, the last year of the war, pay was often twelve months behind.

At the time of the war, privates were paid $5.00 per month. Unskilled laborers could expect to earn from $10.00 to $12.00 per month, making a soldier's salary extremely unappealing — even if the soldier were actually receiving it. But for the soldier with a family to support, and often needing to purchase his own food and clothing, leaving the army and working for higher wages was not only very attractive but necessary for the survival of his family.

In some parts of the country during this time, the expenditures for war greatly benefited the economy. While soldiers were paid barely enough to survive — if they were paid at all — businesses were benefiting. "[T]he nation was in the flood tide of a wartime boom fueled by huge government expenditures and a mushrooming trade that included large exports of grain to the Spanish peninsula and large imports of manufactured goods from the British Empire."[79] This kept the war popular in the western part of the country, and in some other isolated areas that were also experiencing economic prosperity, but this inequity was a contributing factor in desertions.

---

78. Hickey, p. 77.
79. Hickey, p. 107.

During the Revolutionary War, "while some citizens were amassing fortunes from the war, the soldiers were compelled to do without."[80] This situation had not changed thirty years later, and the response of many soldiers to it did not change either.

When civilians are getting rich from the war in which the soldier is not being paid for his life-threatening service, it cannot be surprising if the soldier questions his commitment to the military and the goals it is attempting to attain. This is a problem America still faces in today's military engagements.

LACK OF SUPPLIES

In any circumstances, men and women need certain basic supplies in order to perform their duties. In the battlefield this need is even more critical.

Yet the government seemed to place more emphasis on balancing its financial books than on providing the soldiers with basic necessities. In 1802 the government contracted with civilian agents to provide the needs for the armed forces. Although the government reestablished the quartermaster and commissary departments in March of 1812, shortly before war was declared, "it was months before either department was staffed and operational, and the authority granted to each was vague and overlapping. Even when operational the supply departments were woefully inefficient, and troops in the field frequently had to go for months at a time without shoes, clothing, blankets, or other vital supplies."[81] As a result, for much of the war many soldiers lacked these basic supplies. At one point, General Peter B. Porter was forced to halt a march of troops to Canandaigua because of insufficient tents and related equipment.[82]

Shortly after war was declared, General Van Rensselaer described the conditions of his troops. "Some were without shoes, they lacked all types of supplies, including ammunition."[83]

In the summer of 1813, militiamen at Wilmington had to be housed in the residences of private citizens because they did not have enough tents. Others who were fortunate enough to have tents cooked on kettles borrowed from residents. With conditions such as this it is not surprising that one Captain

---

80. Edmondson, p. 124.
81. Hickey, p. 78.
82. Skeen, p. 118.
83. Skeen, p. 98.

reported that twenty militiamen deserted in a single evening.[84] In February of 1814, "Captain William King reported that the Twelfth and Fourteenth regular regiments lacked arms and equipment, as well as clothing, tents and medical supplies."[85]

It should be noted that these problems plagued the army during the American Revolution and had not been resolved in the thirty years since the conclusion of that war. In April of 1778, "Washington informed the president of Congress that doctors had attributed the loss of hundreds of lives to the dearth of clothing, and he added, "I am certain Hundreds have deserted from the same cause."[86]

That soldiers in these circumstances recognize that the military is not providing for their basic survival needs as well as they could do themselves, is not surprising. Their decision to desert to provide for themselves should also not be surprising.

LACK OF FOOD

The responsibility of feeding the troops was outsourced to private contractors. This had disastrous effects as the contractors often provided poor quality provisions, or provisions in inadequate amounts, in order to show a profit.

Because of this, food was in very short supply at different times during the war. One officer reported that his troops were literally starving. Another, General Edmund P. Gaines, said that inadequate amounts of food and bad food "had done more to retard American operations than anything else."[87]

ILLNESS

Disease was rampant and the bad food did not help. "Epidemic diseases such as dysentery, typhoid fever, pneumonia, malaria, measles, typhus, and even smallpox were common and often fatal."[88] Fevers raged out of control, with no

---

84. Skeen, p. 129.
85. Skeen, p. 101.
86. Edmondson, pp. 114 — 115. Original spelling, grammar and punctuation maintained.
87. Hickey, pp. 78-79.

known remedy. The cases of soldiers who were ill were greatly compounded by the medical practices of the day. The known drugs at this time in history generally provided no benefit, and often caused death.

Citizens of frontier America generally received medical treatment at home. Wives and mothers were accustomed to providing both medical treatment and first aid. With death all around them, some soldiers simply returned home for treatment.

POOR LEADERSHIP

As has been noted, the entire administration of the War of 1812 was an exercise in incompetence. Among militiamen, conspicuous failures of leadership and other factors rendered them incapable of defending the frontier.

"The principal reason for America's failure was poor leadership. The administration's strategy was ill-advised, the War Department failed to give proper direction to commanders in the field, and most of the army's senior officers were incompetent."[89]

Although this is a point that is not widely taught in elementary and high schools, the war did not represent a great victory for the US. The country had to look to the peace treaty ending the war, signed in Ghent, Belgium, for victory.

> In the military and naval campaigns, the record of the United States during the war of 1812 was decidedly mixed. There were some successes...and some failures....[I]n the peace negotiations, however, the nation's record was much better, not because of what the envoys won but because of what they avoided losing. It was in Ghent, Belgium...that the Unites States consistently outmaneuvered the enemy, and it was here that Americans could claim their most significant victory.[90]

The reasons for this non-victory can be traced at least partly to leadership problems. An incident that occurred in 1813 is typical of the leadership and decision-making abilities of those in charge:

> According to J.I. Stull, captain of the Georgetown Rifles, a force of approximately 120 men, he appealed to [Secretary of War John] Armstrong to release some of the rifles in the Washington arsenal. Armstrong refused, insisting that the rifles were intended for the northern army and could not be spared. Consequently, when the rifle companies were called out after the British landed, they were forced to take muskets, and they were further delayed in procuring ammunition and flints. As for

88. Hickey, p. 79.
89. Hickey, p. 90.
90. Hickey, p. 281.

the rifles that Armstrong refused to release, Stull noted, "It was understood and believed that those very arms...were destroyed by the British on the 25th August."[91]

Armstrong had strongly resisted additional fortifications for Washington, D.C. as the focus of war shifted toward that region. His position seemed to have been driven by the financial constraints he was under, and the high cost such fortifications would incur. While he may have been correct in that regard, he did not accurately gauge the feelings of the citizenry. As a result, he was blamed for the fact that the British burned the city, and after that incident local militia refused to take orders from him. He soon resigned in disgrace.

Examples of poor leadership were shown repeatedly by General Alexander Smyth. Among his other responsibilities, Smyth was in charge of two aborted attempts to invade Canada. Although many militiamen refused to cross the river, insisting on their legal right to remain on American soil, Smyth had obtained an adequate number of them who were willing to cross the border into Canada. After having boldly declared that his troops would quickly defeat Canada, he called off the scheduled attacks. "In the aftermath of Smyth's cancellation of the invasion, large numbers of militiamen deserted. Some 600 Pennsylvania militiamen deserted within twenty-four hours, and nearly that many left in the next few days."[92] Several officers also deserted at this time.

> "Shortly thereafter Smyth stole back to Virginia using back roads. Without even the courtesy of an investigation, he was dropped from the rolls of the army...."[93]

Training and leadership were sadly lacking throughout the war. In September of 1814, a skirmish between militiamen and a British advanced party ended when the militiamen fled. "A mitigating circumstance explaining the militia reaction was that New York dragoons, who wore red coats, were on the heights watching the enemy, and the militiamen mistook them for the enemy attacking in their rear."[94] Since militiamen were notoriously poorly trained and incompetently led, this is not surprising

It was not uncommon for troops to mutiny against incompetent leaders; nor was it uncommon for mutiny to lead to desertion.

---

91. Skeen, p. 132.
92. Skeen, p. 104.
93. Hickey, p. 88.
94. Skeen, p. 116.

INADEQUATE WEAPONRY

In some regards the army did better at producing arms during the War of 1812 than it had done during the American Revolution. Two armories — at Springfield, Massachusetts and Harpers Ferry, Virginia — were already in service at the start of the war, and others were built during the war.

But having the supplies and getting them to the soldiers in the field were not the same thing. In July of 1814, Major General Duncan Cameron complained of the problem of arming a battalion of militiamen. He said that although they would have rifles, "the number of those I fear will be few; and indeed I am apprehensive that they will be very deficient in arms — of ammunition they will have not to carry from home...."[95] If not for the fact that many soldiers owned rifles of their own, many more would have been unarmed. "The standard weapon of issue during the war was the .70-caliber smooth-bore musket — a muzzle-loaded flintlock that fired a soft lead ball weighing about an ounce. Its effective range was only 100 yards, and it misfired about 15 percent of the time."[96] This too was repeated from the Revolutionary War when many soldiers were sent into battle without guns or ammunition.

Punishments for desertion, as in other wars, were arbitrary. The following story took place shortly after the battle of Buffalo, in 1814:

> Desertions became so dangerous an element that stern measures had to be adopted to combat it. One of the deserters apprehended was deprived of all pay, and made "to march from right to left through the ranks of the Brigade and then from left to right in front of the same with his hat off and hands tied behind him, followed by music playing the Rogue's March; to sit an hour straddle of one of the cannons when the same is mounted with a label pasted on his hat crown in front, with this inscription in large letters, viz: "I became a Substitute for Speculation and am now punished for desertion," and at the expiration of the hour to be drummed out of camp." "This was done, March 31st, at 11 o'clock, and was the most ignominious punishment inflicted at all of the many courts-martial in that winter's camp on the Eleven-mile creek."[97]

Not all punishments were this benign. Others included public penance, paddling, or depriving the deserting soldier of pay that was due him. Congress outlawed whipping in 1812, so officers invented punishments as they saw fit. "In

---

95. Skeen, p. 129.
96. Hickey, p. 79.
97. Hill, Henry Wayland, Ed. 2002. Municipality of Buffalo, New York, A History. 1720-1923. Page 1.

more serious cases, the offender might be branded on the face, his ears might be cropped, or he might be executed."[98]

As in the Revolutionary War, a belief that executions would have a deterrent effect remained common. In February of 1814, a public execution was held.

> During the time we remained at Buffalo, five men were sentenced to be publicly shot for the offence of desertion. They were dressed in white robes with white caps upon their heads, and a red target fastened over the heart. The army was drawn up into a hollow square to witness the example that was about to be made of their comrades who had proved recreant to the regulations of the service. Five graves were dug in a row, five coffins placed near them, also in a line, with distance between coffins and graves to enable the criminals to kneel between them. About twelve men were assigned to the execution of each offender. Their guns were loaded by officers, and they were not permitted to examine them afterwards until they had fired.
>
> All things being in readiness, the chaplain made a prayer, the caps were pulled down over the eyes of the poor culprits, and the word of command given: "Ready! Aim! Fire!" They all fell! Some into their graves, some over their coffins. One struggled faintly and the commanding officer ordered a sergeant to approach and end his misery. He obeyed by putting the muzzle of his piece within a yard of his head, and discharging it. This quieted him perfectly!
>
> At this time one of the condemned slowly arose from his recumbent position to his knees and was assisted to his feet. His first remark was, "By God, I thought I was dead." In consequence of his youth and the peculiar circumstances of his case, he had been reprieved, but the fact was not communicated to him until this moment. He had anticipated execution with his comrades, and when the report of the guns took place, he fell with them, though not a ball touched him. The platoon assigned to him had guns given to them, which were not charged, or at least had nothing but powder in them.[99]

In the evidence regarding desertion during the War of 1812, three main issues are demonstrated:

1) Soldiers who deserted generally did so for legitimate reasons. While they may have been inspired to enlist by high thoughts of patriotic duty or may have been drafted to fight for their country, they often were not provided the means to do so and were not equipped with the basic necessities of survival. Additionally, many worried about their families back home, who had no means of support while their husbands and fathers were in far off battlefields. Add to these conditions the suffering from exposure to heat and cold, illness and

---

98. Hickey, p. 76.
99. War of 1812: People and Stories. http://www.galafilm.com/1812/e/people/ hanks_memoirs4.html. Accessed October 6, 2005.

wounds with little or no means of relief, and desertion becomes a reasonable, sensible course of action.

2) The government continued the practice started during the Revolutionary War of using the cruelest methods of dealing with deserters. The official tally of executions for desertion during this war is 181: three in 1812, 32 in 1813 and 146 in 1814.[100] How many others may have been executed without official sanction is unknown. And execution was only the cruelest and most inhumane of the punishments routinely administered: men were subjected to humiliations that are difficult to imagine, including face branding and having their ears clipped.

Those in charge continued to believe that public punishment was justified and served as a deterrent to others who might desert. The fact that the rate of desertions did not diminish throughout the war years while the number of executions increased indicates that execution was not an effective deterrent.

3) Lastly, and perhaps most importantly, the reasons for desertion during the War of 1812 were most often rooted in government and military policies and/ or inadequacies. No man would be expected to remain in the employ of a company that did not pay him as promised for long periods of time. Yet the US government expected that in this war. No employer would realistically assign a man to difficult and dangerous tasks without providing him with the tools to accomplish them. The US government, in the War of 1812, did just that.

Executing a man for deserting when he has done so rather than starve to death cannot be seen as fair. Branding his face or cropping half the hair on his head when he deserted because he had not been paid in months, and needed to support his family, shines a different light on the "disgrace" of desertion. The disgrace is not that of the deserting soldier; rather, disgrace falls upon a government and administration that starts a war (whether for a just cause or not) and attempts to wage it on the backs of men who want no part of it, and without providing them with the basic needs.

The consequences of war are astounding, and too infrequently considered. In 1814 Rev. John Strachan, of Upper Canada, offered his church as a hospital to the British army.

> Faced with ministering to large numbers of patients, a great many of whom Strachan wrote were "sadly mangled" from their battlefield injuries, and having to bury as many as six or eight souls a day during particularly grim periods, he

---

100. Hickey, p. 222.

lamented: "I wish that those who are so ready stirring up wars would traverse the field of battle after an engagement or visit the hospitals next day and they would receive a lesson that might be very beneficial to them in future."[101]

Rev. Strachan's words, spoken nearly two-hundred years ago, are as apt and true today as they were in 1814.

---

101. Benn, Carl. 2002. *Essential Histories: the War of 1812*, p. 78.

CHAPTER 3: THE MEXICAN–AMERICAN WAR

Throughout the first half of the nineteenth century America grew in economic and military power. Along with this came the concept of Manifest Destiny. This belief that it was the divine purpose of the United States to run roughshod over anyone and everyone else captured the imagination of many Americans.

Mexico, meanwhile, which had gained independence from Spain and established its own constitution in 1824, was struggling with a wide range of internal problems. Violent revolts led to changes in leadership, military leaders competed with civilians for power, and conservatives and liberals could not come to any workable consensus for a viable government.

With Mexico attempting to stabilize its government and society, its advantages and vulnerability did not go unnoticed.

> The new nation drew the eyes of the major European powers and of an expanding United States. "'[T]he weakness of Mexico and the rumors of the great wealth that lay hidden and undeveloped in the north of the country invited a race for power on the continents," notes historian David Pletcher. "Britain, France and Russia all turned their attention to Mexico, and unfortunately not with Mexico's best interests in mind."[102]

Particularly appealing were the northern provinces of Mexico, the areas now comprising Texas, California and New Mexico. Seeking to defend its territories from foreign conquest, the Mexican government encouraged citizens to settle there; but Mexicans did not appear to find any advantage in doing so. The

---

102. Christensen, Carol and Thompson Christensen. 1998. *The US Mexican War*, p. 14.

"North Americans," however, saw it as a golden opportunity for individual and collective prosperity and many of them did establish themselves there.

Mexico tried to counter this influx by encouraging Europeans to settle in Texas, offering property and exemption from taxation. These enticements brought new settlers, but they had no loyalty to Mexico and its constitution. In 1827 a small group of settlers rebelled and attempted to establish the separate nation of Fredonia. "Defeated almost immediately, the Fredonian revolt nonetheless inspired US newspapers to rally round its 'freedom fighters.'"[103]

Mexico's relations with its province of Texas continued to worsen, culminating in the convening of the Texas Convention of 1836. On March 2 the delegates at the convention voted to create an independent nation of Texas. Mexico was defeated in battle but never recognized Texas as anything but a province in rebellion.

In March of 1845, nine years after Texas declared itself independent, the US offered it statehood.

> When the United States offered Texas statehood in March 1845, Mexico responded by breaking off diplomatic relations and withdrawing its minister from Washington. Mexican governments had declared repeatedly that annexation of Texas would be an act of war. In an effort to avert the conflict, President Jose Joaquin de Herrera offered to recognize Texas as a separate nation if it chose independence over annexation to the United States. But Texas refused the offer, voting on July 4, 1845 to become the twenty-eighth state in the Union.[104]

In addition to the United States' annexation of Texas, several other factors conspired to make war inevitable. First were those internal to Mexico. Herrera, who had been in office for only a short time, had been named president after the overthrow of Antonio Lopez de Santa Anna who had been an extremely controversial leader. During the election of 1845 Herrera was opposed by several candidates and although he won, he was never able to establish a successful government.

Mexico faced severe economic and social problems. Herrera knew that a war with the United States would only worsen them. Yet he received no support from the Mexican Congress in his efforts to avoid war. Any overture toward peace with the United States, including the possibility of negotiations, put him and his government at risk of being overthrown.

---

103. Christensen, p. 19. This theme of supporting every scurrilous guerrilla movement that seems to have some advantage, for the United States has continued it into the twenty-first century. See chapter 13 Summary and Analysis.

104. Christensen, p. 46.

Another major factor was lodged in America's White House. "President Polk held the niceties of diplomacy in contempt."[105] With this attitude, war with Mexico was only a matter of time.

In Mexico, General Mariano Parades was a popular and ambitious member of the military class. In 1844 he deposed Santa Anna. Now, with the crisis with the United States brewing, and Herrera wanting to avoid war if at all possible, the powerful Parades marched his troops into the capital. Faced with the real possibility of civil war, President Herrera resigned, giving the government to Parades.

Now in power, Parades wanted nothing short of an immediate military victory. He would not back down, as Herrera had wanted. With Parades' obstinacy and Polk's arrogance there was no way of avoiding war. In January 1846, the US declared war on Mexico.

As in America's earlier wars, desertion rates in the Mexican–American war were high; in fact they approached the highest records of previous wars.[106] Additionally, as with previous wars, it is difficult to obtain an accurate number of the rate of desertion, partly because of different ways of measuring it.

There are three ways in which the rate of desertion is generally discussed. "The first is to compare the number of desertions to the aggregate strength of the army, the second is to compare it to the number of enlisted men in the service, and the third is to compare it to the number of enlistments during the period."[107] With this in mind, the following estimates are revealing. From a total of 26,992 enlisted soldiers, 2,849 deserted during the war. The rate of volunteers who deserted — 3,900 out of 59,000 — was somewhat less.[108] Another estimate puts the total at 14%.[109] Other estimates indicate that anywhere from 9,000 to 10,800 soldiers deserted.[110] "Of these, less than 100 were actually court-martialed and convicted.[111] Regardless of which count is most accurate, there can be no

---

105. Christensen, p. 49.

106. Because of inaccurate and limited records, the exact number of desertions is unknown.

107. McDermott, John D. "Were They Really Rogues? Desertion in the Nineteenth-Century US Army." *Nebraska History.* Winter 1997. Vol. 78, No. 4, p. 166.

108. Foos, p. 2002. *A Short, Offhand Killing Affair*, p.109

109. McDermott, John D. "Were They Really Rogues? Desertion in the Nineteenth-Century US Army." *Nebraska History.* Winter 1997. Vol. 78, No. 4, p. 166.

110. King, Rosemary. 2000. Border Crossings in the Mexican American War. *Bilingual Review, Vol. 25*, p. 1.

111. Hogan, Michael. 1997. *The Irish Soldiers of Mexico,* p. 19.

question that desertion was a significant issue during the Mexican–American War.

The reasons for this discrepancy between the volunteer force and the "regular" army become clear once the significant differences between the two forces are understood. In volunteer troops, officers were selected by popular mandate. Under these circumstances, the officers were far more likely to treat the enlisted men as citizens and as social equals. While this was perceived to have had detrimental effects on the effectiveness of the volunteer forces, it probably contributed to a reduced desertion rate among them.

Yet one must ask: is a military force effective if morale is so low as to contribute to a high desertion rate? It would seem that having soldiers remain present and willing to fight as directed would be more effective than a more highly trained force, a large portion of which must be expected to be absent at any time.

Another significant difference was the ability of volunteers to leave the military at will.

> A fundamental privilege of the volunteer, was the right to abrogate his oath of service if he felt the terms of that service did not live up to promised standards. Regular army deserters went about with a bounty on their heads, payable to anyone willing and able to turn them in. Volunteers in most cases could desert with impunity.[112]

Soldiers of the regular army had no legal means of redress for any injustices or difficulties they experienced. Desertion was their only option.

The reasons for desertion were many, and as will be seen they did not differ significantly from those of the earlier US wars. They included the following:

- Harsh conditions;
- Poor leadership;
- Corporal punishment;
- Lack of belief in the cause;
- Lack of basic rights as American citizens;
- Poor wages; and
- Discrimination.

Each of these factors will be examined separately, but it is important to recognize that in many cases there were overlapping causes that added up to persuade the men that desertion was the only rational choice open to them. A study of each condition follows.

---

112. Foos, pp. 100-101.

HARSH CONDITIONS

In any war the foot soldier endures unspeakable hardships. Soldiers in the Mexican–American War fared no better. Desertions began even before war was declared. Because of the difficulties in camp, desertions were constant throughout the prewar months. Illness was rampant on the battlefield; men who did not die from sickness were often left permanently debilitated by it. At one time shortly before the declaration of war, illness, mainly dysentery and fevers, was so prevalent that one-sixth of the soldiers were on sick report, and approximately one-half suffered from some degree of illness

That the men were susceptible to these and other illness is not surprising considering the conditions under which they lived. "The tents provided by the Quartermaster were worn and rotted and had been condemned by a board of survey."[113] In addition, the Quartermaster had neglected to provide floors for them, requiring the men to sleep on the ground. Weather conditions were such that the temperature could drop from ninety degrees to below freezing in a matter of hours. Soldiers slept in mud or on frozen ground. There was little wood available for fires, and the men were without horses or mules to carry what could be found.

"General Winfield Scott observed of the volunteers that they neglected basic camp routine, including trenching, stacking of arms and the securing of dry bedding. Scott claimed that the volunteers 'lose or waste their clothing, lie down wet or on wet ground — fatal to health....'"[114] As indicated by General Scott, the health of the soldiers was compromised not only by the lack of supplies, but also by the individual neglect of the soldiers. Volunteers had a more democratic form of organization, and in general were less disciplined, less well-organized, and apparently lacked leaders willing or able to appropriately guide or motivate them to better behaviors.

The unsanitary conditions of service meant that almost as many men fell to smallpox, yellow fever, cholera, dysentery, and typhoid as to enemy bullets.[115]

With suffering and certain death facing them, often before they ever set foot on the battlefield, desertion for many of these soldiers was a reasonable, sensible decision.

---

113. Foos, p. 18.
114. Foos, p. 90.
115. Cramer, Marc. 1996. "The Fighting Irish of Mexico," *America*, Vol. 48, p. 1.

Some soldiers were sent to remote outposts where their tasks consisted of hard labor: building bridges, hewing wood, quarrying stone, etc. For many recruits this was not what they expected when they enlisted to "defend the country," and these assignments were a rude awakening.

"One of their officers noted that 'great complaint is made that the volunteers will scarcely work; daily labor was not embraced in their conception of war; it goes some way to prove that democracy and discipline — of the military sort — are not entirely congenial.'"[116] It seems somewhat incongruous that regulars, who were expected to perform these and any other duties as ordered, were disdained by many, yet the volunteers were more highly respected and even granted the right to depart from the military at any time.

POOR LEADERSHIP

Leadership problems plagued the army for a variety of reasons. They appeared to start close to the top.

> A US Army lieutenant, present on the Rio Grande in the months leading up to the outbreak of war, denounced the harsh conditions for officers and men. He accused the War Department and the administration of depraved indifference toward the troops. Not having seen a paymaster in many months, they were compelled to borrow from "Shylocks in search of victims that pollute the camp."[117]

In addition, rapid promotion of officers came as a result of education, not ability. Thus, unqualified men found themselves in positions of leadership for which they had education but no experience and little ability. Coupled with this were the class differences that were prevalent at the time. Although an officer's salary did not come close to matching that of the social elite, his education allowed him to be considered a gentleman.This enabled officers to move in the most popular circles of wealthy society during peacetime. Once in the field, these same men were forced by necessity out of the elite circles to which they'd quickly become accustomed, and thrown into almost constant personal contact with enlisted men, who they considered their social and economic inferiors.

This feeling of superiority was not lost on the enlisted men. Officers missed few opportunities to remind recruits of their inferior position in society, and they were clearly held in disdain. "It was generally accepted among the elite

---

116. Foos, p. 89
117. Foos, p. 19.

political class that regular soldiers constituted a servile and degraded class of men, who fought for pay and not out of patriotism."[118] It may be true that many men enlisted for the promised financial benefits, as men have done since professional armies first began and as they are still doing in the Iraq War. But those who held them in such contempt were often members of the elite political class who did not see any need for they themselves to demonstrate their patriotism by military service.

Individual leaders also demonstrated their incompetence, often repeatedly. One example is Colonel William S. Harney. The colonel had been reprimanded twice for disobeying orders. In addition, he had a reputation as an arrogant and aggressive officer. At one point he was recalled to Washington for court martial as a result of disobeying a direct order from his commander. His actions at the battle of Cerro Gordo on April 16 demonstrate his disregard for the men under his command.

> He continued his attack beyond the point to which he had been ordered, and then was pinned down. Fortunately for him and his men, when darkness fell he was able to withdraw. Harney seemed to have a penchant for disobeying orders. He appeared to have learned nothing from the escapade, which brought him trouble in Washington. Nor would this be the last time that he placed his men in jeopardy.[119]

Also,

> [c]ourt martials regularly doled out whippings and other corporal punishments and ritual humiliations to common soldiers, and this severity maintained the unbridgeable social gulf between officer and enlisted man.[120]

The attitude of some officers was described by a soldier from Texas. "[I]n our Texas war, an officer was no better than a private...but here if we speak to one of these d — — -d regulars who has a strap on his shirt or one of our own officers familiarly or pretend to dispute his word or differ with him we are treated like dogs. Bucked, bucked sir, and I assure you Texans will not be bucked."[121]

Without a deep sense of trust and commitment between officer and soldier there will be no sense of loyalty to the officer. Men in the artificial context of the field of battle are equals in a deeper sense than might be found in most other situations. If this equality is not recognized by those mandated to

---

118. Foos, p. 33.
119. Hogan, p. 69.
120. Foos, p. 22.
121. Foos, p. 90.

lead, their leadership will never be accepted by those who are to follow. Desertion in such a case becomes the only alternative for many.

It should be noted that incompetence and arrogance were not restricted to US military leadership. Santa Anna, who rose to and fell from power numerous times during his long political career, often allowed bravado or wishful thinking to cloud his judgment. Yet he seemed to have at the forefront of his mind the welfare of the men who served under him. Early in 1847, when a loan he requested from the Catholic Church to supply his army was granted but for a lower amount than requested, "he actually provided a large amount of his own money for the provisioning and clothing of his men."[122] Such an action, if representative of his general method of operation, may also have motivated some American soldiers to desert to the Mexican side.

Corporal Punishment

Punishment for desertion during the Mexican–American War reached new heights in cruelty.

> A favorite practice [of officers punishing captured deserters] was bucking, that is, tying a soldier in a cramped position, with a wooden pole running under his knees and through his elbows; he could be left like this for hours, sometimes at intervals over several consecutive days. Deserters and other serious offenders were made to wear iron collars with spikes, or a ball and chain, and subjected to hard labor. Desertion during wartime was punishable by hanging, but more commonly by a combination of branding, flogging and imprisonment.[123] [And] Regular army officers were notoriously quick to resort to the lash or other humiliating physical punishments against miscreant soldiers.[124]

Other punishments included having the soldier lie spread eagle in the blazing sun, sometimes for several days in a row. Face branding was a popular punishment: "HD" for habitual drunkards, "W" for anyone who was, by some arbitrarily-determined standard, deemed worthless, and a two-inch "D" for deserters. These marks remained for life.

A main duty of officers was the discipline of soldiers. This they took seriously, not hesitating to implement the most draconian methods as described above. The following example was not uncommon: "One of our Boston recruits

---

122. Hogan, p. 47.
123. Foos, p. 25.
124. Foos, p. 13.

was gagged with a bayonet, his teeth broke and loosened, and his mouth cut severely."[125] This sounds more like an injury inflicted by an enemy than a disciplinary measure from the soldier's own commanding officer.

The soldiers created a song of sorts that described their feelings about the cruelty they witnessed and experienced:

> Sergeant, buck him and gag him, our officers cry,
>
> For each trifling offense which they happen to spy,
>
> Till with bucking and gagging of Dick, Pat, and Bill,
>
> Faith, the Mexicans' ranks they have helped to fill.[126]

Obviously, soldiers themselves were not blind to the link between excessive corporal punishment and desertion to the enemy side. Some asserted that "[a]ristocratic, cruel behavior was the source of the troubled state of the army, not individual recruits."[127]

The general (if vague and unconvincing) notion that desertion is the result of a character flaw on the part of the man who deserts is here contradicted once again. Under such conditions, desertion is a show of strength of character, not weakness. It is not a character flaw to leave cruel, unjust circumstances when such behaviors are inflicted upon men who have chosen, either freely or under duress, to serve their country in the military.

LACK OF BELIEF IN THE CAUSE

Perhaps more than in any previous war, in the Mexican–American War lack of belief in the cause was a major reason for deserting. The war was not universally supported; Ulysses S. Grant — later US president — referred to it as "the most unjust war ever waged by a stronger against a weaker nation."[128] Abraham Lincoln and Henry David Thoreau were also vocal opponents, and a strong anti-war sentiment was active throughout the country, although it never attained a majority status.

Atrocities perpetrated by the Americans on Mexican civilians also led to desertions. General Winfield Scott's troops engaged in various unspeakable cru-

---

125. Foos, p. 104.
126. Cramer, Marc. 1996 "The Fighting Irish of Mexico." Cramer, Marc. *America*, Vol. 48, p. 1.
127. Foos, p. 104.
128. Hogan, p. 20.

elties. "His men would also engage in many reprehensible acts and depredations against Mexican civilians; Mexican women would be assaulted; churches and Catholic convents would be bombed and looted."[129]

Before invading Veracruz, Scott bombed the city for six days, sending approximately 1,340 shells raining down on it every 24 hours. Of the estimated 1,100 Mexicans killed, at least 500 were civilians. During this prolonged period of bombing, foreign consuls and the bishop begged for a reprieve so that women, children and foreign nationals could be safely evacuated. However, their pleas had no visible impact on Scott, who continued the bombing with no pause.

This bombardment was widely reported in the US and Europe and gave strength to the American peace movement. Thoreau refused to pay taxes and later wrote "Civil Disobedience" based on the slaughter of Veracruz.

Desertion during this war took a different turn. "The distinctive crime of the Mexican War, however, was desertion to the enemy, a crime...that suggested forces of attraction — on the part of the enemy — as well as the negative factors that drove recruits away from the US Army."[130] The San Patricios, an American battalion that deserted to the Mexican side, is described in detail in the section on discrimination below.

LACK OF BASIC RIGHTS AS AMERICAN CITIZENS

One fundamental irony has plagued the US fighting forces since the American Revolution and still plagues the US military to this day. Fighting in the name of "liberty," those in the military have to forego their own liberties for the duration of their term of service.

This problem manifested itself in several ways during the Mexican–American war, as it does in each war and in peacetime.

A recruit from Louisiana stated the following: "We are worse off than slaves; confined within narrow walls; very few liberties allowed us. There is a great deal to be seen in this city and much to please the fancy of any free man; but as a soldier I can appreciate nothing."[131] Had this young soldier been a civilian, a variety of entertainments and experiences would have awaited him while vis-

---

129. Hogan, p. 63.
130. Foos, p. 105.
131. Foos, p. 103.

iting Mexico City. Apparently he felt these could be accomplished in safety, but as a soldier they were all forbidden.

In more important ways than entertainment were soldiers during the Mexican–American war deprived of rights and privileges that their civilian counterparts enjoyed. "The army tried to keep them isolated as much as possible from mainstream society, with its expectations of political and economic rights."[132] Such rights are for American citizens, not American soldiers.

During the Mexican–American war, professional "camp followers" appeared with great frequency. These included gamblers, prostitutes, sellers of liquor, and others who preyed upon the soldiers, taking advantage of their loneliness, boredom and the poor conditions under which they lived. In at least one reported situation, "[t]hese professional camp followers robbed, assaulted, and murdered soldiers, and General [Zachary] Taylor was unable to do much to disperse them, it being a point of military law that civilian crimes be handled by a civil authority. The soldiers, too, were constrained from taking vengeance against the camp followers, by the disciplinary strictures of their service."[133]

The extreme nature of this deprivation of rights is seen when army recruits are compared to so-called 'rented' slaves and others who were hired by the army as laborers. The "slaves were at least separated from the direct paternalism of their owners, and...could engage in various economic activities. The soldiers, on the other hand, were in a close paternal relationship with their officers and were subject at any time to perform any task requested of them, or to endure corporal punishment."[134]

Basic rights afforded US citizens were not granted to soldiers during this period of time. One soldier described the situation succinctly:

> In fact, throughout the American service generally, desertion...is not looked at in the light of a crime by the soldier. This is principally owing to the conviction that they are not treated justly. No great amount of logic is required to perceive that a contract, to be binding must bind both parties; but is would take a good deal to convince the soldier, that he is bound to observe an oath which he has taken under certain implied conditions, which he finds are not observed.[135]

---

132. Foos, p. 24.
133. Foos, p. 18.
134. Foos, p. 23 – 24.
135. Hogan, p. 134.

POOR WAGES

In the country's earlier wars, pay for those who were said to be defending the country had always been insufficient for more than bare existence; in this regard nothing had changed during the Mexican–American war. One report states the following:

> Two deserters, fed up with the abysmal conditions in the Massachusetts Regiment made a difficult trek across the wastes of the Nueces River country to Galveston. "After reaching Galveston, they found Yankees in such demand that they easily obtained employment, one as a school-master, at $60 per month, and the other as a manual laborer, at $45." The choice of wages over the marginal honor attendant upon remaining with their comrades was quite clear, and the information on which to base such a decision readily available for most recruits. The Massachusetts papers circulated this report with little comment, and on the face of the report the deserters were portrayed as having made a sound and sensible choice.[136]

In discussing the enticements that Mexico offered to potential American deserters (money, land, positions of authority in the military), Paul Foos points out that "Most of the enticements held out to the deserters were as illusory as the advance pay and bonuses held out by the US volunteer recruiters."[137] When money is offered for enlisting but is not paid, one must ask if the recruit is obligated to keep his part of the contract. Soldiers opting to desert to the Mexican side could not have known that many Mexican promises were as empty as American ones.

In 1847 there were rumors that wages for privates would be raised to $10.00 a month. This was coupled with uncertainty about the expected length of service. When the wage was confirmed at $7.00 a month, talk of desertion became rampant. How many men deserted as a result of this is not known.

DISCRIMINATION

Religious discrimination against Catholics was all but an accepted military policy during the Mexican–American War. "The army's semiofficial discountenancing of Catholics was one of many grievances soldiers bore, and it was no doubt a factor in desertions."[138] The US military seemed to view the Mex-

---

136. Foos, p. 101.
137. Foos, p. 107.
138. Foos, p. 107.

icans as a fundamentally immoral race and blamed their immorality on the fact that the Catholic Church was the dominant religion of the nation. Some Catholics too bought into this concept, believing that the Catholic Church in Mexico could only be reformed with American Catholic oversight.[139] With this view dominating, crimes against Catholic clergymen and church buildings were rampant, and seldom successfully prosecuted.

Forced attendance at Protestant services also caused problems. "It was common practice to compel soldiers to attend religious service in the army, the chaplain invariably being a Protestant. The blatant unconstitutionality of this practice was slyly evaded in the article of war that 'earnestly recommended' rather than compelled officers and enlisted men to attend divine service."[140]

At this time in history, discrimination against Catholics seemed to be at least the semiofficial policy of the military. Early in the war, while at least one-third of soldiers in the regular army were Catholic, there were no Catholic chaplains. This policy appears to have been at the root of the mass desertion of the San Patricio Battalion. A study of this battalion is included below.

A large number of US army recruits were recent Irish immigrants who had come to America seeking a better life. In the Fifth Regiment of General Zachary Taylor there was an obscure, uneducated private, born Sean O'Raghailligh. However, using the more American version of his name he was better known as John Riley. Riley was to lead a courageous but ill-fated band of US soldiers who deserted to the Mexican side.

The discrimination against Catholics, especially Irish Catholics, in the military must be seen in the context of feelings within the United States.

> The 1830s saw the spread of a particularly vehement brand of xenophobia throughout the United States, fostering an intense distrust of immigrants and a dislike of Roman Catholicism that often culminated in anti-Catholic riots and church burnings in New England. Irish immigrants were openly discriminated against, looked down upon, and labeled "Micks." Nowhere was discrimination more evident than in the armed forces, where an Irishman's chances of becoming an officer were virtually nil.[141]

Yet many Irish Catholic immigrants did enlist, either because they didn't realize the extent of the discrimination or because they needed a job, any job, and this was the one they could get. But it did not take long for them to experience violent persecutions from the men and officers with whom they had com-

---

139. Foos, p. 129.
140. Foos, p. 26.
141. Cramer, Marc, p. 1.

mitted to serve. In addition, the Mexicans offered soldiers double the wages of their American counterparts.[142]

The Irish had come to the US in the first place to escape the cruel oppression of the British government. Many of those who were soldiers during the Mexican–American war saw their newly-adopted nation treating the Mexican people in the same cruel, repressive manner from which they themselves had escaped.

> Soon after enlisting in the US army the San Patricios began to see they were fighting on the side on injustice. They saw the United States carrying out a huge, greedy and cruel land grab, reminiscent of the English occupation of Ireland. The killing, looting, rape and senseless destroying of Mexican civilian property reminded them of the British injustice back in Ireland.[143]

As a result, John Riley led a band of about fifty deserters that eventually swelled to a number of between 200 and 800 — not all of them Irish — forming the San Patricios Battalion.

While the San Patricios are often said to have been mostly Irish, this is probably a result of the prominence of Mr. Riley. The facts do not support the idea that the battalion members were exclusively or even predominantly Irish. Robert R. Miller, a historian on the San Patricio Battalion "looked at a sample of 103 known members of the battalion and found only two-fifths (40) to be Irish born."[144] This would indicate that discrimination against Irish Catholics was hardly the only factor that led to these desertions. The following table lists the birthplaces of the sample examined by Miller.[145]

Country	Number	Percent
Ireland	40	39
United States	22	21
German states	14	13
Scotland	7	7
Mexico	7	7
England	4	4
Great Britain	3	3
Canada	2	2
France	1	1
Italy	1	1
Spanish Florida	1	1
Poland	1	1

---

142. Cramer, Marc, p. 1.
143. Why they defected; http://www.vivasancarlos.com/defected.html. Accessed July 3, 2005.
144. Foos, p. 108.

It appears, however, that America's leaders needed to present some palatable explanation for the desertions of these men, since this represented something that went far beyond the usual seemingly few, isolated cases of desertion. Labeling them as Irish immigrants, "foreigners" with no real loyalty to America, seems to have satisfied the public need for an easy explanation that did not place any blame on the United States.

Mr. Riley, prior to the official outbreak of the war, quickly exchanged his US private's uniform for that of a Mexican officer. "It is worth noting that Riley had earned seven dollars per month as an American private, whereas his pay as a Mexican lieutenant would be fifty-seven dollars monthly."[146] The San Patricios battalion quickly became known as one of the most courageous and efficient organizations on the Mexican side.

The American view of the San Patricios Battalion is far different from the Mexican one. US historical accounts generally refer to the men comprising that battalion as turncoats, traitors, defectors, deserters or drunkards. Regardless of the label affixed, America discounts the bravery and expertise in the art of soldiering that they demonstrated. Yet the evidence, some of it provided by American officers, tells a different story.

Following a particularly cruel slaughter by Texas volunteers, many American soldiers deserted, some to the Mexican side. Major Luther Giddings of the Ohio volunteers commented on fifty Americans who deserted at Monterrey. Said he: "They were to serve with a courage and fidelity in [the Mexican ranks] that they never exhibited in ours."[147]

In early 1847, Santa Anna sought to surprise the American forces at Agua Nueva. His soldiers marched for days with little food or water, and towards the end of the trek, they marched forty-five miles in twenty-four hours, a remarkable feat for men who are rested and well fed, but an incredible one for those who are starving and near exhaustion. When the battle finally started (at a different location because the Americans had moved to a more defensible position), the United States "attacks on the San Patricio gun emplacements on February 23, though steady and concentrated by the Fourth artillery, were unsuccessful. The San Patricio fire, on the other hand, was accurate and deadly."[148] The American

145. Miller. Robert Ryal. 1989. *Shamrock and Sword: The Saint Patrick's Battalion in the US – Mexican War*, p. 175.
146. Miller, pp. 29 – 31.
147. Hogan, p. 45.
148. Hogan, p. 49.

forces were decimated. Following this battle, approximately 1,500 Americans deserted.

Despite sustaining heavy losses in this and other battles, the number of San Patricios grew until it consisted of two companies by August, 1847. However, they were not sufficient in size or strength to be victorious in the end; they were defeated at the Battle of Churubusco on August 20, 1847. Although they reformed briefly, they never regained their previous numbers and strength.

The cruelty of the treatment they received after their final capture just before the end of the war is exemplified by the trials and sentencing of the surviving members of the San Patricio Battalion.

General Scott arranged two courts-martial and placed in charge of the first Brevet Colonel John Garland; the second was presided over by a Colonel Bennet Riley (no known relation to John Riley). The notorious Colonel Riley was put in charge of executions. All three men were Catholic, at least in name, and all were of Irish descent, although none were immigrants. Scott may have put these men in charge at least partially to present a façade of fairness to the trials.

During the trial, no defense counsel was provided to the prisoners. While counsel is not required it was, at this time, sometimes provided in capital cases. The defendants were left to defend themselves as best they could.

Several used drunkenness as a defense. Although in modern American society this is seldom accepted, it was seen as a legal defense during the time of the Mexican–American War.[149] It appears that the San Patricio defendants used it as a defense in the hope of getting a lighter sentence. "Unfortunately," to all appearances, "the fate of the San Patricios was sealed before they ever set foot in the courtroom."[150]

On September 10, 1847, Riley was whipped with fifty lashes and branded with a two-inch " 'D' on both sides of his face, scarring him for life. In the distance, fifty of Riley's soldiers, mostly Irishmen like himself, looked on with fear, one eye on Riley and the other on the gallows."[151] In all, fourteen men were flogged and branded on that day.

For those observing these punishments — the hangings, floggings and brandings — the horror and disgust were obvious. "The smell of burning flesh and the mangled and bloody back of the San Patricios revolted Captain [George]

---

149. Hogan, p. 165.
150. Hogan, p. 167.
151. Cramer, Marc. 1996, p. 1.

Davis, General Scott's aide-de-camp...."[152] One Mexican editorial read as follows: "Mexicans: these are the men that call us barbarians and tell us that they have come to civilize us. These men who have sacked our homes, taken our daughters from their families, camped in our holy burial places.... May they be damned by all Christians, as they are by God."[153]

Thirty of the remaining men slated for execution were singled out for particular torment under the direction of the notorious Colonel Harney. In his thirty years as a soldier, Harney had earned a well-deserved reputation for brutality.

> During the Indian Wars he was charged with raping Indian girls at night and then hanging them the next morning after he had taken his pleasure. In St. Louis, Missouri, he was indicted by a civilian court for the brutal beating of a female slave that resulted in her death. The choice of Harney as executioner of the San Patricios seemed calculated by the American high command to inflict brutal reprisals on the Irish Catholic soldiers. Harney would not disappoint them.[154]

On September 13, 1847, at dawn, Harney ordered the thirty remaining prisoners to be brought forward. They stood on wagons with nooses placed around their necks. This included one man who had lost both legs and was unable to walk to his own execution. The site of these executions was within viewing distance of the site where the final battle — the outcome of which could not have been in doubt — was to be fought. There the sentenced soldiers watched until finally, at 9:30, the US victors raised the American flag atop Chapultepec Castle. At that point the order was given, the wagons were pulled away and the men were all hanged.[155]

It must be remembered that the San Patricios had been standing, bound hand and foot, each with his head in a noose, for nearly four hours in the burning Mexican sun. When Harney finally gave the order for the hangings to proceed, such was the relief that their sufferings were finally at an end that "some of the men actually cheered as the nooses tightened and the wagons pulled away."[156]

One American biographer put a different, and most unusual, interpretation to their dying cheer. "Just before the traps were sprung, with their last breath in

152. Hogan, p. 177.

153. Hogan, p. 177.

154. Hogan, Michael. The Irish Soldiers of Mexico. http://www.crisismagazine.com/hogan.htm. Accessed on July 10, 2005.

155. King, Rosemary. 2000. Border Crossing in the Mexican American War. *Bilingual Review*, Vol. 25.

156. Hogan, p. 187.

a shout that was heard across the valley, they cheered the flag they had betrayed."[157] There were, of course, no traps to spring; the men were standing on wagons that pulled away when the order was given, leaving them hanging from the beam erected for that purpose. Their shout could certainly not have been heard "across the valley" where heavy fighting continued at the northern end of Chapultepec Park. And since many of the San Patricios had deserted the American army and joined the Mexicans because they believed in the cause for which Mexico was fighting, and then had witnessed the unspeakable brutality inflicted on their comrades, and awaited their own cruel fate, it is difficult to understand how, with their dying breaths, they would cheer their killers.

This brutal sentencing was in violation of the Articles of War and William De Hart's Observations on Military Law, and the Constitution and the Practice of Courts-Martial (1847) that governed courts-martial at that time. Execution for deserters during war at this time was proscribed as death by firing squad; hanging was only for spies or for those committing crimes against civilians, like Harney himself.

For those who deserted before the declaration of war — as many of the San Patricios did — permissible sentencing included only one of the following: branding at the hip, fifty lashes, or confinement at hard labor. Several of the San Patricios received in excess of fifty lashes "until their backs had the appearance of raw beef, the blood oozing from every stripe," according to one American witness,[158] in addition to then being executed. Prompt carrying out of the sentence was also demanded.

> The sentence of the court, according to the Articles of War, should always be carried out promptly. "To prolong the punishment beyond the usual time would be highly improper, and subject the officer who authorized or caused such to be done to charges." In the case of the last of group of 30 San Patricios to be hanged, this Article of War was cavalierly ignored.[159]

Military justice — a euphemism for human injustice — continued; Harney, with his already-disgraceful background and his flagrant violation of the Articles of War through the unspeakable cruelty toward the executed prisoners, was not punished. Rather, within a month he had been promoted to the rank of Brigadier

---

157. Hogan," p. 187.
158. The Irish Soldiers of Mexico. Michael Hogan. http://www.crisismagazine.com/hogan.htm. Accessed on July 10, 2005.
159. The Irish Soldiers of Mexico. Michael Hogan. http://www.crisismagazine.com/hogan.htm. Accessed on July 10, 2005.

General and he participated prominently in a triumphant march into Mexico City.

As noted earlier, American and Mexican perspectives on the San Patricios are diametrically different. In the US they are forgotten, or seen as obscure deserters, worthy of nothing but a shameful footnote in the glorious history of the Mexican–American War. To the Mexicans, however, they are national heroes and are revered to this day.

As has been shown, many of the reasons for desertion that were seen in America's earlier wars were still prevalent in the Mexican–American War. Poor conditions have plagued the US military from the American War for Independence to today; the government has either been unwilling or unable to rectify these conditions. During the Mexican–American War — a clearly imperialist conflict — it appears that as long as the military had sufficient numbers of men to replace those who died, the motivation to improve the soldiers' conditions simply did not exist.

Cruel, inhuman corporal punishments for the most minor infractions have also been a hallmark of the military since the American Revolution. That these draconian practices have not prevented the alleged crimes they purport to punish, and that in fact they lead to desertion, should indicate clearly that they are not effective.

The fundamental problem of the military's removal of basic rights from its soldiers is also an old story, and one that continues to be told today. Those who go to war because they have been persuaded that they are fighting for democracy and freedom (regardless of whether the war being waged has anything to do with those virtues) have every right to expect democracy and freedom for themselves. Many fail to recognize, in advance, the extent of the sacrifice they are making, especially in terms of the rights they have involuntarily surrendered upon entrance into the US military, and they desert seeking to regain those freedoms.

Added to these causes of desertion was the blatant discrimination that foreign-born Americans, and not only Catholics, were subjected to; many of them ended up identifying with the Mexicans whom they perceived as victims of American oppression.

The men who deserted from the US military during the Mexican–American war cannot be seen as cowards or traitors. Those who had signed up for a paid job went to the employer who offered to pay more. Those who were inspired to fight for their values learned that their faith had been misplaced; they felt betrayed by the US. Under the circumstances, they made reasoned decisions.

CHAPTER 4: THE CIVIL WAR

One cannot discuss the causes of the American Civil War without including slavery as a major factor. But slavery must be viewed in the context of the larger issues that led to the war. Rivalry and hostility between the North and South had their roots in the early days of colonization, and these factors eventually led to war.

During the Constitutional Convention of 1787, because of the great disparity in the size of the white population in Northern and Southern states, it appeared that the North would have far more representatives in Congress. This was not acceptable to the South. In order to ensure equal representation with the Northern states, the South eventually accepted the three-fifths compromise, in which five slaves were counted as three free men. This helped to achieve a representative balance between North and South.[160] That white, slave-owing Southerners were willing to agree to this compromise despite their firmly held belief that African-Americans were somehow less human than they, and unworthy of full citizenship, demonstrates how anxious they were to achieve equal representation with the North. It also indicates the rivalry that existed between the North and the South for nearly eighty years prior to the Civil War. The years from 1787 to the outbreak of hostilities saw no lessening of these tensions.

---

160. Fehrenbacher, Don E. and Ward M. Mcafee. *The Slaveholding Republic: An Account of the United States Government's Relations to Slavery*, p. 24.

As the population of the country shifted in the first half of the nineteenth century, Northern population increased as dramatically and Southern population decreased. "In 1800 half of the population of the United States had lived in the South. But by 1850 only a third lived there and the disparity continued to widen."[161] This was due at least partly to the increased industrialization of the North; people from the South went North for employment, and immigrants chose Northern states for the same reason. Because of this, representation of Southern states in the House of Representatives dwindled while Northern representation — and therefore power — increased.

In the presidential election year of 1860, Stephen Douglas was the nominee of the Democratic Party. The nomination of Douglas, a Northerner, was rejected by the Southern states, which nominated Kentucky Senator John Breckenridge. This action alone demonstrates the lack of unity in the country during this volatile period: the South viewed itself as sufficiently independent to nominate its own candidate.

The Republicans nominated what might be seen as a compromise candidate, Abraham Lincoln. Candidate Lincoln did not believe that the government could outlaw slavery, but could do whatever possible to prevent its spread. For the South, any law regulating slavery was viewed as a threat to the Southern economy; slaves worked the cotton fields and were seen as necessary for this work. Northerners for the most part were not concerned about the morality of slave ownership and shared the perspective of economic utility, despite a small but vocal abolitionist movement in the North. Because of Lincoln's position on this important issue, when he was nominated South Carolina announced that it would secede from the Union if he were elected.

Lincoln was elected and on December 20, 1860, South Carolina seceded from the Union. Within one month, Mississippi, Alabama, Florida, Texas, Georgia and Louisiana followed.

On April 12, 1861, weeks after Lincoln's inauguration, the first shots of the Civil War were fired. A Federal ship on its way to resupply Fort Sumter was fired upon by the Rebels. Lincoln called for 75,000 troops. Tennessee, Virginia and Arkansas immediately chose sides and left the Union. The Civil War had begun.

---

161. Scott, John. 2005. Justifications for War. http://www.v7n.com/forums/showthread.php?t=18431&page=1 Accessed October 21, 2005.

Almost from the start desertion was a problem for the Union.[162] "During the Civil War the 'unconquerable desire' of men to return to their homes was observed on a massive scale."[163] It is impossible to determine with close accuracy the number of soldiers who deserted from the Union Army. Part of the reason stems from the difficulty of knowing exactly how many men enlisted. The total number of enlistments during the war has been estimated at 2.8 million,[164] but probably at least half a million were reenlistments.[165]

US Provost Marshal General James Fry estimated that there were approximately 200,000 deserters between 1863 and 1865. This is deserters and not desertions; the number of desertions would necessarily be much higher since many men deserted multiple times.[166] Fry himself acknowledged that the records at his disposal were far from accurate.

A report issued shortly after the First World War states that the highest desertion rate in US history occurred during the Civil War; in 1865, according to this report, the desertion rate was 45%.[167] One of the many difficulties in determining an actual number is the impossible task of distinguishing who actually deserted and who was absent due to another, legitimate, reason. And even within this context there are more difficulties.

Many men went on leave authorized by company officers who had no right to authorize leave.[168] Would they be considered deserters, when it was their understanding that leave had been granted, and they did not know that their authorization was invalid? Another question concerns ill and injured soldiers. Many men who became sick or were injured on the march simply went home. Of those, some returned to the battlefield after their convalescence and some did not. Would those who did return properly be considered deserters during their time at home? Other soldiers with properly authorized furloughs never returned from them. At what point would they be classified as deserters? These questions

---

162. Desertion was also a major issue for the Confederacy, but that is beyond the scope of this work.
163. Moore, William. 1975. *The Thin Yellow Line*, p. 158.
164. Heitman, Francis B. *Historical Register and Dictionary of the United States Army*, Vol 2. Wash, DC: GPO 1903. RefColl, p. 285.
165. Livermore, Thomas L. 1957. *Numbers & Losses in the Civil War in America, 1861-65.* Bloomington: Indiana UP, 1957. E491L78, RefColl, p. 1
166. Cashin, Joan E. 2002. *The War was You and Me*, p. 264.
167. Humber, Robert C. 1942. Absences and Desertions During the First World War. *A.W.C. Historical Section, Study No. 34*, p. 6.
168. Lonn, Ella. 1998. *Desertion During the Civil War*, p. 145.

greatly compound the difficulty of tracking the number of deserters during the Civil War.

Records from the war indicate that desertion rates averaged 5,500 per month, peaking at 10,692 in October 1864.[169] So, while the exactness of these numbers cannot be confirmed, the evidence suggests that desertion presented a major problem to the Lincoln administration during the Civil War.

Pinpointing the official policy of the US government pertaining to desertion during the Civil War is also difficult. The policy changed repeatedly depending on varying circumstances (See Table 1 at chapter end). According to policy, desertion was a capital offense; that never changed but it was seldom enforced. Execution was only one of several possible punishments. Desertion so severely depleted the armed forces that capturing the deserters and forcing them back into military service was seen as preferable to executing them.

In 1861, the Lincoln administration offered $30.00 to anyone who apprehended a deserter. Desertion was rampant and that amount was soon reduced to $5.00, presumably as an economy measure. However, it was soon after raised again, to $10.00, and finally in September of 1863, two years after the policy was implemented, the reward was raised back to $30.00. It seems that the lower rewards did not provide sufficient motivation to apprehend deserters.[170] Regardless of the amount of the bounty, it did little over the long term to address the problems of desertion.

The problems of recruitment during the Civil War had many causes. For many Americans, the need to provide for their families and the desire to remain at home with them kept them from enlisting. The government's efforts to mandate recruiting with the threat of a draft only strengthened resistance to the military.[171] One such government effort was the establishment of the Militia Act on July 17, 1862. This act ordered states to upgrade their militias by recruitment. If recruiting efforts were unsuccessful, a draft was to be instituted, requiring service for a period of nine months.

The threat of a draft may have been made for a different purpose. It was believed by many government officials that the suggestion of conscription in itself would motivate men to enlist. If this was the reason for the threat, it did not have the desired effect. The Militia Act met with strong resistance. The citi-

169. Lonn, pp. 151-152.
170. Alotta, Robert I. 1978. *Stop the Evil*, p. 86.
171. For additional information, see *The New York City Draft Riots: Their Significance for American Society and Politics in the Age of the Civil War*; Iver Bernstein (Oxford, 1990).

zenry did not believe that conscripted service would only last nine months; they believed the men would be required to remain for the duration of the war. Military service was considered noble, but only if performed voluntarily. Conscription was thought to be undemocratic and thus un-American.[172]

In this context, "many white Northerners compared the draft to slavery. Civilians and soldiers both used the analogy repeatedly, declaring that the draft was a form of bondage appropriate for the 'old world'...or decried it as an attempt to 'enslave the white man.' Others compared military life to slavery...."[173]

The Emancipation Proclamation itself, issued on September 22, 1862 to become effective on January 1, 1863, caused tremendous resentment and led to more desertions. Bigotry was common at this time and soldiers felt that Lincoln only freed the slaves to either provide more soldiers for the army or to fill the jobs the recruits had left behind.[174] "Certain Democratic newspapers provided open justification for desertion, telling their readers that volunteers had been deceived and that the enlistment oaths were dissolved by the Emancipation Proclamation."[175] The encouragement of the press along with the deeply held attitudes of some soldiers worked effectively to increase desertions.

Once the recruits faced the horror of battle, any thoughts of the glory of war — still prevalent during this time period — evaporated. The horrific suffering they saw repulsed the men, many of whom had only joined for the promised financial bonus, or bounty (see Table 2, Federal Bounties Offered and Table 3, Other Bounties Offered), that was usually not delivered. Following battle, as the seriously injured crowded into hospital tents for whatever treatment might be available, the less seriously hurt and the ill contended with their difficulties as best they could. The problem of illness among soldiers during the war cannot be minimized; disease killed more Union soldiers than Confederate bullets did.[176] Many men, desperate for relief from their suffering and unable to find it on the battlefields, simply went home.

The draw to return home was twofold for many of the soldiers. They needed medical attention and home was the best place to get it. And many of them had left their families nearly destitute; when they left for military service they expected to send home money provided by the government. But in most

---

172. Alotta, p. 4.
173. Cashin, p. 269.
174. Alotta, p. 28.
175. Alotta, p. 77.
176. Alotta, p. 30.

cases the government never paid the promised money. This presumably absolved them of their obligation to the military, and it surely left them with the duty to return home and provide for their families. These two factors were far stronger than any rhetoric coming from political leaders.

While cowardice is often cited as the only reason for desertion, it must be remembered that self-preservation is the strongest urge in man. For Union soldiers, conditions for going to war could hardly have been worse. Often they were sent into battle with little training and without guns, or with guns with no ammunition; fear in this circumstance is completely understandable. They usually had bayonets, but these were little more than worthless against the bullets of the Confederate soldiers. Add to that a lack of uniforms, inadequate footwear and limited amounts of food, and flight can be seen as having little to do with cowardice. Any honest soldier will recognize some fear. Yet when properly trained, motivated by the cause and outfitted with the necessary equipment — if not to preserve his/her life and accomplish battle goals then at least sufficient to give him a "fighting chance" — that fear can be controlled. Many valiant soldiers have voluntarily fought in "suicide" missions, knowing that they have little or no chance of surviving but believing that they might at least accomplish the goal, whether that is to defend his comrades in retreat, to inflict significant damage on the enemy, or achieve some other goal; but to be thrown into battle with little or no training and no useful weaponry is a pointless sacrifice. Flight is then the best and most reasonable path to take.

The soldiers of the Union Army were, for the most part, raw recruits. They lacked military discipline and required competent leaders who they could trust to make them effective soldiers. In many cases this leadership and the trust it should have engendered were tragically lacking. An example during the battle of Fredericksburg in late 1862, although extreme, is telling. Confederate General James Longstreet described the aftermath thus:

> The [Union] army had fallen... like the steady dripping of rain from the eves of a house. Our musketry alone killed and wounded at least 5,000; and these, with the slaughter by the artillery, left over 7,000 killed and wounded before the foot of Marye's Hill. The dead...were piled sometimes three deep, and when morning broke, the spectacle that we saw upon the battle-field was one of the most distressing I ever witnessed. The charges had been desperate and bloody, but utterly hopeless. I thought, as I saw the Federals come again and again to their death, that they deserved success if courage and daring could entitle soldiers to victory.[177]

---

177. Alotta, p. 60.

Many of the bodies had been stripped by Confederate soldiers, themselves in need of warmer clothing. This left the scene even more ghastly, as the bloated and mangled bodies rotted on the ground. "With all the preparations they had made, the medical department never envisioned such carnage as the troops suffered at the hands of the Confederates at Fredericksburg."[178]

While the battle still raged and defeat for the Union was assured, a prominent general, Thomas Francis Meagher, continued his plans for a victory celebration. Arriving during the heat of the battle he could have had no doubt of its eventual outcome. Yet he instructed his men to construct a hall for the victory celebration. The fact that the Union Army was experiencing a horrific defeat only altered his plans; he moved the site of the feast to a smaller, safer location.

With the battle raging and the Union Army being butchered, Meagher and the other officers feasted. The soldiers in the trenches, who were well aware that this party had been scheduled and was being held, referred to it as the "Death Feast." While they fought and died in the horror described above, their leaders ate and drank in the comparative safety of the party room. Even before the battle, while the recruits seldom had any food but hardtack and raw pork, the officers feasted on foods carefully prepared in nearby houses. The party only concluded when artillery shells began piercing the building with regularity.

After this infamous dinner party, the officers dispersed. Some returned to their men on the battlefield, some left Fredericksburg, and some left the army. Meagher went to New York on a leave of absence.[179]

Incompetent leadership would have been bad enough, but even an incompetent leader willing to die with his men can be respected. Uncaring, callous leaders were too much for many of the soldiers to bear. With no one else looking out for their welfare, they would rely on themselves. That often meant desertion.

A variety of measures was instituted to prevent desertion and to locate deserters. The motivation for this may have been more to replenish the depleted ranks than to punish law-breakers.

In September of 1862, Secretary of War Edwin Stanton created the role of provost marshal general. Provost marshals traditionally were responsible for protecting the property of citizens along the line of the march. The responsibility of the provost marshal general was to control the troops and enforce discipline; first and foremost, this included watching for and preventing desertions. Each

---

178. Alotta, p. 64.
179. Alotta, 65-66.

provost marshal general appointed special provost marshals in each state, depending on the number of troops within that state. These individuals could earn $1.00 a day. Privates at that time earned $13.00 a month.

The creation of this role did little to prevent desertions or capture men who had already deserted. It seems to have caused more ill-will than anything else; during the war, 38 provost marshal generals were killed during the dispatch of their duties and 60 were injured.[180] Opposition to their activities never diminished.

As the war dragged on and with desertions averaging over 5,000 per month, additional steps were taken to prevent desertions and locate deserters. The Enrollment Act, passed on March 3, 1863, provided for the identification of men who had deserted. The names of men who were known to be present — and the names of those who were not — were culled from field commanders' reports. This information was given by the provost marshal general to the district marshal. The local provost officers then attempted to locate the deserters.

Like the Militia Act before it, the Enrollment Act met with heavy resistance from the citizenry. Opposition to conscription remained strong; the belief that it was un-American was pervasive in many parts of the country. President Lincoln defended the act, stating that "the constitution declares that 'The Congress shall have the power to raise and support armies.'"[181] His quoting the Constitution did little to end the opposition.

In conjunction with the Enrollment Act, and possibly to deflect some of the opposition to it, Lincoln granted amnesty to all deserters, those imprisoned and those still on the run. The motivation for this, again, probably had more to do with needing soldiers than anything else, since recruiting efforts consistently fell far short of goals and desertions continued to deplete the already sparse ranks.[182]

Lincoln may have hoped that deserters would return to the ranks; if nothing else, at least those in custody could be forced back into service. Yet there was little to prevent them from fleeing a second time, which many did.

The problems of apprehending deserting soldiers went beyond the challenge of physically finding them. There were conflicts concerning the jurisdiction over deserters when captured. Initially, provost marshals, in response to

---

180. Alotta, p. 88.
181. Alotta, p. 96.
182. Alotta, p. 80.

state courts issuing writs of habeas corpus, turned their prisoners over to civil authorities. Prisoners often escaped during this transfer. Lincoln suspended the writ "as far as it related to officers and soldiers in the military or naval service of the United States."[183]

At times throughout history the government has believed that execution has a deterrent effect on desertion and periodically has decided to make an example of a deserter. This certainly occurred during the Civil War. The case of William H. Howe[184] is one of the most shocking because everything concerning the arrest, trial and execution of this young farmer strikes even the most casual observer as grossly unfair and is the antithesis of everything the US purports to stand for.

William H. Howe lived in Perkiomenville, Pennsylvania at that start of the Civil War. It is unlikely that the war touched him in any significant way at the start; Washington D.C. and its associated governmental activities were days away by horseback and would not have seemed to the young man to have much relevance to his struggle to eke out a living for his family. But as the rewards for enlisting, or bounties, as they were called, increased, Mr. Howe probably saw this as a means of providing some desperately-needed money for his wife and children. Deciding that his family would benefit more from government aid if he joined the army than by his continuing to work the farm, he enlisted.

The bounty was never paid, leaving his family worse off than before. Howe saw heavy combat in the disastrous battle at Fredericksburg and witnessed the carnage of that engagement. Following this battle, the hospital tents were filled with the wounded and dying. Howe was not wounded but suffered from chronic diarrhea; he'd been afflicted with this for at least several weeks, having between 40 and 60 bowel movements a day. As previously noted, disease, especially diarrhea and dysentery, killed more Union soldiers than Confederate bullets. However, since he was not in obvious pain — there were no bloody wounds upon his body — he could not get any assistance from medics.

Like most of the recruits from rural areas, Howe was accustomed to receiving medical treatment at home. With the horror of the Fredericksburg massacre fresh in his mind, his body racked with pain, and lacking adequate

---

183. Alotta, p. 102. Note: The suspension of some basic rights has been repeated under the guise of national security at other times since then.
184. The story of William H. Howe as related here is taken from *Stop the Evil.*

clothing, shoes and food, William made the same decision as thousands of his fellow-soldiers had already made: he simply went home.

Back in Perkiomenville, Howe's wife nursed him back to health and he went on with his farming responsibilities. It is unlikely that he considered his military obligation incomplete; many of his friends and neighbors had done exactly what he'd done. Unfortunately for him, at this time the push to capture deserters was very strong.

On June 21, 1863, sometime close to midnight, David Y. Eisenberry, an assistant special guard, and Abraham R. Bertolet, an enrolling officer, both clearly drunk, knocked at William's door, seeking to arrest him for desertion. When his wife inquired who was there, Eisenberry gave the name of a friend of William's. Since Mrs. Howe knew this friend and would have recognized his voice, she did not admit him. Eisenberry claimed at the subsequent trial that he then gave his true identity and purpose for being there. Mrs. Howe still refused to admit him. Bertolet then urged Eisenberry to break in the door. In the next few minutes, shots were fired and Bertolet was dead. William fled into the woods but was soon caught and tried for murder as well as desertion.

Reading transcripts from William Howe's two trials, a reader can easily determine that William and/or his wife (if it was one of them who actually fired the bullet that killed Bertolet; it might have been Eisenberry himself) had only fired in defense of their home and children. So, while the charge of desertion may have been justified, murder could not have been.

Yet William was charged, convicted and sentenced to death. For this, his first trial, he was unable to hire a lawyer. The lawyer he wanted, Charles Hunsicker, refused to take the case because it was before a military court. "In his letter to the court, Hunsicker indicated that a lawyer could provide no service to Howe because if an unacceptable decision were reached in a civil court the lawyer could appeal to a higher authority. That was not, he felt, true in a military court."[185] This left William to defend himself. He pleaded guilty to the charge of desertion, but not murder.

During the trial William testified that he shot Bertolet in defense of his home and family. Yet he asked no questions on cross-examination despite damning testimony from several witnesses.

---

185. Alotta, p. 108. Note: See Chapter 13, Summary and Analysis, for contemporary examples of the differences between military and civil justice.

After the prosecution rested, Howe spent the evening preparing a statement of defense. Although uneducated and desperate, he appears to have worked diligently to prepare an honest, straightforward statement. When he presented it the next day he clearly stated that he did not know the intruders who had broken into his house late at night and had no intention other than defending his family.

The verdict was quickly reached: guilty on both counts. A punishment of execution was recommended.

"But the matter was not settled. The papers were forwarded through channels, and the judge advocate general's office was not happy with the manner in which the trial had been conducted. As a result, the verdict was overturned due to 'informality.'"[186]

For the second trial, William hired Edmund Randall, under whom he had served at Fredericksburg. Randall believed in his innocence. But despite Randall's competence and his belief in his client, the second trial seemed more of a mockery of the most basic tenets of justice than the first. Lt. Col. Henry A. Frink was scheduled to preside; Randall challenged this since Frink had originally prepared the charges and specifications against Howe. "The rules of court-martial state that one cause for challenge was prior knowledge of the case which could prejudice the judgment of the officer."[187] Frink convinced the judge that his association with the first trial was minor, and so he was not sufficiently familiar with the case to be prejudiced one way or the other. The challenge was overturned.

In addition there were discrepancies regarding the kind of gun that William owned and the bullet that killed Bertolet; issues concerning a lantern that had been set on a tree stump to illuminate the front of the house (the light it provided could not possibly have shone on the door, if it was placed in the tree stump's position according to witness testimony); there was even some question as to whether this William H. Howe and William Howe, a known deserter, were the same or different people. None of these issues was resolved at the trial.

In spite of these problems, William was again convicted on both charges and the sentence of death was passed.

Randall appealed to the White House, noting the discrepancies listed above and other serious violations and apparently hoping that Lincoln, himself a

---

186. Alotta, p. 116.
187. Alotta, p. 119.

lawyer, would recognize the injustice of the sentence. By this time, executions did not require approval by the president (as had been the case early in the nation's history), but the president had the right to commute a sentence. Randall did not ask that William be released, only that his sentence be commuted to life imprisonment. Hours before the scheduled execution, he received word that his request was denied.

The cruelty and injustice to William continued. The morning of his execution he was housed in a cell where he could watch the building of the scaffold, in violation of military regulations. He was not allowed to see his clergyman until shortly before his execution.

From the limited accounts of the execution, it appears that William went to his death with dignity. The following is the statement he read just before being hanged:

> Fellow-soldiers and officers: I am now about to go before my God, to answer for the crime of having taken the life of a fellow-creature. I bow with submission to my sentence, and fully forgive those who passed it and all who were witnesses against me. They did their duty as well as they could, and I take this opportunity to thank you from my heart, the members of the court-martial who tried me, and especially Captain Clarke, the judge advocate, and Mr. Edmund Randall, my lawyer, for their kindness to me. But as I have to leave my dear children but my record and good name as a soldier, I feel it a duty I owe to them to state now that I never sought the life of the man I killed, and never wanted it; and I feel God will pardon me for taking it as I did. I know my fellow-soldiers and officers in the army never blamed me for leaving, as I was an invalid, and had no hospital to go to in my regiment. And now I am about to leave this life and I commend my wife and little ones to the charity of the world, and as a last request I ask pardon of those I injured, and hope they will forgive me and pray for my soul.[188]

One hundred and forty-three years later one can only speculate on why William H. Howe was one of the 141 of the total number of deserters singled out for execution[189] from among the tens of thousands who deserted. It does not appear that William's desertion jeopardized either the cause or the lives of other soldiers. Surely among those others there were some whose act of desertion more clearly did so. The murder charge was questionable at best.

It seems that the ill-fated young farmer committed several errors of judgment for which he can hardly be blamed. First, he naively believed that the money promised him for enlisting would be paid, thus benefiting his struggling family. He may have expected that he would be provided with food, clothing,

---

188. Alotta, pp. 163 and 164.
189. Cashin, p. 270.

weaponry (he was an expert marksman prior to enlisting) and medical attention when necessary. He may have believed, on some level, although he probably didn't give it a tremendous amount of thought, that what thousands of others were doing without apparent negative consequences would not prove to be a problem for him. He certainly had no clear awareness of the obligation that comes with enlisting in the military, or the fact that some basic rights as American citizens do not follow one into the military.[190]

William H. Howe's execution stands as an example of the kind of travesty of justice that is not uncommon when the government decides to take a stand on desertion. William's was certainly not the only execution for desertion during the Civil War, but one must also consider the pardons Lincoln approved, and the general amnesties he issued. Among these pardons and amnesties, why was William H. Howe executed?

During the Civil War it appears that two wars were being waged by the Union, one against the secession of the South and the other against desertion. When the first war effort suffered because of the lack of men, drastic measures to win the second war were occasionally launched. These measures were consistently ineffective and temporary, but for William H. Howe they proved fatal.

Even an occasional execution did not stem the tide of desertions, because neither that nor any of the government's other efforts addressed the various causes of desertion.

NINE CATEGORIES OF REASONS FOR DESERTION

In her landmark book Desertion During the Civil War, Ella Lonn lists nine categories of reasons for desertion:[191]
1. Pacifism
2. Reluctance to coerce the South by military force
3. Military defeat
4. Delay in paying troops
5. Lack of discipline
6. War weariness

---

190. This deprivation of basic civil rights while serving in the US military has not changed for the better since the Civil War. See Chapter 13 for a discussion on contemporary practices of the military, and a comparison of military justice to civil justice.
191. Lonn, p. 127.

7. Poor caliber of recruits

8. Bounty jumping, and

9. Civilian encouragement.

Throughout her book, Lonn refers to desertion as an "evil" and discusses the "cowardly or traitorous encouragement of desertion by civilians."[192] It is puzzling to hear her describe desertion in these terms when, with only one exception, the reasons that she herself identified for desertion can easily be viewed as valid. She states further that "The draft riots were a distinct abetting of the soldier in refusal to enter upon his military duty."[193] Yet many of the popular newspapers of the day supported not only draft resistance but also desertion. If the press and the general public at that time, understanding the circumstances, thought the men were right to evade, who is to say that they were wrong?

Desertion During the Civil War provides excellent information about the topic, and remains, nearly seventy-five years after its initial publication, the definitive work on the subject. Yet it was written from the same viewpoint that colors most studies of desertion, the one approved by every administration since long before Abraham Lincoln. This point of view denigrates the value of the individual in favor of the state, regardless of the individual's feelings about the goals of any given war. Lonn implies that following incompetent and uncaring leaders into battle is a duty; once a man enlists or is conscripted, he no longer has the right of opinion and independent action.

A closer look at the nine reasons she stated as causing desertion will help to bring this into a more reasonable perspective.

1. Pacifism

Today men and women with deeply held beliefs against war struggle to obtain classification as conscientious objectors. There is no evidence to show that during the Civil War such individual beliefs were given more serious consideration by the government than they are today. Then as now, some soldiers elect to sacrifice citizenship by deserting rather than participate in an activity that violates their deeply-held principles.

2. Reluctance to coerce the South by military force

Men enlisted for a variety of reasons, which often were not related to any belief that it was legitimate to use military force to keep the South within the

---

192. Lonn, p. 142.
193. Lonn, p. 142.

union. A man may have enlisted to earn the promised financial bonus because he was desperate to help his family. Once that agreement had been made and the government fulfilled its part of the bargain, the recruit had an obligation to fulfill his. Yet in most cases the government did not fulfill its responsibility by making the promised payment. One wonders why a man could be considered to have an obligation to stay and fight when his reason for agreeing to do so in the first place had not been actualized.

The military has a long tradition of expecting its members to simply follow orders. This expectation demoralizes any man. Those who do not willingly comply are forced to do so. During the Civil War the army did not have the ability to accomplish this task with the same efficiency it has today. Men of the Civil War held to their ideals no more or less than soldiers today, but did not have the military machine of twenty-first century America to contend with. Desertion without capture was far more likely to occur in the 1860s than in 2005.

3. Military defeat

The horror of war was not anticipated by those required to fight. The following report appeared in the Inquirer on December 23 1862:

> [O]ur men lay in every conceivable shape and attitude; some across each other, some had fallen with outstretched arms, others with hands beneath them, and again some with arms or legs partially upright in the air. I saw two or three with half or more of their heads blown off — one in particular whose body lay half concealed in a ditch, and bore little resemblance to a human being.
>
> Sadder still were the cries and groans of the wounded who had been left on the field and which filled the midnight air with dying supplications....Who can tell his thoughts, whether of home or kindred, wife or loved one, when forsaken, bleeding, dying and lying under the enemy's guns, within hearing distance of both exhausted armies, his sounds of life gradually passing away.[194]

Those who are victorious may be able to come away with some sense of satisfaction, but for the losing side there is unspeakable demoralization. After watching friends and associates die by the thousands, for no apparent purpose or for a purpose with which they did not agree, led by callous officers, it is no wonder that a Civil War soldier saw desertion as a viable alternative.

4. Delay in paying troops

As stated earlier, many men who had enlisted for a three-month period received no pay; they may not have deserted, but the likelihood of their reenlisting was non-existent. Others waited over nine months to receive their pay. For many of these, the realization that they could earn more in civilian life moti-

---

194. Alotta, pp. 68-69.

vated them to desert. They had done what was required to fulfill the contract they had made with the government: they reported as ordered. But the government in many cases did not fulfill its part of the contract. A contract violated by one party is null and void. Many soldiers saw no reason to maintain their agreement under these circumstances.

5. Lack of discipline

General Milroy wrote the following on January 16, 1865 regarding the Fifth Tennessee Cavalry:

> I have tried every means known to me to bring about order and efficiency in the regiment, but have not been rewarded with success, even to this day. The field officers seem to have no conception of their obligations or duties; have no control over their subordinates or men. Officers and men absent themselves without authority whenever they take the notion to visit their homes. The regiment is about 800 strong, and the largest number that can be paraded in camp at any time will not exceed 200. Most of the 600 absentees are unaccounted for.[195]

The discipline required in the military was a new concept for the recruits of the Civil War, and one that many of them were not interested in maintaining. As General Milroy stated, both officers and enlisted men continued to do as they pleased with little regard for the troop as a whole.

> Yet other men deserted because of their inability to adjust to the regimentation of military life, a universal motive among deserters in modern wars, and those difficulties became obvious soon after Northern soldiers arrived at camp. Some men could barely tolerate hauling logs, because that was menial labor, or scrubbing, sweeping, and making beds, because that was women's work, while others could not endure the forced confinement.[196]

With these attitudes, not at all unusual in America of the 1860s, desertion cannot be surprising.

6. The hardships of war

The hardships included exposure to the weather, poor and limited amounts of food, lack of shoes, blankets, tents, etc., and lack of weaponry. One general reported drawing three days' rations during a twenty-day march.[197] Many of the men, after months of service, were shoeless and nearly naked.

No war requiring hand-to-hand combat is without unspeakable hardships. But during the Civil War men by the tens of thousands lacked basic necessities. Yet often, as in the case of the "Death Feast," they could see that those who were

---

195. Lonn, p. 136.
196. Cashin P. 268.
197. Lonn, p. 132.

not risking their lives in the trenches had what they — the foot soldiers — went without. This unfairness could only further damage morale, regardless of how strongly a soldier believed in the cause.

7. Poor caliber of recruits

It is interesting that Lonn identified a problem with recruits who were "noticeably inferior after 1862."[198] At the very start of the war, there appeared to be no shortage of volunteers. This did not last long, as the government increased the numbers required and the populace confronted the reality of military life.

Lonn refers to those whom she classes as "inferior" as cowardly and immoral, and further states that most of them were "foreigners." She concedes that some foreigners served with honor and loyalty, but points out that most of the mercenaries were from abroad, or were from states that had manufacturing plants that hired foreigners. She reports that these states had the highest rate of bounty jumpers.

One can only wonder if their reasons for desertion were any different from anyone else's during the Civil War. They, like their citizen counterparts, may have enlisted with every intention of fulfilling the obligation undertaken in exchange for the bounty; but the bounties were never paid. They may have sustained injuries or suffered from illness with no opportunity for treatment. They may have been so horrified by the carnage they witnessed that they chose to desert. Lonn's assertion that they were morally inferior does not withstand thoughtful scrutiny.

From all evidence it appears that the soldiers considered themselves to have the rights of US citizens. This includes the right (and responsibility) to make decisions for themselves and act upon those decisions. The military universe cannot grant this right, but that is a point that was not well understood by the general public. This deprivation of rights violates basic Constitutional tenets. Civil War recruits had every expectation of maintaining their rights as citizens; in nineteenth-century America it made perfect sense.

8. Bounty-jumping

Of all the reasons for desertion listed by Lonn, this appears to be the one that could most logically be seen as a criminal activity. This is the only reason for desertion that Lonn identified in which the recruit may have enlisted with no intention of fulfilling his obligation. Bounty-jumping refers to the practice of enlisting for monetary benefit, then deserting and enlisting in another regiment

---

198. Lonn, p. 138.

for an additional payment. Although it was not done in significant numbers, bounty-jumping was certainly one cause of desertion.

However, one must consider the possibility that a man enlisted in his home state and then, when the promised bounty was not paid, went elsewhere to try again. In these circumstances, the criminal activity is not that of the recruit, but of the government that refused to pay the promised bounty.

9. Encouragement by civilians

It seems that this topic touches on all the others. That civilians encouraged desertion should not be surprising. Family members wanted to be reunited with their loved ones and they considered it unjust that the soldiers found themselves struggling in conditions so onerous. Without a clear knowledge of the legal consequences of desertion, they worked to find creative ways to help friends and family members leave the military and return home. Few deserters would have been successfully in evading the authorities had they not received assistance in doing so from civilians.

Joan E. Cashin identifies another reason for desertion: "Men who had already enlisted and then left the service did so for the elemental reasons that prompted men in other conflicts to desert, with fear, hunger and combat fatigue leading the way....[T]he Civil War had its share of cowards who were designated as such by the public and the military.[199] Fear is not mentioned by Lonn, although she mentions hunger and alludes to combat fatigue. But her description of all deserters as cowards seems to include an assumption that fear was a major factor — if she does not cite it among the specific reasons she lists, at least it is implied in her beliefs about each deserter's character. But again, to equate being fearful with being a coward is a gross over-simplification.

After deserting, some men went to Canada, some joined the Confederate army, and some eventually rejoined other regiments of the Union Army. But many simply returned home to pick up their lives, as William H. Howe did. Regardless of where they went, it's clear that cowardice generally had little to do with their decision to desert. The threat of execution hung over every man who left. He needed compelling reasons to walk out; and in most cases, they were plentifully available.

---

199. Cashin, p. 265.

UNION POLICY ON DESERTION DURING THE CIVIL WAR

In the following table outlining the Union's legal policies relating to desertion, only the most pertinent aspects of each law or act are included. Where it is specified that a law was "seldom enforced," it indicates just that; the law existed on the books but in actual practice seems to have existed mainly to intimidate soldiers and/or officers into submission. In Number 1, it appears that the military at this time did not want to execute deserters, either due to compassion or the hope that, if merely captured, they would rejoin the depleted ranks.

"Loosely enforced" is a broad concept intended to indicate the inconsistent or low level of effectiveness and enforcement of the policy. For example, in Number 6, military commanders had the responsibility listed, but were either unwilling or unable (or perhaps both) to accomplish this assignment.

"Enforced," indicates that the policy was strictly adhered to. Interestingly, the policies listed as "enforced" do not concern the harsher polices enacted during this time, but rather relate to monetary rewards and administrative procedures.

Table 1: Union Policy on Desertion during the Civil War

	Year	Policy	Enforcement
1	1806*	1. Military Code outlined punishments for desertion, execution being only one of several options. 2. If a soldier or officer aided someone else in deserting, he was treated as if he himself had deserted. 3. Executions of soldiers for desertion had to be approved by the president.	1. Seldom enforced. 2. Seldom enforced. 3. Enforced.
2	1826**	July: The president's approval an execution was no longer required an execution; the commanding general could authorize the execution.	Enforced.
3	1861	The reward for the arrest and delivery of a deserter was $30.00.	Enforced.
4		September: The reward was reduced to $5.00.	Enforced.
5		November 11: the writ of habeas corpus was suspended.	Enforced.
6	1862	April: Military commanders of citizens were made responsible for capturing deserters.	Loosely enforced.
7		June 7: Only the Secretary of War could grant a leave of absence to an officer, except for certain medical emergencies.	Loosely enforced.
8		June 12: All soldiers physically able were ordered to report to their regiments by August 11.	Not enforced.
9		September 8: Secretary Stanton denied a request to grant leniency to deserters in Canada.	Enforced.
10		September 24: Office of provost marshal general created.	Enforced.
11		November: Officers deserting were discharged dishonorably and without pay.	Loosely enforced.
12	1863	In accordance with the Conscription Act, absentee officers could be reduced in rank and ordered to serve three years or for the duration of the war.	Loosely enforced.

13		March 3: The Enrollment Act centralized reporting of deserters.	Loosely enforced.
14		March 10: Clause in the Conscription Act: all deserters who reported for duty by April 1, 1863 would not be punished beyond loss of pay for time of desertion.	Enforced.
15		April: Invalid Force established (later renamed Veterans Reserve Corps). This group worked with arresting deserters and draft resistors, and guarding deserters and/or escorting them to the front.	Enforced
16	1864	February: The punishment of all deserters currently sentenced to death was reduced to imprisonment for the duration of the war.	Enforced.
17	1865	February 8: Deserters had to make up in service the time lost during their desertion.	Loosely enforced.
18		March 3: 1. Deserters were given 60 days to turn themselves in, or face loss of citizenship. 2. An officer who knowingly mustered in a deserter was to be dishonorably discharged	1. Not enforced. 2. Not enforced.

*This is the date the policy was established that was in effect at the start of the Civil War.
**This was a small but significant amendment to the Military Code of 1806.

Table 2: Federal Bounty Offered

Year	Bounty	Monthly Pay	Payable When
1861	$100.00	$13.00	Upon honorable discharge
1862	$100.00	$13.00	$25.00 at time of mustering; balance at honorable discharge.
1864	$300.00	$16.00	$25.00 at time of mustering; balance at honorable discharge (new recruits only).
1864	$400.00	$16.00	$25.00 at time of mustering; balance at honorable discharge (new recruits only).

Table 3: Other Bounties Offered[200]

State	Bounty
Maine	$10.00
Massachusetts	$12.00 per month relief funds
New Hampshire	$17.00 (only briefly offered)
New Jersey	$6.00 per month
Connecticut	$300.00
New York	$75.00
Vermont	$7.00 per month
Wisconsin	$5.00 per month

---

200. Lonn, p. 140.

CHAPTER 5: THE PHILIPPINE-AMERICAN WAR

The ink was not yet dry on the Treaty of Paris ending the three-month Spanish-American War (see Chapter 12, Other Conflicts; Peacetime Desertion) when the first shots of the Philippine-American war were fired.

The war with the Philippines resulted directly from the outcome of the war with Spain. When the United States defeated Spain it demanded possession of Guam, Puerto Rico and the Philippines. The US had occupied Manila since August 13, 1898, the day before Spain requested a peace treaty after suffering crushing defeats in the Caribbean. Spain was willing to concede Cuba and Puerto Rico, but wanted to retain the Philippines. This was under discussion until December 10 of that same year, when the Treaty of Paris was signed, under which Spain was forced to surrender the Philippines along with Guam and Puerto Rico. "Under this treaty, Spain recognized the independence of Cuba, and ceded to the United States Puerto Rico, Guam, and the Philippines. For these concessions the United States paid a compensation of 20,000,000 dollars.[201]

However, the treaty had to be ratified by the US Senate in order to take effect, and although it was eventually accepted, it was not without significant opposition. The newly formed Anti-Imperialist League, with such prominent members as former President Grover Cleveland, Andrew Carnegie and Mark Twain, opposed annexation of the Philippines. African-American citizens were

---

201. Mowat, R. B. 1925. *The Diplomatic Relations of Great Britain and the United States*, Page 282.

also vehemently opposed to the annexation of the Philippines. According to The Boston Post:

> On July 17, 1899, in anticipation of the coming presidential election, a meeting of Boston blacks was held to further the influence and organization of anti-imperialist sentiment in the black communities of the nation. This meeting adopted the following resolutions.
>
> Resolved, That the colored people of Boston in meeting assembled desire to enter their solemn protest against the present unjustified invasion by American soldiers in the Philippine Islands.
>
> Resolved, That, while the rights of colored citizens in the South, sacredly guaranteed them by the amendment of the Constitution, are shamefully disregarded; and, while the frequent lynchings of negroes who are denied a civilized trial are a reproach to Republican government, the duty of the President and country is to reform these crying domestic wrongs and not to attempt the civilization of alien peoples by powder and shot.
>
> Resolved, That a copy of these resolutions be sent to the President of the United States and to the press.[202]

The Filipinos themselves were resisting the US occupation, and many Americans saw that as a clear reason to oppose the annexation. Nevertheless, on February 6, 1899 the US Senate ratified the Treaty of Paris and the Philippines legally became a US possession.

The Filipinos resented the American presence and were outraged that Felipe Agoncillo, special envoy from Emilio Aguinaldo y Famy, who was leading the Filipino rebellion against Spanish rule,[203] was denied any participation in the meetings of the Treaty of Paris. Spain, with no input from the Filipinos, had surrendered their nation to a foreign power.

> When President William McKinley announced America's intention of keeping the Philippines, he referred to the situation as "benevolent assimilation." The "Benevolent Assimilation Proclamation" ... was announced in the Philippines on January 4, 1899. It stated clearly the intention of the United States to stay permanently in the Philippines.... In the same proclamation, General Elwell Otis was named the commander of American ground forces in the Philippines, which was to "extend by force American sovereignty over this country."[204]

One may well wonder how "benevolence" and "force" are compatible, but this did not seem to trouble the US government. As the American occupation

---

202. Schirmer, Daniel B. and Stephen Rosskamm Shalom. *The Philippines Reader: A History of Colonialism, Neocolonialism, Dictatorship, and Resistance.* (Boston, 1987), p. 32.

203. Keenan, Jerry. *Encyclopedia of the Spanish-American and Philippine-American Wars,* (Santa Barbara, 2001), p. 3.

204. Bautista, Veltisezar. 1998. *The Filipino Americans: From 1763 to the Present.* Page 63.

unfolded, benevolence proved to be an empty word while force took center stage. The racist practices of the US in the Philippines were among the most shocking the world had ever known.

Two days prior to the ratification of the Treaty of Paris, an incident occurred that is generally marked as the start of the Philippine-American War. It must be remembered, however, that the US had invaded the Philippines as part of the Spanish-American War and was already occupying Manila. But on February 4, 1899, a confrontation between two US soldiers and three Filipinos near Manila resulted in the deaths of at least one of the Filipinos. Fighting immediately started and the United States was once again involved in war.[205]

The reports of this incident that reached the US placed all the blame on the Filipinos. Prior to this the citizens of the US seemed divided on the issue of the annexation of the Philippines. However, once the American press reported that Filipinos had opened fire on Americans, the tide in the US turned. On February 6, the Treaty of Paris was ratified by a vote of 57 to 27.

Desertion quickly became an issue, as it had early on in each of America's wars. Again the reasons were not significantly different from those cited in earlier wars.

HORROR OF WAR, AND APATHY TOWARD THE CAUSE OF THE WAR

1. Horror of war

In few wars did American soldiers participate in such ghastly deeds as during the Philippine-American War. Perhaps because of William Howard Taft, the first civil governor general referred to the Filipino people as his "little brown brothers'[206] many American soldiers seemed to perceive the Filipinos as somewhat less than human. Official policies resulted in the most horrifying scenes of carnage.

> On the eve of the Samar campaign, the war was clearly degenerating into mass slaughter. It was hardly precise to call it "war" any longer. The Americans were simply chasing ragged, poorly armed bands of guerrillas and, failing to catch them, were inflicting the severest punishment on those they could catch — the people of the villages and barrios of the theater of operation. US commanders were becoming increasingly outspoken about the true nature of their policy. (Major General Adna R.) Chaffee wrote in September, "...we are dealing with a class of people whose character is deceitful, who are absolutely hostile to the white race and who regard

---

205. Bautista, page 63.
206. Smith, Robert Aura, 1958. *Philippine Freedom, 1946 – 1958.* Page 31.

life as of little value and, finally, who will not submit to our control until absolutely defeated and whipped into such condition."[207]

The Samar campaign was the responsibility of Brigadier General Jacob Smith. At the start of the campaign he issued very direct orders to the soldiers under his command: "'Kill and burn, kill and burn, the more you kill and the more you burn the more you please me.' It was, said Smith, 'no time to take prisoners,' war was to be waged 'in the sharpest and most decisive manner possible.' When asked to define the age limit for killing, Smith gave his infamous reply: 'Everything over ten.'"[208]

This was, certainly, an extreme case, but not unique as incidents related by various soldiers who witnessed and/or participated in atrocities shows:

> Anthony Michea of the Third Artillery wrote: We bombarded a place called Malabon, and then we went in and killed every native we met, men, women, and children. It was a dreadful sight, the killing of the poor creatures.[209]

Captain Elliot of the Kansas Regiment wrote this about the Caloocan fight:

> Talk about war being "hell," this war beats the hottest estimate ever made of that locality. Caloocan was supposed to contain seventeen thousand inhabitants. The Twentieth Kansas swept through it, and now Caloocan contains not one living native. Of the buildings, the battered walls of the great church and dismal prison alone remain. The village of Maypaja, where our first fight occurred on the night of the fourth, had five thousand people on that day - now not one stone remains upon top of another. You can only faintly imagine this terrible scene of desolation. War is worse than hell.[210]

Burr Ellis, of Frazier Valley, California, narrated what he did in Cavite.

> They did not commence fighting over here for several days after the war commenced. Dewey gave them till nine o'clock one day to surrender, and that night they all left but a few out to their trenches, and those that they left burned up the town, and when the town commenced burning, the troops were ordered in as far as possible and said, "Kill all we could find." I ran off from the hospital and went ahead with the scouts. And you bet, I did not cross the ocean for the fun there was in it, so the first one I found, he was in a house, down on his knees fanning a fire, trying to burn the house, and I pulled my old Long Tom to my shoulder and left him to burn with the fire, which he did. I got his knife, and another jumped out of the window and ran, and I brought him to the ground like a jack-rabbit. I killed seven that I know of, and one more, I am almost sure of: I shot ten shots at him running and knocked him

---

207. Francisco, Luzyiminda. 1973. The First Vietnam: The US–Philippine War of 1899; *Bulletin of Concerned Asian Scholars*, Vol. 5, p. 15.

208. Schirmer, p. 17.

209. Bautista, page 67.

210. Bautista, page 67.

down, and that evening the boys out in front of our trenches now found one with his arm shot off at the shoulder and dead as h___. I had lots of fun that morning....

From Fred D. Sweet, of the Utah Light Battery, came these words:

> The scene reminded me of the shooting of jack-rabbits in Utah, only the rabbits sometimes got away, but the insurgents did not.[211]

The first two anecdotes indicate some remorse for the actions, or at least some sense of compassion for the victims. The third openly expresses the man's enjoyment in performing this slaughter. The fourth seems flippant and lacking in any compassion.

> It should be remarked that not all of the US soldiers reveled in the bloodlust of their commanders. Many were repulsed by what they had witnessed and experienced in the Philippines and were anxious to expose American policy upon their return to the United States. Others took to drink or went mad. Alcoholism and insanity followed venereal disease as the major cause for the reduction in available US manpower in the Philippines. Desertion was difficult due to geographical factors, but incidences of officers being shot in the back "by snipers" were not unheard of, and a handful of Americans actually joined with and fought with the guerrillas.[212]

It should be mentioned that Smith and some others were court-martialed for the massacre they ordered. But Smith's sentence was later reduced by President Theodore Roosevelt — one of the architects of the Spanish-American War which resulted in the Philippine-American War — and Smith was not dismissed from the service but placed on the retired list.[213] His second in command, Major Littleton W. T. Waller, was later charged with murder, but was acquitted.[214] At that, not all the men under his command followed his orders. "As the Judge Advocate General of the army observed, only the good sense and restraint of the majority of Smith's subordinates prevented a complete reign of terror in Samar. Still, the abuses were sufficient to cause outrage in the United States when they became known near the end of March 1902."[215] About one third of the population of Samar had been killed during this campaign.

At least partly as a result of scenes such as these, by 1901 American soldiers had begun deserting to the Filipino side. "On June 21, some of the American sol-

---

211. Bautista, p. 68.
212. Francisco, p. 8.
213. Keenan, p. 370.
214. Keenan, p. 27.
215. Philippine History Group of Los Angeles. The Balaniga Massacre: Getting Even. http://en.wikipedia.org/wiki/Balangiga_Massacre. Accessed October 10, 2005.

diers defected and joined the Filipinos. Among the deserters were Privates John Wagner, Edward Walpole, Harry Dennis, John Allance, and a certain Private Meeks. These men apparently felt outraged by the inhumane treatment of the Filipinos by their fellow Americans."[216] This is a switch from many other US wars when American soldiers simply left the service, but is similar to circumstances in the Mexican–American War (see Chapter 3, Mexican–American War). A disproportionate number of African-American soldiers deserted and joined the Filipinos, often feeling a close bond to their cause.

> African American soldiers who joined the insurgents not only received high-ranking military commissions but also enjoyed the respect of their new colored comrades. Not the least of their contribution to the insurgent army was the training they provided in the proper use of firearms. American troops who encountered insurgents trained by deserters were singularly impressed by the improvement in "the accuracy of their gunfire."[217]

One African-American who deserted to the Filipino side was David Fagen of the Colored 24th Infantry, who accepted a commission as an officer in the Filipino army. Treated poorly while he was fighting for the Americans, Corporal Fagen urged others to join him after his defection. General Frederick Funston put a $600.00 bounty on his head. "Next to Aquinaldo[218], he was the most despised insurgent in the eyes of the American officer corps in Luzon...."[219] Funston made every effort to capture him, saying that Fagen was "entitled to the same treatment as a mad dog."[220]

2. Apathy toward the war

Although there was some initial enthusiasm for the annexation of the Philippines and the subsequent war as a result of the press reporting of the shootings of February 4, not all soldiers were invested in the war.

---

216. Philippine History Group of Los Angeles. War for Independence: The View from a Small Town. http://www.bibingka.com/phg/cabugao/default.htm. Accessed October 10, 2005.

217. The Philippine Revolution and the Philippine-American War. Through my Grandfather's Eyes: Ties that Bind: African American Soldiers in the Filipino War for Liberation. Anthony L. Powell. http://www.boondocksnet.com/centennial/sctexts/powell98a_d.html. Accessed October 10, 2005.

218. Emilio Aguinaldo y Famy, the Filipino rebel leader.

219. Welch, Richard E. Jr. *Response to Imperialism: The United States and the Philippine-American War. 1899 – 1902*, p. 113.

220. Gatewood, Willard B., Jr. 1975. *Black Americans and the White Man's Burden, 1898-1903.* Page 289.

James A. Reid, a Colorado volunteer, had this to say: "We are not nearly as anxious to fight these people as some of people may think we are, and we do not enter any of the fights with the same spirit we did when fighting the Spaniards. If a vote was taken to take us home now or wait six months and discharge us here with our travel pay and finals, which would amount to nearly five hundred dollars, I do not believe that ten percent would be willing to stay, so you see how the men look at this addition to the United States....There have been about one hundred and twenty-five killed and three hundred wounded all together, and, when you consider that these beastly islands are not worth one American life, you can see what they are costing."[221]

Sergeant Arthur H. Vickers of the First Nebraska Regiment said, "'I am not afraid, and am always ready to do my duty, but I would like some one to tell me what we are fighting for.'"[222]

This is only a small sampling, but the Philippine-American war was just one of many to show that Americans are often hesitant to fight a war against a nation that does not appear to have any significant ill will or aggressive inclination toward the US. In order to make the sacrifice to leave loved ones and risk their lives in the military, people generally must have a motivation beyond the sense of duty to do whatever the government demands. In this example (and how many others?) the initial skirmish that officially opened the war was given extensive and skewed press coverage in the US, resulting in a great increase in hostility towards the Philippines and enthusiasm and support for the war, but none of that was long-lasting. And it is sometimes those who do not have to fight a war who are most interested in waging it.

The strategic and economic importance of the Philippines to the US, considered great during the occupation, proved inconsequential. Even Theodore Roosevelt, who doggedly pursued the war with Spain that culminated in the war for the Philippines, wrote in 1907 that "'from a military standpoint the Philippines form our heels of Achilles,' and that in case of war with Japan it would take an army as large as the German army and a navy the size of the British navy to prevent their capture."[223] That other US imperial adventures had the same result has been amply demonstrated.

---

221. Bautista, p. 66.
222. The Philippine-American War. http://www.historyguy/PhilippineAmericanwar.html. Accessed July 20, 2005.
223. Morris, Richard B, William Greenleaf and Robert H. Ferrell; *America: A History of the People*, Volume 2 – From 1865. (Chicago, 1971), p. 487.

CHAPTER 6: WORLD WAR I

The underlying causes of World War I provide a lesson for all future generations, a lesson that is often ignored. While the assassination of the Archduke Franz Ferdinand of Austria-Hungary may have been the catalyst for war, the conditions for it were being created for years before this assassination occurred. Four main factors can be identified as preparing Europe for war.[224] Although these will be discussed separately, the relationships between them can be clearly seen.

Militarism: Britain, Germany and France all competed to have the largest, strongest and most advanced military systems in the world. Each increase in the military strength of one nation caused the others to further strengthen their own armies and navies. The arms race of the 1950s and 1960s between the US and the Soviet Union parallels this pre-World War I military buildup.

Alliances: Countries that later became embroiled in World War I had previously established protective alliances among themselves. This was done for mutual and shared protection, but in practice simply pulled other countries into war when one felt threatened. At the start of the war, two major alliances existed. The Triple Alliance was composed of Germany, Italy and Austria-Hungary. In opposition to this was the Triple Entente, made up of Britain, Russia and France.

Imperialism: Many of the world's most powerful nations in the pre-World War I years had extensive empires, with colonies in Asia, Africa and elsewhere.

---

224. This discussion is based on information found in *The Oxford Illustrated History of the First World War*, p. 9 – 25.

The others, most notably Germany and Italy, sought to compete in this arena also.

Nationalism: The first three issues listed above enabled national leaders to encourage and foment strong feelings of nationalism and patriotism. It was this attitude that led these nations to seek to be the number one military and indus-trial power in the world, and that sparked constant competition.

On June 28 of 1914, a young Serbian anarchist named Gavrilo Princip shot and killed Archduke Franz Ferdinand and his wife Sophie of Austria-Hungary as the royal couple traveled through the streets of Sarajevo during a state visit. They were on their way to a local hospital to visit two officers injured in an assassi-nation attempt made earlier in the day.[225]

Almost immediately Austria-Hungary demanded concessions from Serbia, which granted most but not all of them. This was unacceptable to Austria-Hungary, which declared war on Serbia exactly one month after the Archduke's assassination. Serbia was aligned with Russia, which prepared to assist in Serbia's defense. Germany, allied with Austria-Hungary, declared war on Russia. The Great War, as it was called prior to World War II, had begun.

America did not enter the war until April 2, 1917. This was America's first major foray into international politics, which represented a shift from its recent tradition of isolationism. Prior to World War I, America's wars were waged due to internal problems (e.g. the Civil War) or its own imperial designs — usually but not always restricted to the Americas — or due to issues with other coun-tries that directly affected the United States.

Among Americans there was great hostility toward Germany for sinking the Lusitania two years before, and the Sussex in 1916. But the final insult came in 1917, when the US intercepted the so-called Zimmerman note. In this doc-ument, Germany secretly tried to create an alliance with Mexico, and offered to assist Mexico in retaking New Mexico, Arizona and Texas, which had been lost to the US seventy years earlier. The German foreign office proposed to Mexico "[t]hat we shall make war together and together make peace."[226]

Americans may have been particularly sensitive to this. In the early part of 1916, Mexican bandit Pancho Villa killed nineteen Americans on a train in Mexico, and then raided a community in New Mexico and killed several more.

---

225. Gilbert, Martin. *The First World War*, (New York, 1994), p. 16.
226. Gambone, Michael D. 2002. *Documents of American Diplomacy: From the American Revolu-tion to the Present*. Pp 170 - 171.

US President Woodrow Wilson called out the troops in what became known as the Mexican Punitive Expedition of 1916-1917.[227] Although this ended without war (and without the capture of the notorious Mr. Villa), it may have left Americans feeling particularly hostile toward Mexico.

However, there were other reasons for America to enter the war, as well. When the US declared war one theory blamed corporate interests. The US economy had gradually become dependent on the war, and an Allied defeat would have proven to be a financial disaster for America.[228]

Indeed, one may well wonder if Germany's aborted alliance attempt with Mexico, along with its sinking of the Lusitania and the Sussex in and of themselves would have been seen as sufficient reason for entering the war.

Whatever the real reasons may have been, beyond the incidents that stirred the public's outrage, in the spring of 1917 America was once again at war.

With war inevitably comes desertion, and American soldiers' reasons for illegally leaving the military still had not changed significantly. The horrors of battle, the need to provide for families, the hardships of war and the clash with personal convictions are factors common throughout desertion's history.

But one change that came with World War I is the government's definition of desertion, and its efforts to prevent it. During World War I, three types of status were distinguished as offenses that related to, and included, desertion. They are as follows:

1. Absent without Official Leave (AWOL);
2. Straggling; and
3. Desertion

ABSENT WITHOUT OFFICIAL LEAVE

> This offense, in many instances, is, in reality, desertion. However because of the exigencies of the service, such as frequent changes among officers and organizations, the necessary technical proofs are not always available, so the offender, who is in reality a deserter, is often convicted of absence without leave only.[229]

---

227. Taylor, Maureen. 2004. Rhode Islanders and Pancho Villa. New England Ancestors.org.   http://www.newenglandancestors.org/education/articles/research/localities/ rhode_island/across_border.asp (accessed October 29, 2005).

228. Strachen, p. 147.

229. Humber, Robert C. 1942. Absences and Desertions During the First World War. *A.W. C. Historical Section, Study No. 34*, p. 1.

The offense is lawfully punishable in war by any penalty short of death.[230]

STRAGGLING

Straggling is the offense of wandering away from the rest of the troop.

According to some, "This offense is in reality absence without leave in its most serious form, induced mainly through cowardice or through lack of physical and moral stamina to endure great hardships or death itself....[T]here is no record of the numbers of such offenders, but it is known that there were many."[231]

It should not be surprising that when faced with certain or near-certain death, most people will do almost anything to save their lives. This is hardly the same thing as "lacking physical and moral stamina."

Devotion to the cause is surely one of the noblest virtues. A more glorious calling can hardly be imagined than the dedication of one's life, to the point of death, to something one believes in. However, one cannot help but wonder if perhaps in some cases it is those who do not attempt to save their own lives who suffer from some defect of character. Not all American foot soldiers who served in World War I can be expected to have been completely devoted to the cause; of over 10 million who were inducted, 2.8 million were drafted.[232] Such selfless devotion might play a part in voluntary enlistment, but has little to do with soldiers who were conscripted.

Further, it is not unreasonable to question the motives and character of those who send others into life-threatening situations while they themselves remain in relative safety.

DESERTION

The denigrating of the characters of those who deserted (which seems to have begun in the US during the War of 1812) reached new heights of exagger-

---

230. Humber, p. 1.
231. Humber, p. 3.
232. Eisenhower, John. 2002. *Yanks: The Epic Story of the American Army in World War I.* (New York) p. 25.

ation and distortion in World War I. A government report serves as an excellent example:

> "The most fundamental cause appears to be due to the individual character of the deserter.
>
> "Among the principal causes mentioned in various reports of commanders on the subject are the following:
>
> 1. Mental deficiency and ignorance.
>
> 2. Lack of moral character and stamina.
>
> 3. Unwillingness to submit to military discipline and restraint.
>
> 4. Public attitude towards desertion and deserters.
>
> 5. To evade the consequences of a crime.
>
> 6. Involvement with women.
>
> 7. Addiction to the use of drugs and excessive use of intoxicants.
>
> 8. Home sickness.
>
> 9. Cowardice.
>
> 10. Mishandling of men by officers and noncommissioned officers.
>
> 11. Home conditions, such as poverty or illness in family."[233]

Unfortunately, the report that lists these reasons does not give details. But a closer examination of each puts them into a more reasonable perspective.

1. Mental deficiency and ignorance.

These appear to be two completely different topics. One who is mentally "deficient" can hardly be held responsible for his actions. No amount of education will help a person overcome such a deficiency. Optimally, such people are trained in some trade and housed in supervised living situations where they can lead as fulfilling and productive a life as possible, although this does not seem to have been the case during the years of World War I. However, there was an awareness of these problems. The review of the court martial of Private Leo Claist stated that the accused "had, in his youth, suffered an injury to his head....Also that he had been a sufferer from a mental disease."[234] The report

---

233. Humber, p. 5
234. Shaw, LT R.C. 1919. Analysis of the Causes of 200 Desertion Cases. Army Chief of Staff, Entry 8, #1050, Records of the War Department General and Special Staffs (Record Group 165), p. 1.

states that this information, though vital to determining guilt and penalty, was only mentioned incidentally in an unrequired letter from Private Claist's company commander. Why this level of specific, pertinent information was not required for all those accused of desertion must be questioned.

It could be stated that there has been a change since the time of World War I, and the military is now more careful about screening so that those individuals who have handicaps that would make them unfit for military service are not inducted. This is a worthy goal but such screening cannot ensure that no person with either mental handicaps or emotional/psychological problems is admitted, or that a person who develops such problems while in the service will be handled appropriately. Studies have indicated that some mental problems, including schizophrenia, could be precipitated by military combat.[235] Yet other than serving his or her required time in the military, as unsuited as he/she may be, such a person can only expect to be discharged to a prison following the commission of some crime.

Ignorance is another topic altogether. Ignorance among recruits can be overcome by providing information. The report does not indicate what information is lacking.

In a separate report, ignorance is classified as "Ignorance of the Seriousness of Offense."[236] That report indicates that in many such cases there are mitigating circumstances. It states, in part, the following:

> No attempt was made to include here cases where the deserter acted under the belief that a minimum of punishment would be inflicted, but only cases where, as a result of ignorance of the Articles of War or brevity of service, there was no conception of the corpus of the offense.[237]

In each case it appears that a "blame the victim" mentality was in force during World War I. A man who committed the "crime" of desertion because of his mental incapacity was still guilty. The reason may have been mental "deficiency," but the verdict remained "guilty."

2. Lack of moral character and stamina.

It is interesting that lack of character or stamina should be given as a major reason for desertion, since such a judgment can only be subjective; there is no

---

235. Bemak, Fred, and Lawrence R. Epp. Transcending the Mind-Body Dichotomy: Schizophrenia Reexamined. *Journal of Humanistic Counseling, Education and Development*, Vol. 41, 2002.

236. Shaw, p. 3.

237. Shaw, p. 5.

tangible evidence that could prove a "lack of moral character and stamina." Here we see a prime example of the military using demeaning and degrading terms to describe men who wish to control their own lives.

Rather than viewing desertion as demonstrating a "lack of moral character and stamina," one could see it as showing the strength to leave a dangerous and intolerable situation despite massive pressure to stay.

This same report says that during war, there is a change in the kind of man who enlists. War entices a "[h]igher type of enlisted [man] and consequent rise in moral standard."[238] The report does not suggest the basis for this judgment of an increased moral standard, and since desertion occurs in every war, and often at just as high a rate later in the war as in the beginning, there does not appear to be significant evidence supporting this claim.

3. Unwillingness to submit to military discipline and restraint

It is patently unfair to expect draftees to submit to the regulations of the military. They are being forced into a situation not of their choosing, taken from all that they have chosen, taught to overcome the deep-rooted abhorrence of killing, and put into life-threatening situations, often either repeatedly or for extensive periods of time, or both. They are restricted from seeing family and other loved ones, and enjoying the normal pursuits of everyday life.

Expecting this of those who enlist is also unfair. Few people fully understand what the US military expects in terms of discipline and restraint. While most countries teach a man how to be a soldier, the US breaks the man to create the soldier.[239] No man or woman accepts the destruction of all he or she believes in without resistance. Sometimes that resistance takes the form of desertion.

Additionally, an individual's personal circumstances may change; a soldier may marry, have a child, or lose a parent. The military makes no allowance for a change in circumstances. A civilian can quit his job or relocate to another area of the country or the world, if he so desires. A soldier has no such rights.

> [T]he draft delivered a massive lesson that contradicted some of the most hallowed American social values. It taught young men and their families that individuals were not always masters of their fate, and that they could not always shape their destiny through self-reliance.[240]

---

238. Humber, p. 7

239. Rising-Moore, Carl and Becky Oberg. 2004. *Freedom Underground* (New York), p. 89.

240. Cooper, John Milton Jr. 1990. *Pivotal Decades: The United States, 1900 – 1920,* (New York), pp. 271-272.

The conditions to which US soldiers were subjected by the military itself were enough to cause problems. Soldiers "were packed like sardines on the transports which ferried them across the Atlantic to Europe. Many found conditions on board...more intolerable than those in the trenches.[241]

Once they arrived, even before battle they found things going from bad to worse. As in earlier wars, disease, unsanitary conditions and poor food in meager quantities met the new soldier.

> The suffering he most commonly endured derived from more banal things, such as being perpetually at the mercy of the elements, a poor diet, the filthy grime, and the ubiquitous "cootie" or louse. The stench of living and dead bodies, the appalling noise and excruciating boredom, added to the awful purgatory.[242]

And that was before they got to the trenches, where conditions were unspeakably horrific. Young men plucked from farms and cities were thrust into situations they could not have imagined in their most frightening nightmares. But even the initial conditions were often sufficient to cause morale to drop and men to question their reasons for being in the war.

4. Public attitude towards desertion and deserters

> It is believed that public opinion regarding desertion in general has a profound effect upon it. It is a recognized fact that a large number of people are sympathetic toward those evading capture for any crime. Naturally more sympathy is felt toward those escaping from military service, which offense they do not regard as a serious crime but rather as the man's right to quit employment.[243]

Note the government's own statement acknowledging that desertion is often seen as a "...man's right to quit employment." The military allows no provision for resignation.

It's also noteworthy that this government study says that more sympathy is "naturally" felt towards deserters. One wonders why the government fights so tenaciously against the "natural" inclinations of the populace.

During times of war there is sometimes an adjustment in this attitude, at least initially. Often when the country first embarks on war the public, in a fervor of patriotism, condemns desertion and deserters. However, as has been

---

241. Mead, Gary. 2000. *The Doughboys: America and the First World War* (New York). Caption under photograph 25.
242. Mead, p. 191.
243. Humber, p. 7.

shown in the previous chapters, this attitude does not last, and successful desertion often relies on civilian assistance.

Support for deserters may have been high at least partly as a result of opposition to the war.

> Few Americans knew clearly why they were at war. President Wilson made the initial choice to go to war for honor and to secure larger ideals, but his job of educating the public had just begun. Mobilization required more than massing troops and materiel; it also required instilling morale and a sense of public purpose.[244]

5. To evade the consequences of a crime.

Of the nine major reasons listed for desertion in Chapter 4, on the Civil War, bounty-jumping was indicated as the only one in which the soldier may not have intended to fulfill his obligation. As such, it could reasonably be seen as the only type of desertion that is in fact a crime. At first glance, desertion to evade the consequence of criminal activity might be seen in the same light. The deserter in this case has left his responsibilities only to protect himself from lawful prosecution. However, "crime" must be put in its proper context.

A record of court-martials from World War I reveals an interesting fact: "most court-martial convictions were for offenses that were crimes only in military society."[245] The same behaviors performed by a civilian are not considered crimes. Therefore, a soldier may engage in an activity believing — without even thinking about it — that he still has the same rights he held as an American civilian. However, he may quickly learn that certain behaviors that are performed with impunity as a civilian result in arrest and incarceration in the military. That a man thus accused decides to desert can only be seen as reasonable. What kind of fair treatment can be expected when he finds out after the fact that what he is accused of having done is considered a crime?

Certainly, some soldiers in World War I, and other wars, desert to evade the consequence of a real crime. But these should not be lumped together with the many who may desert because they find that some activity they could perform freely as a civilian is suddenly a crime. More than evading the consequences of a crime, this could be seen as fleeing a patently unjust situation.

---

244. Cooper, pp. 268-269.
245. Keene, Jennifer Diane. 1994. Intelligence and Morale in the Army of a Democracy: The Genesis of Military Psychology during the First World War. *Military Psychology*, Vol. 6, 1994, p. 246

The study that made this finding also concluded that "There were ... unappealing aspects of military life that appeared to drive soldiers to rebel."[246] One must wonder why that conclusion was only drawn after exhaustive research into court-martial records, when it must appear obvious to the most casual, unbiased observer.

6. Involvement with women.

Like the other categories, little information is given about this topic. But it can only seem natural that men living with other men and spending all their time in the company of men would seek female companionship should the opportunity arise. Arriving in Europe and learning that prostitution was legal in France, the troops found opportunities were plentiful.

> The French embraced the inevitable and established a system of licensed brothels behind the front lines.... For the first four months after arriving in France the doughboys [American soldiers] were not under any formal ban from visiting brothels. This changed once [General John J.] Pershing realized how serious a problem VD was for the British and French, who both lost millions of troops' days each year as a result of sexually communicable diseases. Doughboys were then formally banned, on pain of severe punishment, from visiting brothels.[247]

Despite General Pershing's concern for the welfare of the soldiers — or the need to have soldiers ready and able for combat — the men in the trenches crawled out whenever possible to enjoy the comforts and pleasures of the opposite sex.

> Being barred from bordellos is one thing, abstinence is another. There is no way of quantifying how many doughboys had sexual relations with prostitutes or those who did not charge for the service, but it is evident from the archives that the typical AEF soldier had a normal inclination to indulge this need whenever possible.[248]

The information compiled by the government does not specify if these men who deserted due to "involvement with women" left permanently, or simply took extended periods of leave.

7. Addiction to the use of drugs and excessive use of intoxicants

It is difficult to assess the claim that addictions led to desertion in World War I in light of the increased understanding of addiction that has been gained in the latter part of the twentieth century. And the information documented by

---

246. Keene, p. 246
247. Mead, p. 201.
248. Mead, p. 202.

the military does not provide any useful guidelines for doing so. One could reasonably ask if the soldier turned to drugs or alcohol to provide relief from the horrors of war experiences. Winston Churchill, in commenting on the book The Secret Battle by A.P. Herbert, said this:

> [it was] one of those cries of pain wrung from the fighting troops by the prolonged and measureless torment through which they passed; and like the poems of Siegfried Sassoon should be read in each generation, that men and women are under no illusion about what war means.[249]

One description of a July 1, 1916 battle is as follows: "Wounds and death were the fruit of it, and to those who outlived it an accursed memory of horror."[250]

Another battle, three days later, produced this report by poet Siegfried Sassoon. There were "three very badly-mangled corpses lying in [a trench]; a man, short, plump, with turned-up moustaches, lying face downward and half sideways with one arm flung up as if defending his head, and a bullet through his forehead. A doll-like figure. Another hunched and mangled, twisted and scorched with many days' dark growth on his face, teeth clenched and grinning lips." Then, at noon, closer to the front line, he passed "thirty of our own laid out by the Mametz-Carnoy road, some side by side on their backs with bloody clotted fingers mingled as if they were handshaking in the companionship of death. And the stench undefinable."[251]

When this scene is multiplied by tens of thousands, few human beings can withstand the emotions that must certainly be triggered. The degree and intensity of stress experienced by soldiers in combat cannot be explained or understood fully by anyone who has not experienced it. One thing that studies have shown is that many people resort to drinking or drug use as a coping mechanism.

Military women and men are subjected to a wide range of stressors as part of their military work assignments and duties. Such stressors may be associated with the physical or mental challenges of their jobs, demands placed on them because of a shortage of other personnel, exposure to trauma associated with combat, or conflicts between military and family responsibilities. In addition, military women may experience stress associated with being a woman in a predominantly male environment or because of sexual harassment they may

---

249. Gilbert, p. 169.
250. Gilbert, p. 261.
251. Gilbert, p. 263.

encounter. Military personnel are also likely to experience the same stressors as other people outside the military, including the press of family and work responsibilities and uncertainties introduced by changing economic conditions.

Several decades of research also point to the multidimensional nature of reactions to stress and to the fact that such reactions may vary by gender. Numerous studies have reported strong relationships among stress, alcohol consumption, and emotional problems, with particularly robust connections between stressful life events and depression for women and stress and alcohol abuse for men. Exposure to traumatic stressors has been strongly implicated in the elevated rates of substance abuse and dependence among veterans.[252]

And then, some soldiers may abuse drugs and/or alcohol simply to deal with the loneliness of being far from home and loved ones.

8. Homesickness

As has been shown in earlier chapters, homesickness or related feelings can be a frequent cause of desertion. Men who are taken away from all that is familiar and thrust into extremely difficult, often life-threatening situations, will normally long for home. But homesickness is not simply a longing for home; a study of college students can be used to compare entry into the military.

> The transition to university life is often looked upon as a positive event. However, the changes that result can at times be stressful for the student, as he or she leaves existing sources of social support behind. Commonly, this stress creates feelings of homesickness and the intense desire to return home. While initial feelings of homesickness are obviously common for most, if not all, new students, prolonged feelings often prove to be problematic. Burt (1993) showed that persistent feelings of homesickness can lead to a lack of concentration and ability to perform, along with absent-mindedness and cognitive failures. Thus, homesickness in college students is an issue that must be taken seriously, for it can influence one's level of success in adapting to their new lives as collegians.[253]

This study concerns college students. However, many parallels between young adults entering college and young men entering the military can be found. As with college students, the new soldier leaves behind existing sources of social support. The response to this loss is the same in the soldier as in the student: feelings of homesickness and a sometimes overwhelming desire to return home.

---

252. Bray, Robert M., John A Fairbank and Mary Ellen Marsden. 1999. Stress and Substance Abuse among Military Women and Men. *American Journal of Drug and Alcohol Abuse, Vol. 25*, p. 1.

253. Johnson, James. E. *Homesickness in Socially Anxious First Year College Students.* College Student Journal, Vol. 37, 2003.

If these feelings persist, the soldier will demonstrate the same symptoms experienced by college students: lack of concentration, absent-mindedness, cognitive failures. Those who experience homesickness might notice an increase in depressed feelings, anxiety, obsessive thoughts and physical ailments. And while the military attempts to create a new support system for the soldier, it is often not sufficiently satisfying to ameliorate homesickness and its accompanying symptoms.

Homesickness is no longer viewed as something only experienced by a child when first going away to camp. The Textbook of Clinical Psychiatry describes it as a manifestation of separation anxiety.

> Homesickness can strike any of us when we have moved to new surroundings and are being called upon to meet our needs in a different way and with different people. Each of us has a different tolerance for change and learned different methods for coping with unfamiliar surroundings. Homesickness can be a general term that represents grieving, feeling sad, feeling loss of meaning, fearing change, anticipating disappointment, or being lonely. Sometimes it can become a more serious depression if the person cannot begin to meet his/her needs for love and belonging with new people.[254]

It is not hard to imagine the difficulty a soldier has in meeting "his/her needs for love and belonging" when on the battlefield. When we remember that a soldier, despite the best efforts of the US military, is first and foremost a human being — a man or woman — and only secondly a soldier, the need for that human contact and acceptance is not puzzling.

9. Cowardice

One cannot dismiss cowardice as a factor in desertion, but as indicated by the US government itself, this is only one of several reasons for desertion. Yet as mentioned in a previous chapter, there might be a fine, or possibly invisible, line between cowardice and the instinct for self-preservation. Anyone thrust into a life-threatening situation will certainly have thoughts on how best to protect him/herself. This may be especially true of a conscripted soldier, one who is simply following the rules of society without giving them much thought. When faced with mortal risk, and having no conviction in the cause he is forced to fight for, he may see desertion as an option. Cowardice may have nothing to do with it. Rather, lack of belief in what he is doing, coupled with feelings of self-preservation, may be the overriding factors.

---

254. Homesickness, 2004. University of Missouri – Rolla. http://campus.umr.edu/counsel/selfhelp/vpl/homesickness.html. Accessed October 20, 2005.

Additionally, a soldier may flee battle not due to cowardice, but to avoid killing. In spite of intense training by the military to see the 'enemy' as somehow less than human, not every soldier can buy into that idea. The thought of taking life may be so abhorrent that the soldier leaves the field of battle, risking the death penalty rather than kill. The military may misclassify this as cowardice.

The horrors of World War I cannot be exaggerated; only those who actually witnessed them can have any reasonable conception of their impact. "The destructiveness of the First World War, in terms of the number of soldiers killed, exceeded that of all other wars known to history."[255] An estimated 15,000,000 people, including at least 5,000,000 civilians, died in the war.[256] Gary Mead shares a tale that shows some of that horror:

> In October of 1918, shortly before the war ended, Private Albert Ettinger was in a foxhole. Needing a match he quickly ran to an adjacent foxhole, which had two men in it, one of whom was Color Sergeant Bill Sheahan. Ettinger retrieved a match and quickly returned to his foxhole. Moments later a shell landed in the adjacent foxhole. Rushing to the site, Ettinger found the second soldier, now missing both legs. There was no sign of Sheahan.
>
> Everyone was mystified as to what had happened to Sheahan. I told Tom Fitzsimmons he had been in that hole, because I had spoken to him only a few minutes before the shell exploded. At dawn we started to look around and soon came across what appeared to be a piece of roast beef strapped by a web belt, and the initials "W.S." were burned into the belt. That was the mortal remains of Bill Sheahan.[257]

Cowardice certainly caused desertions, as the study indicates. But nowhere in the study are the horrors of war even considered as a reason for desertion. That these horrors might be far more horrific than many a soldier could have anticipated, that many a soldier might decide he could not uphold his end of the bargain, cannot really be considered surprising.

10. Mishandling of men by officers and noncommissioned officers

A government report of 1919 states that one method of desertion prevention is "Intelligent and just handling of the soldier by officers and noncommissioned officers."[258]

This implies that there was a problem of mishandling of men, and such mishandling has manifested itself in ways that are shocking by any standards.

---

255. Gilbert, p. 540.
256. Gilbert, page xv.
257. Mead, p. 326.
258. Humber, p. 9.

World War I produced such cases as these: a recruit refused to surrender his cigarettes to an officer and was sentenced to twenty years at hard labor. For being "disrespectful" to an officer, a soldier received five years in prison. A young soldier, for being AWOL for twenty-seven days, was sentenced to forty years in prison. Another AWOL soldier was sentenced to life in prison. Thirteen Negro soldiers were convicted of murder and executed two days later — four months before their "appeals" were processed in Washington.[259]

Leaders demonstrated their incompetence in battle as well as in their individual dealing with soldiers, as is revealed in a comment concerning battles in the fall of 1918. "[T]here is no avoiding the fact that the green AEF divisions thrown into this battle were revealed as grievously inexperienced and sometimes poorly led. Casualties were unexpectedly heavy."[260]

Leaders stood aloof from the soldiers they led, causing resentment among the troops. While this was not uniform throughout the military, it occurred sufficiently to be noticed by other officers. Leadership as a cause for or factor in desertion has been discussed in previous chapters. Like other issues leading to desertion, the US military has consistently failed to address and rectify this problem.

11. Home conditions, such as poverty or illness in family.[261]

From the Revolutionary War to the present, concern about conditions back at home has always been a factor. A soldier's need to provide for and protect his family often outweighs any other obligation. At great risk to themselves, soldiers frequently leave the military to return home to help resolve family problems.

At the start of World War I, trade with Europe, which up to that time had been a great source of revenue — and thus employment — for Americans, decreased to a fraction of what it had been prior to the war. Jobs disappeared, [*NO*] and this may have encouraged some men to enlist. Once the war began, and fewer men were available for domestic employment, women began entering the work field. However, then as now their salaries were significantly less than those of men. This hardship may have influenced some men to desert and return home.

Jobs increased ε start of WWI

---

259. Sherrill, pp. 73 – 74.
260. Mead, pp. 303 – 304.
261. Humber, p. 5.

A study of two hundred desertion cases that were tried between April 6 and November 30, 1917, added several reasons for desertion. The following table summarizes the study: [262]

	Principal Cause	Number of Cases	Percentage of Total	Culpability	
				Positive	Mitigating Circumstances
1	Cowardice	4	2	4	
2	Degeneracy	3	1.5	3	
3	Desire for Active Service	9	4.5		9
4	Drug Addiction/ Drunkenness	44	22	30	14
5	Enemy Affiliations	3	1	2	
6	Entanglement with Women	6	3	1	5
7	Family Troubles	7	3.5		7
8	Fear of Medical or Surgical Treatment	6	3		6
9	General Dislike of Service	8	4	6	2
10	Incorrigibility	10	5	10	
11	Money Fines	4	3	4	
12	Subnormal Mentality/ Insanity/Ignorance of Seriousness of Offense	36	18.5		36
13	Trouble with Superior Officer	13	6.5	6	7
14	Unpopularity with Associates	3	1.5	2	1
15	Obscure	31	15.5		
16	Influenced by Associates	1	0.5		1
17	Homesickness	9	4.5	1	8

In order to facilitate comparisons between this list and that referenced above, the following separate categories have been combined: "Drug Addiction"

---

262. Humber, p. 3.

and "Drunkeness" as one category, and "Subnormal Mentality," "Insanity" and "Ignorance of Seriousness of Offense" as another category.

This report adds several categories:

- Desire for Active Service
- Enemy Affiliations
- Fear of Medical or Surgical Treatment
- Incorrigibility
- Unpopularity with Associates
- Obscure, and
- Influenced by Associates.

Other categories listed are named differently but are analogous to classifications in the first list:

"Degeneracy" equates to "Lack of moral character and stamina;"

"General dislike of service" equates to "Unwillingness to submit to military discipline and restraint," and

"Money fines" roughly equates to "To evade the consequences of a crime."

One additional category is worthy of note, although mentioned only incidentally in the report:[263] poor leadership and training, especially within the militia, which have plagued the military since the American Revolution. The report, in discussing how little soldiers understood of the Articles of War, states: "Particularly was this so with regard to units mustered into the Federal service from the National Guard, where lax discipline and poor instruction in military regulations was the contributing cause of many desertions."[264]

Even in a glowing description of troop behavior, poor leadership has been noted. A description of the 26th American Division, one of the first to reach France, shows the lack of experience and the potential jeopardy this placed the soldiers in:

> It had more experience in trench warfare than any other American Division, except the 1st, but it had never had any opportunity to train in liaison work under conditions of open warfare. Its staff personnel had seen many changes, and had not developed that machine-like certainty of action so necessary in handling 25,000 men in the presence of the enemy. [T]he lack of instruction and experience in troop leading placed officers at a disadvantage when troop leading of a high order was demanded by the complexity of the maneuver.[265]

---

263. Humber, p. 2.
264. Humber, p. 2.
265. Liggett, Hunter. 1925. *Commanding an American Army*, p. 51.

The same report states that in the week between July 18 and July 25, 1918, the 26th Division "lost through all causes about 4,000 officers and men, of whom 600 were killed."[266] How many of these deserted, if any, is not specified.

The symptoms of poor leadership are obvious even among the leaders' peer group.

> Some men are so constituted by nature that success gives them what is known as the "big head." They at once become inflated by an exaggerated idea of their own importance. One of the signs of this condition is the assumption of an overbearing manner. Were the effects not so serious upon others, this state of affairs would be laughable. Invariably, men of this type are correspondingly depressed when affairs do not go right. They go at a step from bombastic optimism to despair. They are unfit for the command of others.[267]

The government's attempts to prevent the reasons for desertion during World War I seem sadly misplaced in the light of even its own acknowledged reasons for desertion.

> The Government has made strenuous effort to better the condition of the soldier, especially during wartime, with respect to his living conditions, dress, pay, enjoyment and contentment. There is little more which can be done for the soldier, and there is no justifiable reason for him to desert.[268]

It seems a bizarre juxtaposition to invoke "enjoyment and contentment" in the context of military life. Soldiers are separated from loved ones, deprived of the basic right and dignity of making decisions for themselves, thrust into life-threatening situations and treated as any other tool in a well-oiled war machine. This is not compatible with the pursuit of "enjoyment and contentment."

The efforts of the military, although possibly well intentioned, do not address the causes of desertion.

For example:

> With a view to promoting morale, health, and efficiency, and to diminish the temptation to be absent without leave and to desert, a Leave Area system on a duty-status was established in France for the American Expeditionary Forces. The finest French recreational resorts, with all their accessory attractions, were leased and organized into leave centers to which soldier(s) could go at Government expense.[269]

The same document that details this information includes a discussion of the "luxurious hotels frequented in ordinary times by wealthy vacationists..." and

---

266. Liggett, p. 52.
267. Liggett, p. 159.
268. Humber, p. 5.
269. Humber, p. 2.

"the best food and service...."[270] Yet when we review the reasons for desertion, as identified by the government, it does not appear that pampering soldiers in French luxury for a week and then flinging them back into the foxholes of war addresses any of them in any way. It may at first appear somewhat puzzling that the study states that these measures would eliminate any "justifiable reason" to desert when the measures in no way address the major reasons for desertion. But the reasons for desertion as described herein cannot be eliminated without a fundamental change in the US military, to include allowing soldiers to maintain their rights as US citizens while in the military, and treating them as human beings first and soldiers second. It would also help if the US desisted from imperial ventures whose objectives are often, at best, poorly understood by those forced to carry them out, and at worst are abhorrent to them.

It was in World War I that the idea of morale, and the need to keep up the spirits of the soldiers, was first conceived. The Morale Division was created as the result of the efforts of individuals who believed that military commanders did not appreciate the human component in the army. Some military officials recognized the enormous challenges of incorporating millions of soldiers into what had previously been a peacetime, defensive army and preparing them to fight a war on foreign shores. Reports of dissatisfactions among French and British troops strengthened the recognition of the need to improve the morale of the American soldiers, and hopefully prevent some of the problems the other countries were experiencing within the ranks.

The political maneuverings that were required before the top brass accepted the importance of the psychology of the soldier need not be documented here. There was strong resistance to the concept of considering the soldier's thoughts and emotions. Eventually, in 1918, Colonel Edward L. Munson of the Medical Corps, the Director of Medical Officers' Training in the Office of the Surgeon General, convinced Assistant Secretary of War Frederick Keppel of the need for some kind of psychological intervention.

> In his initial memo, Munson (1918) highlighted the consensus emerging among intelligence officers that many recruits seemed unclear about the purpose of the war. Wondering how dedicated even knowledgeable conscripts were to a war they had been drafted to fight, Munson predicted that a morale crisis was imminent once the United States began to sustain the kinds of losses suffered by the European armies during their first year at war.[271]

---

270. Humber, p. 2.
271. Keene, p. 245.

It should not be surprising that the efforts of these psychologists were not universally accepted by those in military leadership positions who did not see soldiers as men, but rather as tools for war. "The empathetic perspective that morale advocates offered often annoyed more traditionally oriented military officials who dismissively accused them of trying to turn military training into summer camp."[272] Denied permission by Commander-in-Chief John J. Pershing to observe and treat men in the American Expeditionary Forces, they had to content themselves with monitoring training camp problems. For many young soldiers, the seeds of discontent that may eventually lead to desertion are sown there.

Jennifer Keene cites the following scene:

> Sent to Camp Meade, Maryland, to observe the Army's induction procedure firsthand, Captain E. R. Padgett (1918) watched hundreds of drafted men arrive each day and stand for hours in the summer sun with their suitcases, satchels, and bundles lying on the ground near their feet. "Some of these draftees were laughing [and] joking, [but] others (many, many of them) were sullen, subdued, sad," Padgett (1918) reported to his superiors in the Morale Division, "and I saw a good many of them who were having a hard time (and not always successfully) in keeping the tears back". At a loss to explain why these men seemed so resentful of being called into service, Padgett noticed that many of the noncommissioned officers monitoring each line of recruits had large, loosely furled American flags under their arms. These were, Padgett (1918) realized "evidently flags taken from the drafted men as they came into camp; evidently flags used by groups of drafted men from the same respective towns when they marched down to the depot amid the cheers and applause of their fellow townsmen, who gave them a good "send-off." Then, when they hit Meade, the first crack out of the box, they were let down with a thud and their flag taken away from them.[273]

For many recruits and draftees this was their first taste of military discipline and the lack of freedom it brings. For these men the flag was a cherished symbol of the sacrifice they were making on behalf of their beloved country, presented to them by loved ones they were leaving and might never see again. To have that country thank them with such a slap in the face could not have been easy to accept.

Padgett and his associates recognized the problem and recommended a solution; however, how it was to be implemented was never explained.

> From their own newly assigned vantage points, Morale Division psychologists, welfare workers, and intelligence officers concurred that receptions like these sent a terrible message to new recruits. Padgett (1918) recommended that "we could at

---

272. Keene, p. 247.
273. Keene, p. 246.

least implant among them the idea that they are not conscripts, taken in the draft, but men selected through the draft to serve the Government, and therefore, they have been honored — which to most of them, I dare say, is a brand new idea."[274]

How the Morale Division employees thought they could convince draftees that they were a select and honored group, chosen among all others, when almost all others were also chosen — and when they were about to be treated to a relentless campaign in boot camp that did anything but honor them — was never made clear.

Despite its limitations, the work of the Morale Division was at least a step toward the recognition that soldiers were men first and soldiers second. This was a step, however, in a very short walk.

> When Assistant Chief of Staff, Brigadier General William Hahn (1921), reviewed the final desertion study in 1921, he agreed that the basic "problem consists of creating a state of mind where the men want to do what the commander wants them to do". Hahn's receptivity to probing the psychology of the soldier was, however, atypical of postwar commanders' reaction to the Morale Division's crime studies.[275]

Even Hahn's purported receptivity is dubious; "creating a state of mind" does not seem to indicate independent, thought-out decision-making. It seems more like thought reform. "[T]hought reform programs... appear to be designed to destabilize the subject's most central aspects of the experience of the self. The newer programs undermine a person's basic consciousness, reality awareness, beliefs and world view, emotional control, and defense mechanism."[276] As newly recruited or drafted soldiers are isolated from all that is familiar, indoctrinated with the philosophies of the military and taught to rely on only each other and their superior officers for information and support, the thought reform principles noted above seem to be in full effect.

The general philosophy of punishments for desertion during World War I are best described in a letter from the Judge Advocate General of the Army to the Secretary of War, dated March 10, 1919:

> No one can approach the subject of sentences for desertion in time of war without keeping in mind the solemn and terrible warning recorded expressly for and benefit by Brig. Gen. Oakes, acting assistant Provost Marshall General for Illinois,

---

274. Keene, p. 246.
275. Keene, p. 247.
276. Singer, Margaret Thaler, PH. D., Richard Ofshe, Ph.D. Thought Reform Programs and the Production of Psychiatric Casualties. http://www.refocus.org/mental.html. Accessed October 29, 2005.

as set forth in his report printed in the Report of the Provost Marshall General for the Civil War. In impressive language he lays the following injunction upon us.

"Incalculable evil has resulted from the clemency of the Government towards deserters. By a merciful severity at the commencement of the war the mischief might have been nipped in the bud, and the crime of desertion could never have reached the gigantic proportions which it attained before the close of the conflict. The people were then ardent and enthusiastic in their loyalty, and...were fully prepared to see that deserters from the Army would be remorselessly arrested, tried by court martial, and, if guilty, be forthwith shot to death with musketry.

"Arrest, trial, and execution should have been the short, sharp, and decisive fate of the first deserters."

This solemn warning was naturally in our minds at the opening of the present war. But, in spite of its urgency, it was decided to exhibit our faith in the American people.... We believed that the "short, sharp, and decisive fate of the first deserters" should not be the extreme penalty as urged by Gen. Oakes. And it is a fact that the (approximately) 3000 convictions for desertion, during the war, the sentence of death was imposed in only 24 cases, and in every such case it was commuted or remitted.[277]

There were 5,584 men charged with desertion during World War I, and 2,657 convicted.[278]

Additionally, between April 6, 1917 and November 30, 1918, 4,316 soldiers were AWOL.[279] It is also worth noting that not all young men who chose not to be involved in the military deserted; many avoided being drafted. "The rate of evasion ran at around 11 percent, or about 340,000 men in the course of the war."[280] Of nearly 65,000 who applied for conscientious objector status, nearly 21,000 served in non-combat roles. There were some 4,000 more, who refused to participate at all. They "suffered imprisonment and often harsh treatment at the hands of military authorities."[281]

World War I is unique in American experience in that there were no official executions for desertion. Anecdotal evidence that some men were shot by other soldiers at the moment the desertion was occurring is unreliable, although the possibility cannot be entirely discounted.

World War I also had the lowest recorded desertion rate: in 1919 only two out of one thousand soldiers deserted.

---

277. Humber, p. 9 (emphasis in original).
278. Humber, p. 6
279. Mead, p. 207.
280. Cooper, p. 272.
281. Cooper, p. 273.

It was also after World War I, and based on information gleaned from court martials for desertion during the war, that some measures approaching fairness were introduced. During the court martials for desertion in World War I the age of the soldier was not required information. Although the fact that the accused was a "youth" was sometimes mentioned, of the study of the two hundred cases referenced herein, the age of the accused is known in only nineteen of them. Of those nineteen, the average age is 19.5 years. Of those whose age was known, the youngest soldier accused of deserting was 15![282] Certainly some mitigating circumstances should be seen in such cases.

One might say that mitigating circumstances are present in most, if not all, cases. But the extreme youth of a soldier who deserts should have an impact on the judge when sentencing. While the US remains, in 2006, the only industrialized nation on the planet that still executes minors, a teenage soldier who deserts probably was not in a position, indeed should not have been put in a position, to cause serious jeopardy to others by doing so.

The US military's experience with desertion during the Great War appears to have taught it little. Although the government made attempts to identify the causes of desertion, these efforts were made within a predefined mindset: those who desert are in some way inferior to those who do not. Whether it is caused by a dubious moral character, association with women, or criminal activities, men who unlawfully leave the service are seen as separate from and inferior in some basic way from those who don't.

Yet evidence to the contrary is readily available, even within the information contained in the government's own studies. As has been shown in relation to the Great War and earlier wars, it is not the soldier that is to blame, but how the institution of the US military is now, and always has been, constituted. Without fundamental change that allows a man or woman to be, first and foremost, a human being, and a soldier only by chosen occupation, the military will continue to struggle with desertion.

---

282. Humber, p. 2.

CHAPTER 7: WORLD WAR II

No fiction writer could ever have invented the horror of World War II. This conflict, which lasted almost six years, engulfed much of the world and killed over 56,000,000 people, over half of whom were civilians. The war started when Germany invaded Poland on September 1, 1939, but the causes of the war predated that event by several years.

The factors leading to this war were extremely complex and will not be detailed here. The following discussion provides a summary of four of the main reasons, but is not intended to be exhaustive.[283]

- Hitler's Goal. Adolph Hitler had come to power in Germany and sought imperial power. He wanted to dominate not only Europe, but also the entire world. This would only come in violation of the Treaty of Versailles, signed in 1919, after the First World War. This treaty severely limited the size of the German military.

- The Goals of Germany's Allies. Italy sought a Fascist-Roman empire in the Mediterranean and Africa, and Japan wanted to extend its empire to China and Australia. Additionally, Germany, Italy and Japan were hostile to the Soviet Union and Communism.

- The Passive Attitude of Other World Powers. Great Britain was sympathetic to Germany's efforts to recover some of its losses from the first World War and, until March 1939, appeased Germany by allowing it to take aggressive actions in Europe. The US at that time had chosen a policy of isolationism, and France could not rely on either the US or Britain for assistance against Germany.

---

283. Martel, Gordon. 1999. *The Origins of the Second World War Reconsidered*; A.J.P. Taylor and the Historians, p. 7.

• The League of Nations, founded after World War I, was ineffective. The concept of such an organization was new, and nations still suffering from the first World War were not interested in having it monitor or regulate their activities if the League's regulations were at odds with their own nationalist goals.[284]

America's entry into the war was cautious. Four days after the invasion of Poland, the US declared its neutrality. But in November, the Neutrality Act was passed by Congress that allowed the US to send arms and other aid to Britain and France.[285] In June of 1940, the US switched from a policy of neutrality to one of non-belligerency, which was defined in part as assisting victims of aggression.[286] One month later, on July 19, President Roosevelt signed the Two Ocean Navy Expansion Act, which started a large-scale expansion of the Navy, and opened the door for the US to declare war on either Germany or Japan, or both.[287] On September 16 of that same year, the president signed the Conscription Bill; the draft started on October 29. These and other steps prepared the country for war.

On December 7, 1941, Pearl Harbor was bombed. The following day the US declared war on Japan, and America was once again at war.

Desertion during World War II was no less a problem than in previous wars. Desertion rates peaked at 6.3% in 1944, but dropped to 4.5% the following year.[288] During the war, 21,049 US soldiers were sentenced for desertion, and 49 of them received death sentences.[289] The highest rate of desertions occurred the same year in which more soldiers were actually being discharged from the Army for psychoneurosis than were drafted.

The reasons for desertion during World War II were not significantly different from those in previous wars.

1. Inability to adjust to military life;

---

284. Martel, p. 7

285. Armstrong, Hamilton Fish, and Allen W. Dulles. 1939. *Can America Stay Neutral?* Pages 72 – 74.

286. Walker, George K. Information Warfare and Neutrality, *Vanderbilt Journal of Transnational Law*, Vol. 33, 2000.

287. Copes, Jan M. and Timothy J. Runyan. 1994. *To Die Gallantly: The Battle of the Atlantic.* Page 4.

288. Chambers, (John Whiteclay II. Ed. 1999. *The Oxford Companion to American Military History.* New York: Oxford UP). Jian, Chen. China's Road to the Korean War: The Making of the Sino-American Confrontation, p. 212.

289. Vance, Laurence M. 2005. The Execution of Eddie Slovik. http://www.lewrockwell.com/vance/vance34.html. Accessed on October 10, 2005.

2. Disagreement with or apathy towards the reasons given for going to war;

3. Incompetent leaders;

4. Horror of war, and

5. Family considerations.

A closer look at each factor adds to understanding; it must be remembered while studying these reasons that some of them overlap, and some might affect a single 18-year-old or a married 25-year-old in considerably different measure. For example, a man might have difficulty adjusting to military life because it separates him from his family.

INABILITY TO ADJUST TO MILITARY LIFE

There has not been a war in which this factor has not led to desertions. In order to fully understand why this is the case, the mentality of the military must be understood.

> [A]ll modern armies are essentially totalitarian enterprises. Once you sign up for them, or are drafted, you are a slave. The penalty for becoming a fugitive is death. Even now, the enforcements against mutiny, desertion, going AWOL, or what have you, are never questioned.
>
> This is remarkable, if you think about it. Imagine that you work for Wal-Mart but find the job too dangerous, and try to quit. You are told that you may not, so you run away. The management catches up to you, and jails you. You refuse to go and resist. Finally, you are shot. We would all recognize that this is exploitation, an atrocity, a crime, a clear example of the disregard that this company has for human life. The public outrage would be palpable. The management, not the fleeing employees, would be jailed or possibly executed.
>
> In what other occupation in the country are there severe penalties, including prison and in some cases execution, for 'desertion,' i.e., for quitting the particular employment? If someone quits General Motors, is he shot at sunrise?[290]

This may, at first glance, seem an extreme comparison, but the fact that it is valid should be shocking. During World War II not only did the military have this power over soldiers, in over 10,000,000 cases it forced men into this position. Of those, approximately 2,600,000 were trained for combat.[291]

---

290. Rothbard, Murray N. 2002. *For a New Liberty: The Libertarian Manifesto*, Revised Edition, pp. 78–79.

291. Huie, William Bradford. *The Execution of Private Slovik* (Yardley, 2004) p. 11.

The military makes little or no concession for a man or woman's individual characteristics; individuality has no place in the US military. The soldier brings certain characteristics to the military situation; these interact with the objective characteristics of the military situation in some complicated way. This interaction determines the relative strength of the soldier's avoidance tendencies (i.e., his tendencies to reject or avoid military life) as opposed to his inhibitory tendencies (i.e. his tendencies to accept military life and conform to military rules, which inhibit the AWOL response).[292]

A man or woman's history, interests, experience, aptitudes, etc. play no part in his or her role in the military. If by chance a soldier is assigned to a duty for which he or she has an interest it is merely that: chance.

The conditions of war are seldom related beyond heroic deeds or major disasters. But many soldiers experienced neither. What they did experience was fear, filth and hunger.

> The hole had become crowded with personal trash. The mud didn't help. Neither did the smell. Our sweaty bodies, rarely washed. Stained underwear, as soiled today as yesterday, and unchanged. Our excrement, a daily problem, never solved. All the sour run-off of ordinary life. None of it could be avoided.[293]

Those who enlisted may have had a variety of reasons for doing so that were unrelated to the war. One anecdote may be instructive.

> Prior to my enlistment, there was no burning desire to become a part of the military. In fact it was the least desirable choice. Because of the hopeless attitude on 9 December 1939, I acted on an impulse and joined the Army Air Corps. This was not without the aid of an alcoholic beverage. There was an immediate feeling of being imprisoned once I become sober but there was no way of undoing that which had been done. This imprisonment due to a signed contract was to last at least four years.

> An individual, in order to function adequately in the work force, should be free from the bondage created by emotional instability. I was unaware of the conflicts which prohibited me from feeling good. After a few days in the Army Air Corps, I was made painfully aware of the fact that there were several reasons why I had a completely hopeless feeling. Having no previous knowledge of life in the military I felt trapped. I had no inkling of how to cope with a set of circumstances which were a part of military tradition.

> In the Air Force as in any other career, the underlying goal is to feel good. Without accomplishing this, some individuals begin to look for alternatives. Those who do not feel good about themselves or their relationship with others, often search for an effective method to cope with anxiety and tension. I had the constant and pain-

---

292. Osburn, Hobart G. and Charles Brown. 1954. 'A Preliminary Investigation of Delinquency in the Army.' US Army Military History Institute, p. 12.
293. Kotlowitz, Robert. 1997. *Before Their Time*, p. 120.

ful feeling of depression and lacked the tools to experience the ordinary pleasures of life. Alcohol became a means to adjust to the Air Force and society.[294]

The factors listed herein include feelings of imprisonment, unfamiliarity with the demands of military life, depression, anxiety and tension. Each of these alone could lead a soldier to desert; together they may create an overwhelming need to depart from the military, using any means possible.

Men and women who have spent their lives exercising their freedom of choice in employment, living arrangements, friends, etc. will not easily adjust to being plucked from all that is familiar and thrust into routines of mind-numbing activities followed by the constant horrors of war (described below). With no lawful means of escape, many during World War II elected to take an unlawful means: desertion.

DISAGREEMENT WITH OR APATHY TOWARDS THE WAR

There is little evidence to support any suggestion that a significant number of Americans did not support the causes of this war. As word of the horrors of the Nazi regime, sympathy for the British, and fear of the development of an overwhelming European power seeped into America's consciousness, it was easy to motivate the populace. But such outrage does not always translate into a desire to take a personal role in overcoming the wrong.

In his memoir, Robert Kotlowitz states the following:

> In 1943, I was a pre-med day student at Johns Hopkins University, in Baltimore, Maryland. Half the student body at Hopkins during World War II was pre-med; it was a respectable way of evading the draft. But I was a fraud on campus, and not the only one. I didn't want to be a doctor.[295]

However, Mr. Kotlowitz did not object to being drafted. He believed in the war and considered its cause to be just.

Men still in school, with young families or starting on promising careers, had little desire to disrupt their lives and risk everything at unfamiliar sites in foreign countries. That millions did so is commendable, although most of them did so under the duress known as conscription, or the draft. They went when

---

294. Alcohol, Alcoholism, and the Air Force. http://www.jimmydoolittlemuseumpromotions.com/chapter7.htm. Accessed July 8, 2005.
295. Kotlowitz, p. 3.

called, but did not volunteer to do so. Thousands who were called made the decision to leave the field of battle.

Additionally, approximately 12,000 men were classified as Conscientious Objectors, "primarily from the three historic peace churches — the Brethren, Mennonites, and Quakers — and also from other denominations."[296] They served in other areas related to the war effort, often through Civilian Public Service (CPS), including work in devastated European cities at the close of the war.

Although it is a small number, some men refused any participation in the war effort. Even with the knowledge that they faced prison, they chose to live by their deeply held principles. Said one:

> I was influenced by my exposure to the lies and failures of World War I and the examples of persons who fought in that war or went to prison for resisting it. A second influence included my visits to Nazi Germany in 1936 and 1937 when I was anti-Nazi and the US government, banks and major corporations were supporting Hitler.[297]

Another young man from that era, Bronson P. Clark, reported on his own actions in 1942:

> Even though I knew I would not accept CPS, having been denied conscientious objector status by my draft board...I wanted to establish that I was a CO first for future treatment within the prison and parole system.[298]

Mr. Clark and other men had clear reasons for refusing participation in Civilian Public Service. At one point he was attached, by leg iron, to Charles Butcher, a Harvard graduate and past editor of the Harvard Crimson. Mr. Butcher filed a lawsuit in an attempt to prove that CPS camps were being operated by Gen. Lewis B. Hershey and other military officers, and not under civilian control as provided by law. Mr. Clark, who was denied CO status, also mentioned that he later learned that his local draft board had denied all CO applications.

While he was in prison Mr. Clark's first child, a daughter, was born. He wrote a letter to her from prison in which he said, in part: "Our principle must be

---

296. We Won't Go: Narratives of Resistance to World War II, the Korean War, the Vietnam War, the 1990 – 91 US- Iraq War, and the 2003 – US-Iraq War; Staughton Lynd, ed. http://www.unitedforpeace.org/downloads/wontgo5-24.doc. Accessed July 12, 2005.
297. Gara, Larry and Lenna Mae Gara. 1999. *A Few Small Candles: War Resisters of World War II Tell their Stories*, p. 20.
298. Gara, p. 3.

to build, not destroy, to create, not to crush. If in any way I have helped these immortal truths, then my being in prison is a thing I hope you shall be proud of."[299]

The treatment these men received would not have surprised resisters from earlier wars, but it would have surprised most citizens. One man talked about his confinement in "the Hole," "a completely bare, isolated cell with only a floor drain for a toilet. I was permitted no reading or writing material and had neither a bed nor a mattress. Each evening a guard brought a blanket and took it away in the morning."[300]

This same man was later confined to the Hole for four days. He had developed the habit of early rising to meditate on his cot. "A rule-conscious lieutenant...ordered me to stop the practice. If I wanted to meditate, he said, I should go to the recreation room. I made the mistake of questioning the logic of his order...."[301]

These men, some of them Harvard educated, some married, with children, endured prison rather than compromise their principles.

INCOMPETENT LEADERSHIP

The Peter Principle states "in a hierarchy, every employee tends to rise to his level of incompetence,"[302] and further that they will remain there until retirement. This is as true in the military organization as it is in any other. It is far worsened in combat when lives are at stake.

While there has been no widespread study of leadership difficulties during World War II, some anecdotal evidence exists. The report of Pierre A. Rinfret is one such example.

Rinfret was a Canadian citizen but a US resident when he was drafted in 1942 at the age of 18. He was seriously wounded in battle, spent several months in hospital and was discharged in November of 1945. His brother Allen Herve Rinfret was killed in battle, and Pierre believes it was due to command incompetence. His version of the story follows; grammar and punctuation are his own:

---

299. Gara, p. 16.
300. Gara, p. 84.
301. Gara, p. 84.
302. Peter, Laurence J. and Raymond Hull. 1969. *The Peter Principle*, page 25.

"My brother was killed as a result of command stupidity.

"His company was in reserve about a thousand yards behind the front. They had been relieved for a rest from combat. They were in a chow line when an enemy barrage came in. He was killed where he was standing.

"He died needlessly and foolishly as a result of some stupid officer deciding to have a chow line close to the front!

"How dumb can you be?

"How do I know all this? His combat buddies told me!

"BUT — IT WAS WORSE THAN THAT.

"The 10th Mountain Division, to which my brother belonged, landed on the beaches of Kiska (one of a chain off of Alaska). They fought the enemy for weeks and progressed to the middle of the islands. The shelling was very heavy and fire fights were numerous. There were no Japanese on the Island!

"They had pulled out several weeks earlier and the American troops were fighting each other! The Japanese were long gone but no one knew it until the American troops faced each other.

"Talk about command stupidity and incompetence!"

He talks further about a childhood friend.

"One of the people I grew up with was named Matty Sigmann and he was killed as he was descending from a truck loaded with replacements which was being unloaded right at the front! They never had a chance! They were killed before they ever got off the truck!

"They died in vain.

"Confusion and chaos were the norm."

Direction from those in leadership could not always be expected. "[W]e were never but never briefed on where we were going, what to expect to find in front of us nor where our own troops might be. It was just a horde of soldiers moving forward until they engaged the enemy."[303]

Rinfret, who was a member of the 104th Infantry Regiment, does not restrict his criticisms to that organization. His writings detail other such situations.

Another apparent weak link in military leadership was Rear Admiral Richmond Kelly Turner. Some accounts seem to indicate that his peers and subordinates spent almost as much time and effort preventing his potential disasters

---

303. The 104th Infantry Regiment of the 26th Infantry Division; Peter Rinfret. http://www.rinfret.com/ww2.html#anchor45432. Accessed August 6, 2005.

as they did following his orders. His record appears spotty at best, ranging from brilliant to incredibly stupid. A description of the man and a few anecdotes from his career illustrate his character and some of the problems he caused.

> Kelly Turner was a loud, strident, arrogant person who enjoyed settling all matters by simply raising his voice and roaring like a bull captain in the old navy. His peers understood this and accepted it with amused resignation because they valued him for what he was: a good and determined leader with a fine mind — when he chose to use it.[304]

> Rear Adm. Richmond Kelly Turner, commander, South Pacific Amphibious Force, alone of the navy leaders, displayed the same type of bold aggressive leadership that characterized King. Unlike King, however, he was possessed of a colossal ego that sometimes led to decisions that ignored the dictates of ordinary common sense.[305]

Arrogance, brilliance and ego, when combined with a tremendous amount of power, greatly increase the risk of disaster. In Turner's case, these forces combined to bring that disaster.

> Turner lays himself open to the charge that, like so many inexperienced commanders, he failed to employ all weapons available to him: specifically, the more than fifteen scouting planes of the cruiser force. Had they been sent out to scour the area south of Rekata Bay at sunset, they could not have failed to locate the oncoming enemy force before nightfall, as it was only a comparatively short distance northwest of Savo Island. Instead, these planes, many with tanks filled with gasoline, remained on their catapults or on deck and became gigantic infernos when ignited by the first enemy projectiles, adding more death and horror to this indescribably dreadful night. In short, Turner had ample means of his own to detect Mikawa's approaching cruisers, but he failed to use them.[306]

A leader who is completely competent yet arrogant impedes his abilities by losing the respect of the soldiers he is to lead. One officer was compared favorably with many others:

> I had the feeling that he never lied, especially to himself. (I wanted to be like that.) Also, I knew that he treated everybody in exactly the same way — I mean everybody. And, far more rare than you might think, he didn't compete with his men in the third platoon, did not compete with them, malign them, laugh at them, or condescend, as we saw all around us all the time in other platoons, in other companies. Rocky had once said. 'Don't worry your asses about F. J. Gallagher. He's not a man who will leave his wounded on the battlefield.'[307]

---

304. Carey, Neil and Merrill B. Twining. 1996. *No Bended Knee: The Battle for Guadalcanal. The Memoir of Gen. Merrill B. Twining, USMC (Ret.).* p. 43.
305. Carey, p. 70.
306. Carey, p. 71.
307. Kotlowitz, p. 128.

When men and women are subjected to the harsh, unspeakable conditions of combat they have a right to expect that those who lead them into battle will recognize their worth and their willingness to sacrifice their lives. When personal dignity, possibly the last thing a soldier has to cling to in the unspeakable horror of combat, is violated by those who should most respect it, another reason for desertion is provided to the soldier.

HORROR OF WAR

As mentioned previously, World War II was the most horrific war that had ever been waged, engulfing much of the world and causing the death of tens of millions of people, many of them civilians. American soldiers — many of them still in their teens — were as unprepared for what they had to face as were the soldiers of any nation. No one could have anticipated the experiences of the most destructive conflict in the history of the world.

Even before they saw combat, the soldiers endured suffering, but it could not prepare them for what was to come. "Life at war for the American GI was essentially long hours of hard physical labour, painful slogging under heavy weights and tedious boredom — interspersed with moments of sheer gut-wrenching terror."[308]

> Life consisting of moving from one foxhole to another had a wide variety of survival concerns; enemy bullets, bayonets and bombs were the worst, but not always the most constant.
>
> No matter what the weather, dehydration was always a concern. Marching made them sweat, and combat left them cotton-mouthed and croaking. Water was often what they could dip out of a shell-hole. Treated with iodine or halezone tablets to kill the bugs. It tasted...well, it tasted like nectar if you were parched and shaking after a firefight.
>
> Of course, there was always French wine or Dutch beer to be liberated if a GI was storming through Europe. If he was island-hopping in the Pacific, a little Japanese sake was said to help kill the intestinal worms that infiltrated through cuts, jungle sores or shrapnel wounds.[309]

They were surrounded by death. The life expectancy of some soldiers going to the front was measured in minutes. "All the replacements, or so it

---

308. GI Joe: US Soldiers of World War Two; Captain Dale Dye, USMC (Retired). http://www.bbc.co.uk/history/war/wwtwo/us_soldiers_01.shtml. Accessed August 15, 2005.
309. GI Joe. Accessed August 15, 2005.

seemed, were as green as could be and most of them did not even have the most rudimentary training. They were cannon fodder and they were killed almost as soon as they arrived in combat."[310]

For many soldiers fear was an almost constant companion. Anyone when thrust into a situation unlike anything they could ever imagine and facing death around every corner will experience fear. There was "the chemical excess of our own pungent fear, which, like a dog, I could sniff out and clearly identify."[311]

That fear manifested itself in a variety of ways. "Johnson was beginning to show nerves for the first time since I had known him, snorting like a horse as we squatted there in the hole...."[312] One can only wonder what such a level of constant, mortal fear does to a person.

Near the conclusion of one horrific battle, one soldier writes, he knew that to stay alive he had to play dead; Germans were still nearby and he had no other choice. He remained as a corpse for hours, slowing his breathing, heartbeat and pulse so any casual onlooker would think him dead.

As he lay there he saw some of the wounded men from his unit.

> By then, fifteen feet away, Johnson was begging for water, whimpering softly into the mud without stopping — an animal's sound that came from deep in his larynx, with no recognizable human overtones. It was not possible to help him. That I swear. It was not possible to help anyone. Ralph Natale, alongside Brewster, was convulsing from his wounds. Ira Fedderman, somewhere ahead of Bern, whose helmet I could no longer see, was calling for his mother, the saddest call of all. So were others.[313]

The carnage soldiers experienced is beyond description. On January 12, 1945, the United States Office of War Information gave the following stunning figures for the number of American killed or missing on all fronts since Pearl Harbor, and Hitler's declaration of war against America, three years earlier:[314]

Known Dead	Missing and Presumed Dead
138,393	73,594

---

310. The 104th Infantry Regiment of the 26th Infantry Division; Peter Rinfret. http://www.rinfret.com/ww2.html#anchor45432. Accessed August 6, 2005.
311. Kotlowitz, p. 104.
312. Kotlowitz, p. 106.
313. Kotlowitz, p. 140.
314. Gilbert, Martin. 1989. *The Second World War*, p. 629.

The study cited earlier found certain data from which it derived what can best be seen as a questionable conclusion. Part of the findings of this study "...show that the delinquents more frequently reported combat duty than did the controls. These data tend to support the hypothesis that combat experience may increase the likelihood that a man may go AWOL, perhaps because of possible disorganizing effects of combat duty, or because of the combat veteran's intolerance of 'stateside' garrison duty."[315]

One implication seems to be that the combat veteran is so disappointed with the boredom and routine of stateside duty that he is anxious to return to the violence, carnage and risk of the battlefield. The conclusion does not suggest that the combat veteran is so horrified by what he has seen and experienced that he will do anything to avoid being sent back to the front.

The traumatic effects of battle during World War II have been studied in some depth. The term 'psychological casualty' refers to those who experienced severe levels of post traumatic stress disorder (PTSD), or what was formerly referred to as 'shell shock' or 'battle fatigue.' These terms were vaguely defined, but PTSD has been more carefully identified.

It is estimated that "during World War II, the United States suffered an average of one diagnosed psychological casualty for every four wounded."[316] However, it is believed that this condition has been vastly underreported and may actually be four times as high.

The factors leading to this condition were many and varied, and almost constant for much of the war.

> [T]here were many factors preying on the emotional stability of the men. The tension of suspense in one form or another was among the most serious; waiting to be killed, for death had begun to seem inevitable to many, and some walked out to meet it rather than continue to endure the unbearable waiting; waiting for the next air raid and the minutes of trembling after the final warning; waiting for the relief ships; waiting without acting through the jungle nights, listening for the sounds of Japs crawling, or for the sudden noise that might herald an attack; waiting even in sleep for the many warning sounds. The fears were numerous: of death, of permanent crippling, of capture and torture, of ultimate defeat in a war that was starting so badly ... [as well as] fear of cowardice ... and of madness.[317]

---

315. Osburn, Hobart G. and Charles Brown. 1954. "A Preliminary Investigation of Delinquency in the Army," US Army Military History Institute, p. 70.

316. Marlowe, David H. 2001. *Psychological and Psychosocial Consequences of Combat and Deployment: with Special Emphasis on the Gulf War*, p. 49.

317. Marlowe, p. 49.

In 1944, those determined to be psychological casualties were described thus:

> [They were] reduced to a pitiable state of military ineffectiveness after prolonged exposure under severest tropical conditions to exhaustion, fear, malaria, and sudden violent death at the hands of an insidious and ruthless enemy.[318]

For those who have never experienced these conditions it is impossible to accurately imagine them. For many soldiers these conditions were part of life for weeks or months; as indicated, some men chose to end the unbearable torment of waiting to die by simply dying. It must not be surprising that others opted to preserve their lives by deserting.

Family Considerations

Millions of men forced from home and family cannot all realistically be expected to embrace the cause they have been coerced to defend. Similar to the military's complete disdain for any individual characteristics is its refusal to recognize the supremacy of a man's duty to his family. That some men prioritize service to country above duty to family is not to be argued here; that is a choice that anyone is free to make. But as some freely make that choice, others see their family responsibilities as taking precedence over those connected to the military.

During World War II women who previously had had no intention of employment outside the home entered the workforce simply because the men who had performed those jobs were at war. Although this was seen as a duty — done out of the desperate need to keep the country going — the attitudes of society did not encourage this except in these extraordinary circumstances. That some men wanted to reenter their own roles as 'breadwinner' or 'head of the house' was a typical feeling during the decade in question. For some, that need and desire was great enough for them to choose to desert.

Despite the fact that 49 deserting soldiers were sentenced to death, execution was only carried out in one case. The execution of Pvt. Eddie Slovik has been studied and analyzed for sixty years. The circumstances surrounding his induction, the nature of his 'crime' and the purpose of his sentence have all been questioned and examined over the years.

Eddie Slovik was born in Detroit, Michigan on February 18, 1920. His life from the start was unhappy; in a letter to his wife dated October 23, 1944, Mr.

---

318. Marlowe, p. 49.

Slovik said "Everything happens to me. I've never had a streak of luck in my life."[319] He spent most of the years from the age of 17 to 22 in prison for a series of minor crimes: embezzling less than $100.00 from an employer over a six-month period, petty larceny, etc.

At the start of the war, Mr. Slovik's draft classification was 4-F, indicating he was ineligible for service. This was a result of his arrest record, which started at the age of 12. By the time he was 22 he'd spent over four years in jail. In November of 1943, the year he was paroled, he married Antoinette Wisniewski.

It appeared at that point that Mr. Slovik's life had taken a turn for the better. Marriage to Antoinette seemed to provide him with a sense of purpose and stability that had previously been lacking. Their first year of married life was probably the happiest of Mr. Slovik's short life.

Shortly before his first wedding anniversary, Mr. Slovik was reclassified 1-A. This could have been simply because of the army's needs for bodies, and one that had served prison time suddenly became acceptable. After basic training, in August of 1944 he said good-bye to his beloved Antoinette and sailed for France. He would never see his wife again.

In France, Mr. Slovik was part of a group of twelve reinforcements assigned to Company G, 109th Infantry Regiment, US 28th Infantry Division. While en route to the unit, Slovik and a buddy, private John Tankey, hid during an artillery attack. Now separated from their unit, they found a non-combat Canadian unit the next morning, which they unofficially remained with for the next six weeks in a rear area. Tankey wrote to the 109th explaining their absence and the two privates reported to their unit on October 7. No charges were filed.[320]

If Mr. Slovik did not know prior to this experience that he was not cut out for the life of a soldier, he learned it now.

The following day Mr. Slovik admitted to Captain Ralph Grotte, his company commander, that he was too scared to serve in a rifle company. He requested reassignment to a rear area unit. He stated clearly that he would run away if assigned to a rifle unit, and asked Grotte if that would be considered desertion. Grotte told him it would, in fact, be desertion, and refused his request for reassignment.

While simply explaining what he could and couldn't do, and how he would handle the situations he might be placed in, Mr. Slovik unwittingly pre-

---

319. Huie, p. 150.
320. Huie, pp. 120 – 128.

pared his own death warrant. On October 9 he told an MP that he would desert if sent into combat. He reiterated this confession with a written document. He was told no consequences would be issued if he destroyed the note and returned to his unit. He refused this offer and damned himself further with an additional letter stating that he understood the consequences of his actions.

His introduction to war was particularly shocking, and this may certainly have influenced his actions. "What Slovik ... saw was mile after mile of charred, gutted, mangled wreckage; men, horses, wagons, trucks, tanks ... a charred body, ghostly, looking almost alive, still sitting at the burned off steering wheel of a charred truck."[321]

Mr. Slovik probably never believed he'd be executed; he had no reason to. Edward Needles, who was a sergeant based at the division stockade where Mr. Slovik was confined for court martial, reminisced about him years later.

> "I remember one day in particular. A couple of other kids who had taken off were having their court-martials, and Slovik was waiting for them to come back.... These other kids came back and they were happy as hell.
>
> "'How much didja get?' Slovik hollered at 'em.
>
> "'Twenty years,' they hollered back, and they seemed happy.
>
> "'I'll settle for twenty years right now,' Slovik said. 'How long you think you'll have to stay in after the war's over?'
>
> "'Aw, maybe six months,' one of the kids said."[322]

Mr. Slovik's reaction was not significantly different from that of many other soldiers. What made him different was his decision to act autonomously and assert himself. This action eventually proved fatal.

> The military needed an example, and Eddie was in the wrong place at the wrong time. Following his execution, one of the witnesses, Lt. Colonel James E. Rudder, sent a message to his regiment. It reads, in part, as follows: "I saw a former soldier of the 109th Infantry shot to death by musketry by soldiers of this regiment. I pray that this man's death will be a lesson to each of us who have any doubt at any time about the price that we must pay to win this war. The person who is not willing to fight and die, if need be, for his country, has no right to life."[323]

---

321. Huie, p. 127.
322. Huie, p. 151.
323. Huie, p. 117.

The question remains sixty year later: why was Eddie Slovik executed? "There were an estimated 20,000 American deserters clear back in Paris, most of whom would pay no greater price than a dishonorable discharge."[324] Eddie Slovik was an obscure private; he had no position of authority. His desertion did not jeopardize the lives of other men, or put at risk any secret strategy. He deserted before he ever reached the company to which he was assigned. "Among those who evaded combat were about forty thousand who were believed to have 'taken off' or 'bugged out' or 'deserted before the enemy."[325] Yet these received sentences ranging from confinement at training centers or dishonorable discharges on one end, to twenty years or death on the other. However, each of these death sentences was later changed to a less heinous one. Why was Eddie Slovik's 'crime' so much more serious that he deserved to die?

As has been noted, the main motivation of what is called military justice is not justice. In most cases it is discipline and control, and this was true in Eddie Slovik's case. "The United States didn't shoot him as a punishment; that isn't the first purpose of military justice. His execution was staged as a hoped-for deterrent."[326] Certainly at this time in history the United States was desperate to keep its soldiers in the field, but the execution of an obscure young man — an execution that was not widely publicized — could hardly have had the desired effect. It must also be remembered that Mr. Slovik was originally classified 4-F, making him ineligible for service.

> During the Second World War, when free America mobilized its manpower against totalitarian challenge, one youth out of every eight was excused from military service 'for reasons other than physical.' They were not the boys with bad hearts, bad eyes, or bad feet, but the boys with bad minds: their number was 1,532,500 — the temperamentally unstable, the maladjusted, the sexually perverted, and the overly nervous. Thus one eighth of the physically-fit products of our little-demanding society were mentally unfit to assume any responsibility whatever in the bloody business of killing the enemy.[327]

Among all these legitimate exemptions, why was there no reason to exempt Eddie Slovik?

---

324. Dzwonkowski, Ron: It's time to pardon Pvt. Eddie Slovik; http://www.freep.com/voices/columnists/erdz27_20010527.htm. Accessed August 12, 2005.
325. Huie, p. 11.
326. Huie, p. 17.
327. Huie, pp. 10 – 11.

The injustice of Mr. Slovik's execution did not stop with his death. Mrs. Slovik, who spent the rest of her life trying to clear her late husband's name, received little information about his death. In 1953 she first met with his biographer, author William Bradford Huie. Said she:

> "I've lived for eight years with little information.... A telegram said that my husband had 'died in the European Theater of Operations.' I send copies of it to Eddie's mother, his sisters, his parole officers. A little later, when I wrote to inquire about the insurance, I got a note saying the insurance would not be paid because my husband had died 'under dishonorable circumstances.' Until now I've never mentioned that note to a living soul. I've kept it inside myself and it's been like a cancer, making me sick."[328]

Mrs. Slovik's efforts on her late husband's behalf were rebuffed by the military for decades. In 1977 her request for $10,000 in life insurance benefits was denied, as were her repeated requests to allow her husband's remains to be brought back to the United States. She died in 1979. Efforts on Mr. Slovik's behalf did not end there. "Bernard V. Calka, a World War II veteran, continued to pursue Slovik's case and, in 1987, the Army finally acquiesced and allowed Eddie Solvik's remains to be returned to the United States to be buried beside Antoinette's."[329] Despite the irregular circumstances surrounding Mr. Slovik's trial and execution it took the Army 42 years to even allow his remains to be brought back to his home country from the isolated section of the Oise-Aisne American Cemetery where he'd been interred, away from the other graves of soldiers who'd died in battle.

Pvt. Eddie Slovik is the only known American soldier executed for desertion in World War II. But the question still remains: Was he indeed the only soldier shot for desertion during World War II?

> "In every Army, there were tens of thousands of soldiers for whom the stress of battle proved too much to bear. Hundreds — even thousands — were shot on the battlefield itself, without a court-martial. They too were victims of war."[330]

Desertion in World War II caused problems for the military as it had throughout each American war. As shown, the issues that led to desertion had more to do with conditions inherent in the military than with the usual reasons given by the government: cowardice and treason. Most of these issues remained unchanged through America's future wars.

---

328. Huie, pp. 18 – 19.
329. Huie, p. 249.
330. Gilbert, p. 636.

Chapter 8. The Korean War

In many ways the Korean War was an extension of World War II, and had its roots long before the start of that conflict. In 1910, Japan annexed Korea and controlled it until the end of World War II. As that war was drawing to a close, and the Soviet Union declared war against Japan, the United States decided to occupy the southern part of the Korean peninsula, south of the 38th parallel. This would include the nation's capital, Seoul. The decision to occupy half of Korea was made due to a fear that Russia might decide to occupy the entire country. The US felt a need to preclude that action, and Russia made no objection to the American decision.[331]

The US quickly installed Syngman Rhee as the leader in the south. Rhee was 70 years old and had lived for many years in the United States. He was knows as an anti-Communist zealot which gave him a high degree of credibility with the American and Korean right.

Russia, north of the 38th parallel, supported 33-year-old Kim Il Sung, who was also supported by many North Koreans and China. Kim had a history as a Korean guerrilla, fighting with Chinese Communist forces against the Japanese in Manchuria in the late 1930s.

Throughout Korea, left- and right- wing factions, once united against the Japanese, were in constant conflict. Much of this centered on the left's vision of reform of the country's land ownership laws, a vision resisted by the right. Current law enabled a small number of the nation's wealthiest citizens to own

---

331. Kihl, Young Whan. 1984. *Politics and Policies in Divided Korea: Regimes in Contest, pp. 5- 25.*

most of the land, forcing many Korean farmers to subsist as tenant farmers. Among Kim's first acts in power was to force through a radical redistribution of land. In the south, the US successfully suppressed the leftist movement.

Rhee was far from a popular leader in Korea, and his standing with the military was extremely low. The amount of desertion from the Korean military in 1949, prior to the start of the war, was excessive.

> [It] must have been one time and one place where there was more desertion to the Communists from non-Communist territory than vice-versa. On 5 May 1949, two whole ROK (Republic of Korea) battalions with their weapons defected. One week later a US-built ROK minesweeper, one of the ROK Navy's largest warships, sailed into the North's Wonsan harbour. To make matters even more galling for Rhee, only 12 days later came yet another defection, as the US-flag freighter, Kimball R. Smith, on loan to the ROK, surrendered at Chinnampo, with two chagrined US Economic Cooperation Administration officials aboard (later released).[332]

> The North Korean army was battle-trained from long assistance given to China's various wars. When the tensions at the 38th parallel finally erupted into gun battles on June 25, 1950, the south was unprepared for the superior equipment, ferocity and tenacity of the northern soldiers. The ROKA (Republic of [South] Korea Army) was outnumbered by 24,000 troops. In addition, the north had 150 Soviet-provided tanks, while the south had none; the north had 200 planes compared to about a dozen available to the ROKA. The range of the north's gunnery was nearly double that of the south's. [333]

This complete collapse of the South Korean army concerned Washington; central to the Truman doctrine was the containment of Communism. At this time there was also a fear that the Chinese government on the mainland, which had driven the Nationalist Chinese from power the previous year, might invade Taiwan, where the Nationalist government had fled. With the South unable to defend itself, the US saw that a war between the two Chinas became more likely. In order to maintain a presence in the area with some appearance of legitimacy, Truman decided to come to the aid of the South. On June 27, 1950, the United States was once again at war.

Desertion plagued the US military during the Korean conflict as it had throughout America's history.

> According to the Pentagon, 46,000 men had deserted from the United States Armed Forces since the outbreak of the Korean War. Of those, only 35,000 returned to duty by their own will or that of the Military Police. In addition, approximately 20,000 men were reported AWOL for one reason or another each month, mostly

---

332. Sandler, Stanley. 1999. *The Korean War: No Victors, No Vanquished*, p. 41.
333. Stueck, William. 2002. *Rethinking the Korean War: A New Diplomatic and Strategic History*. P. 62.

because they were about to be sent overseas. The men out at any one given time would add up to almost two divisions. Nevertheless, the desertion rate during the Korean War was less than half of what it was during World War II.[334]

A study of conditions during the war demonstrates that the same issues that caused desertion in the past remained prevalent. These included the following:

- Disagreement with the purpose of the war;
- Poor leadership;
- Horror at war's atrocities; and
- Family and home concerns.

DISAGREEMENT WITH THE PURPOSE OF THE WAR

In 1950 America was in a period of prosperity. The long years of World War II were behind and many citizens were able to find good employment and start enjoying life. This optimism and prosperity were hardly universal; poverty and racism were still prevalent, but were mainly ignored by middle and upper class white America. A war with Korea was not in the plan. "Few Americans had any idea where Korea was, let alone why it was suddenly necessary to send US forces there to defend it."[335] The seeds of the zealous patriotism bordering on jingoism that infected the 1950s had only been planted; it would be a few years before they bore fruit.

There was little motivation for war among those who would be forced to fight it. "[T]he army in the field was perhaps the most poorly trained and poorly motivated in US history. It had no grand score to settle such as Japan's sneak attack on Pearl Harbor. There were no strong ancestral links to Korea as there were to Europe. The fighting began as another country's civil war."[336]

Nevertheless, President Truman determined that defense of the peninsula country was indeed necessary. This was at least ostensibly in support of the United Nations. U.N. Secretary-General Trygve Lie called the hostilities between North and South Korea, with the assumption that they had been started by the North, a "war against the United Nations" and a "breach of the peace."[337] As a result, "Draft orders were sent to 50,000 civilians in September and again in October; 70,000 more were conscripted in November."[338] Once

---

334. Korean War Educator. 2005. Desertions. http://www.koreanwar-educator.org/topics/brief/p_desertions.htm. Accessed October 28, 2005.

335. Dvorchak, Robert J. 1993. *Battle for Korea: A History of the Korean Conflict*, p. 15.

336. Dvorchak, p. 34.

337. Dvorchak, p. 9.

again, young men starting out in life — beginning higher education, employment or marrying and starting families — were coerced by the government to fight a war with a vague purpose halfway around the world.

Poor Leadership

Quality of leadership is a somewhat subjective topic except when that leadership is extraordinarily good or bad. However, a soldier's perception of leadership can be a motivator in desertion.

A study requested by the Office of the Provost Marshall General on delinquency in the Army was completed in February of 1954. The focus of the study was AWOL and what factors lead a soldier to go AWOL, which is one step below, and often either leads to or becomes, desertion. The study states that "While no direct evidence was obtainable on the actual quality of leadership to which the delinquent and control groups had been subjected, several items were used to explore the soldiers' attitudes toward their leaders."[339]

As noted in previous chapters, a leader who is perceived as caring about the soldiers in his command can expect their loyalty. The 1954 study found that those soldiers who were incarcerated for the offense of AWOL "more often reported that their leaders were not interested in the men."[340] Additionally, these soldiers were unwilling to go to their leaders — officers and non-commissioned officers — and when they did make the effort, they reported more difficulty in being able to see them than the control group (soldiers who were not incarcerated).

It should also be noted that even within the control group only 45 per cent of the men felt that all or most of the officers took a personal interest in their men, and only 38 per cent felt that all or most of the non-coms took a personal interest in their men. This would indicate a somewhat negative feeling toward leadership even on the part of the control group.[341]

Additional information from the study indicates a correlation between negative feelings towards leaders, and general dissatisfaction with all areas of military life: jobs and outfits, routine of life, and discipline.

---

338. Dvorchak, p. 33.
339. Osburn, Hobart G. and Charles Brown. 1954. A Preliminary Investigation of Delinquency in the Army; US Army Military History Institute, p. 55.
340. Osburn, Hobart G. and Charles Brown. p. 57.
341. Osburn and Brown. p. 57.

HORROR AT WAR'S ATROCITIES

The carnage of war takes an incredible toll on those who perpetrate it and those who witness it. Post-traumatic stress disorder, identified only during the second half of the twentieth century, afflicted men and women long before it was formally recognized.

Early on, circumstances for American soldiers in Korea set the stage for the harrowing emotional problems that such carnage brings. The American soldiers were no match for the tenacious North Korean army. Morale was low from the start. One incident that occurred at the end of July 1950, shortly after the United States joined the war, is telling.

> The last of Maj. Gen. Walton Walker's retreating and badly mauled Eighth Army crossed the Naktong River on July 31. This dynamic Texan issued a stand or die order, and through sheer force of bulldog will, he hounded and goaded his demoralized troops to make a fight of it.
>
> 'There will be no more retreating, withdrawal, readjustment of lines or whatever you call it. There are no lines behind which we can retreat. This is not going to be a Dunkirk or Bataan. A retreat to Pusan would result in one of the greatest butcheries in history. We must fight to the end. We must fight as a team. If some of us die, we will die fighting together,' Walker said in a desperate bid to rally his forces.[342]

As Walker 'hounded and goaded' the men under his command to continue to fight, he did not summon some idealistic principle. He did not talk about freedom, self-determination or safety — factors the soldiers themselves were denied since the day of their induction. Rather he said they must fight to prevent being butchered. Anyone might reasonably point out that these soldiers, following the commands of Walker and men like him, had created the danger for themselves. He further seems to indicate some benefit or even glory in dying together in battle. Where was the cause around which dedicated soldiers could rally? Walker, by his desperate attempts to motivate these soldiers, clearly indicates that there simply wasn't one.

In several of America's wars the soldiers enter enthusiastically, willing to either distinguish themselves before God and country, or to defeat what they believed was a real enemy. It is generally only after a period of time — after becoming too familiar with death and carnage — that morale finally breaks. During the Korean War American soldiers reached that point very early.

---

342. Dvorchak, pp. 32-33.

Things did not improve much as the war progressed. Regardless, however, of any country's progress in any war, it is unrealistic to expect human beings to ever become inured to the killing, mutilation and unspeakable suffering that is part of any war. Those who have experienced the smell of burning human flesh, have seen the blood splattered ground, and have heard the pitiable cries for assistance — sometimes begging to be shot in order to end misery — cannot be expected to be happy about the course of the war. Often they know that they themselves have inflicted such misery.

In February of 1951, Corporal Victor Fox of Item Company, 5th Cavalry Regiment, described a scene following the retreat of several thousand Chinese soldiers who were being pursued by the Americans. He said it was a scene of

> "...human carnage right out of hell. All along the flanks of the steep, winding road, I saw the bodies of hundreds of Chinese piled in grisly heaps. Everywhere I looked were these mounds of frozen Chinese bodies lying every which way in their mustard-colored quilt uniforms. Artillery and tank fire must have blasted the Chinese at pointblank range.
>
> "Eighth Army was moving forward again. The advancing troops found signs that the Chinese were being hurt — abandoned gear, bloody bandages and stacks of unburied bodies."[343]

A report from the Associate Press is even more graphic and clearly depicts the suffering of war.

> NORTHEAST FRONT, Korea, Dec. 2 (AP) — Survivors of a Communist ambush said today that fanatical Chinese burned wounded American prisoners alive and danced around the flames "like wild Indians" while the GIs screamed in pain.
>
> Other men of the US 7th Infantry Division said the Chinese threw some wounded soldiers onto a highway and ran over them with halftracks, bayoneted others in the face and machine-gunned their flag of truce when they tried to surrender.
>
> The 7th Division men made a bloody retreat down the east side of the Chosin Reservoir in northern Korea to Hagaru at the southern tip. From there, US Marine and Air Force pilots in probably the greatest mercy flight in history flew 1,000 casualties to rear area hospitals.
>
> One of the three survivors with whom I talked was Pfc. Benjamin Butler, 19, of Browns, Ill., of the 32nd Regiment. He said his group of trucks was attacked around midnight after it ran into a roadblock in the snow-covered hills.
>
> "When some of our guys tried to surrender, the Chinese bayoneted them in the face," he said. "Others waved a flag trying to surrender and the Chinese opened up on them with submachine guns.

---

343. Dvorchak, p. 185.

"After my ammunition was gone, I played dead in the truck. If a man was shot in the leg, they would shoot him again and again and kill him. They took most of the men's clothes and guns....

"They threw about 10 or more into a truck, some naked, some still alive, threw blankets and gasoline over them and set them afire. This bunch took off and we dragged some of them out of the fire.

Butler said while he was playing dead in a truck, a Chinese climbed in and stomped on his face — which showed bruises.

The other survivors with whom I talked were Pfc. Dayle Logan, 19, of Smithers, W. Va., and Pfc. Jackie Brooks, 18, of Richmond, Va., both of the 31st Regiment.

The soldiers, interviewed separately, said the Chinese also bayoneted their own wounded.

Brooks said he was riding as guard on a truck loaded with litter patients.

"We had fought through three roadblocks," he said; "some trucks made it and some didn't. Just after midnight, the trucks ahead of us were shot up and blocked the road. The Chinks started down out of the hills blowing trumpets and whistles.

"Most of them had Thompson submachine guns. A few had .30 caliber carbines with bayonets. The guy in the next truck had a .50-caliber machine gun and I had an M-1 rifle. They killed the machine gunner with a grenade. I got down in the truck body and fired at them. I stayed there till almost dawn.

"They poured gasoline over the truckloads of wounded men and set them afire. I actually saw them do it to four trucks. There must have been about 40 men in each one. Some of them had already been killed by bullets.

"I could hear the men on the trucks screaming 'Help me.' I couldn't do anything. I was out of ammunition by then and there were Chinese between me and the nearest truck.

"They would pour gas on a truck and set it afire and run around it yelling like a bunch of wild Indians. I could see their faces in the light from the flames and they were all grinning and laughing.

"They turned over one truckload of wounded men and ran over several of them with halftracks."[344]

Those who have not experienced the horror herein described may cringe at the thought of it. Certainly feelings of shock and disgust are mingled with compassion for the suffering victims. But for those who were there — those who heard the anguished screams for help of men being burned alive, who watched wounded victims being run over by halftracks and who saw surrendering soldiers machine gunned to death — there can be no forgetting. For those who desert as a result of scenes such as these, and for those who desert before ever

---

344. Dvorchak, p. 133 – 135.

being deployed, having an idea of what awaits them in the field of battle, the label of "coward" has no place.

In every war US soldiers refer to enemy soldiers in some derogatory manner. As shown in the interview referenced above, the Chinese were "Chinks." Asians in general — whether from Korea, China or Vietnam — were referred to as "gooks." Perhaps it is thought easier to kill a "gook," or see their bloody, burned and maimed bodies than it is to kill or see a "person" or "man" in the same condition. However, the incidence of post traumatic stress disorder, barely considered during the Korean War but studied closely following America's later wars, indicates that there is no reduction in the horror of killing, no matter what the victim may be called.

Tens of thousands of American soldiers decided that they either did not want to witness or participate in such atrocities, and deserted prior to deployment. Others left after having these harrowing experiences. In either case, their actions can only be seen as reasonable.

FAMILY AND HOME CONCERNS

In no war has this not been a significant issue in desertions. A soldier, especially in times of war, is usually far from home and loved ones, often for a prolonged period of time. Due to the very fact of war, soldiers do not know if they will ever see their loved ones again, much less when that might be. In the study commissioned by the Office of the Provost Marshall, 59 percent of soldiers incarcerated for AWOL answered "yes" to the following question: "Does your being in the Army cause any special hardships or problems to your wife or family?" For soldiers who served during the Korean War, either in Korea or another location, this is not surprising. "When these men were asked to describe these problems, the most frequent responses were: (a) financial deprivation to the family (45%) and (b) inadequate facilities for taking care of family near the military post, and the impermanency of military life (53%)."[345]

A related factor is the difficulty in obtaining leave. Thirty percent of the incarcerated men reported that they had been refused leave more than twice; fourteen percent had been refused twice. For many men, duty to family is far stronger than an outwardly imposed responsibility to fight a war whose purpose

---

345. Osburn and Brown. p. 71.

is at best, very vague. Without permission to leave, but needing to attend to family matters, deserting is often the only alternative.

The report prepared for the Office of the Provost Marshall presents some predictable findings: AWOL and other activities categorized as criminal by the military are more likely to be committed by younger men, those with less education, from lower socio-economic backgrounds and from dysfunctional families.[346] However, the study did not find cowardice or fear as a motivating factor. "Although avoidance of combat appears to motivate some few individuals, it is not possible to assess the importance of this variable from the present data."[347] The study states that since combat avoidance has a negative connotation, men incarcerated for AWOL may be unwilling to admit it as a factor. "Since 'avoidance of combat' is a socially unacceptable excuse for going AWOL, it is no surprise that almost none of the stockade group gave this as a reason for their delinquency."[348]

However, statistics within the report itself do not seem to support this statement. The questionnaires submitted to both those incarcerated and the control group asked the following: "What do the men in your outfit think of a soldier who goes AWOL?" Fifty-nine percent of those incarcerated and fifty-six percent of the control group responded as follows: "It doesn't make much difference to most of them." The question "What do your parents or relatives think of a soldier who goes AWOL?" produced a somewhat higher negative rating. Thirty-six percent of the prisoners and sixty percent of the control group responded with "They think he doesn't amount to much."[349] So it appears that the negative connotation of AWOL is mixed, at best.

The study also highlighted what the researchers felt was a puzzling finding. One hypothesis said that an increase in the AWOL rate would correspond to an increase in the draftee population. "The assumption was that a disproportionate number of draftees, as contrasted to volunteers, tend to go AWOL. To anticipate one of the findings of the current study, the results indicate a significant tendency for volunteers rather than draftees to be delinquent."[350] Further, "previous studies had indicated that, in terms of military experiences, delinquents are more likely to be volunteers (in contrast to the

346. Osburn and Brown. p. v.
347. Osburn and Brown. p. 76.
348. Osburn and Brown. p. 69
349. Osburn and Brown. p. 70.
350. Osburn and Brown. p. 7.

hypothesis held by some officers), have less service time and less combat experience, and display resentment toward and lack of identification with military life."[351]

This may not actually be as surprising as it first appears. Men who enlist do so by choice; they are exercising their right to make a decision with their lives and their careers after weighing all possible alternatives. Some may be doing so only because they know the draft is inevitable, but their enlistment is still an active decision.

Men who are drafted may have a greater tendency to follow the rules and allow decisions to be imposed upon them. This does not negate their sense of duty, but it does suggest a difference in perception. They are told they must enter the army, so they do so. The former group, those who enlist, proactively decide to take this step in their lives. That they may eventually proactively decide to take the step out of the military, either through AWOL or desertion, is only a logical progression in their demonstrated thought process.

Although the desertion rate was lower during the Korean War than in World War II, a tremendous amount of controversy arose surrounding twenty-three American prisoners of war who chose to remain behind enemy lines.

> [C]ontrary to the 1947 Geneva Convention, which mandated the wholesale exchange of all POWs, President Truman's policy of voluntary repatriation proved highly successful: 47,000 Chinese and North Korean prisoners of war struck a propaganda blow against their Marxist governments by choosing not to return to their homelands.[352]

Yet any propaganda effect that this large number of North Korean prisoners of war who refused to return to North Korea may have had was dwarfed by the refusal of twenty-three Americans who chose to remain in North Korea. Feelings of anti-Communism were rampant at this time, resulting in the witch hunts of Senator Joseph McCarthy a few years later. The term "brainwashing," coined in 1951 by Edward Hunter,[353] was applied almost universally to these men.

During a ninety-day cooling off period during which the twenty-three were held at Panmunjom, two of the men changed their minds and returned to the US Their reward for "seeing the light" of American freedom and justice was

---

351. Osburn and Brown. p. 11.
352. Zweiback, Adam J. 1998 The 21 'Turncoat GIs': Nonrepatriations and the Political Culture of the Korean War. *The Historian, Vol.* 60, p. 1.
353. Zweiback, p. 1.

immediate court-martial and convictions for desertion and related crimes, and long prison sentences. At the conclusion of the ninety-days the remaining twenty-one were dishonorably discharged. While this may have been considered disgraceful, it also meant that should any of these soldiers ever return to the United States, they could not be court martialed.

The reasons for the defection of the 21 were never revealed, but that did not prevent unbridled speculation. One enterprising author wrote about them in 1955 and included in her book the IQ of each soldier. Those with lower IQs, she hypothesized, were unable to withstand Communist mind-control techniques. Those with higher IQs were simply dismissed as rebellious.[354]

A *Newsweek* article reported the following about these men:

> ...[A]n unnamed Indian general at Panmunjom, their chief U.N. custodian during the waiting period ... described the 21 Americans, one Briton, and 327 South Koreans, all of whom rejected repatriation, as "about the sorriest, most shifty-eyed and groveling bunch of chaps he had ever seen." Supposedly these men had betrayed their comrades to curry favor from their captors, and now were afraid to return to America to face expected punishment. Some had even "[fallen] in love with Chinese women." For American readers this last sin was doubly grievous, for the women were both Communists and non-Caucasians.[355]

Only three of the soldiers who remained in the North were African-Americans, and here at least the US press found reason to cheer. The Communist regime had attempted to entice African-American soldiers by reminding them of the racial inequality that was sewn deeply in the fabric of American society. The Saturday Evening Post in its March 6, 1954 issue reported thus:

> It can be positively stated that the commies drew the worst blank of their ideological warfare among the American Negroes held in the POW cages." US News and World Report similarly trumpeted, "American Negro soldiers did not swallow the Communist line on racial equality." Such statements implied that there was no real disadvantage to being black in America, but that the dissimulating Chinese were utilizing false propaganda about American race relations. Further, they implied that black soldiers saw through this ruse because they knew first hand that racial inequalities did not exist.[356]

It should be noted that laws guaranteeing equal rights in the United States were still a decade away, and true equality remains an elusive dream for most, and a frightening nightmare for some.

---

354. Zweiback, p. 1.
355. Zweiback, p. 1
356. Zweiback, pp. 2 – 3.

The theory popular in that time that many emotional problems were traceable to strong, weak or dysfunctional mothers was paraded out and shown off in prominent circles. The same issue of the Saturday Evening Post referenced above, which proudly extolled the American racial equality of the 1950s, "quoted an Army sergeant's explanation for POWs who collaborated during the Korean War: 'These spoiled and pampered kids.... No guts here' — Pate pointed to his belly 'or here' — he pointed to his head. 'Too much mamma,' he finished laconically."[357]

The vilification of the press did not stop with mother-blame.

> In 1954, *Newsweek* reported rumors — denied by the nonrepatriates — that 'about half the Americans were bound together more by homosexuality than Communism.' This statement was credible to Newsweek's readership, for the notion that leftist politics were deviantly unmasculine was preached from the loftiest towers of American academia in the 1950s.[358]

As we consider the limited acceptance that homosexual behavior has achieved at the start of the twenty-first century, it is important to know that attitudes toward homosexuality were far more negative in the 1950s than they are today.

Amid the propagandist babble were some voices of reason.

> As early as 7 May 1953, Republican Representative Edith Nourse Rogers of Massachusetts expressed her anger over the proceedings at Valley Forge, where psychiatrists detained and examined POWs returned in Little Switch. Rogers was upset that soldiers were being stigmatized as victims of brainwashing and probed for signs that the Communists had perverted their loyalties. House Democrat Eugene J. McCarthy[359] of Minnesota drew similar conclusions regarding "debrainwashing" the following week, complaining that "the whole operation begins to look more and more like an atrocity perpetrated by our own officials." He derisively questioned a psychological warfare program that "calls for us to be fanatics." McCarthy was echoed two weeks later by The Nation, which decried the Pentagon's utilization of "political psychiatric therapy" and quoted an army physician who, angered by press reports of brainwashing, stated, "we're not running a damned laundromat here."[360]

Any news about these twenty-one men soon faded into the background as America's attention was turned to another source of the Communist "threat," as

---

357. Zweiback, p. 3.

358. Zweiback, p. 3

359. Note that Senator McCarthy later sought the Democratic presidential nomination on a platform opposed to the Vietnam War.

360. Zweiback, p. 4.

orchestrated by Senator Joseph McCarthy and his infamous Congressional Hearings on un-American activities. It wasn't until 2004 that Korea and desertion once again became prominent in the US news media, with the departure of Charles Robert Jenkins from North Korea.

Mr. Jenkins, as a 24-year-old sergeant with a distinguished record, disappeared from his troop on January 5, 1964 after telling the others he'd heard a noise and was going to investigate. In the subsequent years he appeared in North Korean propaganda films and was labeled a deserter. While in North Korea he married a Japanese woman and they had two daughters. The details of Mr. Jenkins' years in the north will not be recounted here. However, some vital information has been revealed as well as mostly ignored, and it all pertains to desertion.

Initially it was not know whether Mr. Jenkins had deserted or been taken prisoner of war. The US army determined he was a deserter based on letters he'd left behind. However, when told about the content of the letters his family doubted their authenticity; they were signed "Charles" when he always used "Robert." When the family asked to see the letters they were advised that they had been lost; in forty years they have not been found. Other discrepancies greatly trouble the family.

> The Army has finally provided our family with the records of our Uncle, Army Sgt. Charles Robert Jenkins. According to the Army, our uncle left his patrol on the night of January 5th, 1965 and walked across the DMZ into North Korea. No where among the numerous documents is there any reference to the supposed "money problems" or other "difficulties" which led to the supposed desertion of our uncle. Glaring in their absence is the single most important piece of evidence supporting the Army contention that Sgt. Jenkins deserted. The Army is unable to produce the letter and 3 notes purportedly written by our uncle. We find it so odd that the most damning evidence against our uncle is no where to be found.

> The Geneva Convention provides that no determination of desertion can be made until the individual has be(en) questioned in a neutral setting. Yet, no one has ever spoken with Robert. In spite of numerous requests by our government, the North Koreans have not allowed this. If Robert did go to North Korea of his free will, why didn't the North Koreans let him call or write his family? Why won't they allow US investigators to speak with him?[361]

The family also noted that Mr. Jenkins had been home just weeks prior to his disappearance, and was proud of his service. They doubted that any cause would have motivated him to desert just weeks later.

---

361. Jenkins; 2004 .http://www.ipetitions.com/boards/viewtopic.php?topic=2460&forum=6. Accessed on July 7, 2005.

Mr. Jenkins own admission of guilt only further muddied the waters. He claims to have deserted to avoid "hunt and kill" patrols where he did not feel he could lead troops. The repugnance at killing that frequently motivates soldiers to desert is not uncommon.

Additionally, once he left Korea he condemned the regime of Kim Il Sung, and stated he appeared in propaganda movies only under government orders to do so.

Despite a forty-years lapse since his desertion — if desertion it was — and his surrender to US authorities in Japan, the American military was determined to punish him. Following his admission of guilt, the military sentenced him to thirty days in jail, forfeiture of back pay, demotion and dishonorable discharge.

One can only wonder what good such actions accomplish. Mr. Jenkins plans to live in Japan with his Japanese wife and their two daughters. If his disappearance forty years ago jeopardized the lives of other soldiers it was done because he felt he could not competently lead them. Recognizing that he was not qualified to lead men into the kind of battle he anticipated is an example of admirable insight. Refusing to make the attempt to lead in these circumstances is heroic, not cowardly.

Additionally, it was not uncommon for the North Koreans or the Chinese to kidnap American soldiers and through torture and brainwashing, induce them to praise the regime that kidnapped them. Forty years later it is difficult to do anything more than speculate on what may have happened, beginning in the hot, dark jungles that evening.

[handwritten margin note: *WHAT JUNGLES? KOREA?*]

Never before in the history of the United States has a deserter turned himself in after so much time. Yet his age, years in a country he hated, his weakened and unhealthy physical condition meant nothing to the American military. One can say that his sentence was light, but one must wonder why he was given any sentence at all.

As has been mentioned, Mr. Jenkins as a young man was proud of his service to his country, and proudly wore his country's uniform. But when circumstance arose that he felt he could not adequately handle, going to a military supervisor and resolving the issue was not an option. Mr. Jenkins apparently did what so many others in similar circumstance had done before him: he simply left. What makes his story unique is his reappearance forty years later.

There remain more than 8,100 US soldiers missing in action from the Korean War. How many are dead, how many are deserters who have established a new home in Korea, and how many are prisoners may never be known. Yet the reemergence of one man, after forty years, is greeted with hostility by the government. Whatever the truth about Mr. Jenkins disappearance forty years ago, a truth that at this point he himself may not know, the American military determined that he must be punished.

Chapter 9: The Vietnam War

Although the War in Vietnam was the longest and least successful in America's history, pinpointing a starting date is difficult. In 1941, while Vietnam was under Japanese rule, Ho Chi Minh returned to the country disguised as a Chinese journalist after thirty years in exile. He led a nationalist movement that expelled the Japanese.[362] *[handwritten: NO, NO]* France then tried to reclaim Indochina, and attempted to counter the popularity of Ho Chi Minh by establishing what they referred to as an independent Vietnam under Emperor Bao Dai in the south. France also apparently hoped that the US would approve of this choice. *[handwritten: Not the way it was]*

The differences between the revolutionary leader in the north and the hand-picked puppet in the south were stunning. Despite his education, travel and world experience, Minh never lost his peasant appearance and native identity. His obvious devotion "to the Vietnamese people contrasted with Bao Dai's opulent affectations, philandering and record of collaboration with the French and Japanese."[363] The US officially recognized the Boa Dai government in 1950.

[handwritten: JAPS STILL IN VIET ON VJ DAY + 6 MONTHS]

Beginning in 1945 the people of Vietnam, so recently rid of Japanese rule, sought to free themselves from French colonial rule, and their efforts appeared to be gaining success. In May 1950, the US authorized a program to provide economic and military aid to the French, who were struggling to retain control of Laos and Cambodia and Vietnam.[364] That was the start of US involvement in

---

362. McMaster, H.R. 1997. *Dereliction of Duty*, p. 33.
363. McMaster, p. 34.
364. Chambers, p. 758.

Vietnam, an involvement that would escalate over a period of nearly twenty-five years.

In 1954 the French were handed a decisive defeat at Dien Bien Phu. During a peace conference that followed, Vietnam was given independence along with Cambodia and Laos.[365] Vietnam, however, was divided along the seventeenth parallel into a Communist North and a non-Communist south. Elections scheduled for 1956, that would have been a referendum on unification, were refused by the South. America supported the South's boycott. The main reason for this refusal appeared to be the popularity of Ho Chi Minh, the leader of North Vietnam. "President (Dwight D.) Eisenhower wrote later in his memoirs that if in fact the elections had been held, Ho Chi Minh would have gotten 80 percent of the vote."[366] This would have been unacceptable. "It has been a fundamental verity of domestic politics during the cold-war period that an administration must not 'lose a country to communism' on its 'watch.'"[367] It is tragically ironic that Ho Chi Minh did in fact come to power over a united Vietnam, following the deaths of over 58,000 Americans and between 1,000,000 and 2,000,000 Vietnamese citizens.

Ho died in 1969

With Communism seeming to take hold in Vietnam, and the "domino theory" — the belief that if one country became Communist others near it would quickly follow suit — being proclaimed from the halls of Congress and the White House, Eisenhower decided to act. He felt the need to create a viable government in South Vietnam, although how it would have any legitimacy within Vietnam or the world was apparently not considered. He took over the fighting from the French and sent military advisors to train the South Vietnamese army, and authorized the Central Intelligence Agency (CIA) to conduct psychological warfare against the North. US interference in the affairs of Vietnam was now growing.

Subsequent presidents, for a variety of reasons, continued to escalate the war. President John F. Kennedy sent four hundred Green Berets to teach counterinsurgency. His motivation, and that of his successor, Lyndon Baines Johnson, may have been at least partly political. They did not want to appear weak on

---

365. Minahan, James. *Nations without States: A Historical Dictionary of Contemporary National Movements*, p. 540.
366. Werner, Jayne. "A Short History of the War in Vietnam." *Monthly Review*, Vol. 37, June 1985.
367. Pierre, Andrew J. 1985. *Third World Instability: Central America as a European-American Issue*, p. 100.

Communism, which had become a major rallying point within the United States. Kennedy may also have considered the Vietnam question a test of his young presidency and an opportunity to show his resolve against Communism.

A major turning point was the so-called Gulf of Tonkin resolution. This was presented to Congress, the American public and the world as a necessary measure to repel a clear act of aggression against the United States. The facts as then presented were muddied at the time, and subsequent studies have indicated that they were simple untrue. A brief description of those events, as portrayed during the crisis and afterwards, is instructive.

The staging area for the US Seventh Fleet was the Gulf of Tonkin, on the east coast of North Vietnam. On August 2 1964, the US destroyer Maddox was on an espionage mission when it was fired on by North Vietnamese torpedo patrol boats. The Maddox, with supporting air power, fired back, sinking one North Vietnamese boat.

Two evenings later the Maddox and another destroyer, the C. Turner Joy were again in the gulf. It is at this point that things become somewhat less clear.

The captain of the Maddox had read his ship's instruments as saying that the ship was under attack or had been attacked and began an immediate retaliatory strike into the night. The two ships began firing into the night rapidly with American warplanes supporting the showcasing of the American firepower. However, "[m]any later decided they had been shooting at ghost images on their radar. The preponderance of evidence indicates there was no attack"[368]

Regardless of any inconsistencies, this incident, whether real or fabricated, was presented to the world as an act of aggression. Congress quickly met and passed the Gulf of Tonkin Resolution.

The Gulf of Tonkin Resolution allowed the president to take all necessary measures to repel aggression. The following is the complete Resolution:

> Resolved by the Senate and House of Representatives of the United States of America in Congress assembled,
>
> That the Congress approves and supports the determination of the President, as Commander in Chief, to take all necessary measures to repel any armed attack against the forces of the United States and to prevent further aggression.
>
> Section 2. The United States regards as vital to its national interest and to world peace the maintenance of international peace and security in southeast Asia. Consonant with the Constitution of the United States and the Charter of the United Nations and in accordance with its obligations under the Southeast Asia

---

368. Chambers, p. 307.

Collective Defense Treaty, the United States is, therefore, prepared, as the President determines, to take all necessary steps, including the use of armed force, to assist any member or protocol state of the Southeast Asia Collective Defense Treaty requesting assistance in defense of its freedom.

Section 3. This resolution shall expire when the President shall determine that the peace and security of the area is reasonably assured by international conditions created by action of the United Nations or otherwise, except that it may be terminated earlier by concurrent resolution of the Congress.[369]

This was as close to a formal declaration of war as was ever issued regarding Vietnam. For many it was just a formality; the war had been raging for years. By 1964 there were already over 23,000 US soldiers in Vietnam; within a year that had increased to over 184,300.

The draft was a major point of controversy during the Vietnam era. The rules and regulations caused no end of headaches for the military. A report on morale in the services issued in June 1971 stated the following:

Desertion rates regulations established by the government indicate the encroachment on the lives of young American men that the government granted to itself.

College students were eligible for II-S deferments until they fulfilled their degree requirements or reached their twenty-fourth birthday, whichever came first. Initially, it was up to local boards to decide annually whether a student was making satisfactory progress toward a degree. Generally, boards granted a deferment to anyone who could prove that he was enrolled full time in an accredited college or university. However, in early 1966, the Selective Service System initiated the Selective Service College Qualification Test (SSCQT). Any student ranking in the lower levels of their class was eligible for the draft.[370]

The government was not only actually tracking young men to assure that they were registered full time in an accredited institution of higher learning, but also checking up on them to assure their grades met some arbitrarily-set standard. And once the man graduated, he was immediately eligible to be drafted. This degree of surveillance on American citizens by the government — American citizens completely innocent of any wrongdoing — provided these young men with an introduction to the suspension of basic civil rights they would experience in the military.

---

369. Westerfield, Donald L. 1996. *War Powers: The President, the Congress and the Question of War.* Pages 53 – 54.
370. Beckner, Leslie. The Draft during the Vietnam War, http://athena.english.vt.edu/ -appalach/essaysM/draft.htm. Accessed October 11, 2005.

Desertion levels during the Vietnam War caused no end of headaches for the military. A report on morale in the services issued in June 1971 stated the following:

> Desertion rates are going straight up in Army, Marines, and Air Force. Curiously, however, during the period since 1968 when desertion has nearly doubled for all three other services, the Navy's rate has risen by less than 20 percent.

> In 1970, the Army had 65,643 deserters, or roughly the equivalent of four infantry divisions. This desertion rate (52.3 soldiers per thousand) is well over twice the peak rate for Korea (22.5 per thousand). It is more than quadruple the 1966 desertion-rate (14.7 per thousand) of the then well-trained, high-spirited professional Army.[371]

The low rate of desertion from Vietnam[372] — 249 soldiers actually deserted while in that country — does not indicate enthusiasm for the war among the soldiers stationed there. "The comparatively low Vietnam figure was attributed in large part to the dearth of options available to American field troops — Baskir and Strauss quoted one soldier who sardonically asked, 'What are you going to do? Walk through Cambodia?'"[373]

The numbers of men assigned to Vietnam who deserted must be compared to the total number of desertions during the Vietnam era. "Approximately 100,000 US soldiers were discharged for 'absence offenses' during the Vietnam era.... Some soldiers — an estimated seven thousand total — also went 'over the hill' and fled to Canada after receiving orders to report to Vietnam."[374] Many men deserted to Sweden from Germany. Others on leave in Japan deserted from there. Soldiers not assigned to Vietnam may have deserted thinking they'd be deployed there; the number of men sent there escalated dramatically at the peak of the war, and casualties escalated correspondingly.

These desertion numbers, however do not tell the entire story. Although the number of court-martials for desertion during the Vietnam era were comparable or less than in other wars, there were related issues to deal with.

> [T]he military was forced to deal with an alarming number of AWOL and desertion incidents that did not reach the court martial stage for one reason or

---

371. Bloom, Alexander: *Long Time Gone: Sixties America Then and Now*, p. 85.
372. Leonard, Ron. 2000. Vietnam War Statistics and Facts. http://25thaviation.org/id275.htm. Accessed October 11, 2005. *Numbers & Losses in the Civil War in America.*
373. Hillstrom, Kevin and Laurie Colier Hillstrom. 1998. *The Vietnam Experience: A concise Encyclopedia of American Literature, Songs, and Films*, p. 134. This quotation cites *Chance and Circumstance*, by Lawrence M. Baskir and William Strauss.
374. Hillstrom, p. 134.

another. Baskir and Strauss reported that incidents in the Army and Marines in which soldiers were AWOL for more than thirty days rose from about fifteen per thousand troops in 1966 to approximately seventy per thousand by 1972, and that during the Vietnam War the US military experienced approximately 1.5 million AWOL incidents. At the peak of the war, an American soldier was going AWOL every two minutes, and deserting every six minutes. They went on to note that AWOL and desertion offenses accounted for a total loss of roughly one million man-years of military service, and that the Senate Armed Services Committee estimated that in 1968 alone, absenteeism was costing the military the equivalent of ten combat divisions of fifteen thousand men each.[375]

During the Vietnam era over 3,000,000 service personnel were assigned to Vietnam, Cambodia or Laos between 1964 and 1973.[376] "During the five peak years of the war, military desertion rates increased by 400%."[377]

While tens of thousands resisted and avoided the draft, and hundreds of thousands of citizens took to the streets to protest the most unpopular war of the twentieth century, resistance on the part of soldiers took three main forms:

1. Combat Refusal: This is defined simply as a soldier's refusal to obey orders. In extreme cases it resulted in "fragging."
2. Fragging: This is the killing of a superior officer by soldiers under his command. Although the term simply meant that a fragmentation grenade was used in the murder, it later became an all-encompassing term for such an action.[378] In many cases bounties ranging from $50.00 to $1,000.00 were put on the heads of unpopular leaders.[379]
3. Desertion and Absence without Official Leave.

The following table[380] shows the known numbers of each category. Please note that "[f]igures for the Vietnam Conflict are also not known but figures for all US forces throughout the world are known."[381]

---

375. Hillstrom, p. 135.
376. Leonard, Ron. 2000. Vietnam War Statistics and Facts. http://25thaviation.org/id275.htm. Accessed October 11, 2005.
377. Statistics on Decline in Military Status and Discipline during Vietnam Era. http://www.drake.edu/artsci/PolSci/pols124s02/statistics.html. Accessed October 11, 2005.
378. Chambers, p. 279.
379. Bloom, Alexander: *Long Time Gone: Sixties America Then and Now.* P. 85.
380. Fragging and Combat Refusals in Vietnam. http://home.mweb.co.za/re/redcap/vietcrim.htm. Accessed on August 1, 2005.
381. Fragging and Combat Refusals in Vietnam. Accessed on August 1, 2005.

Year	Fragging	"Combat Refusal" convictions	World-wide figures for US Forces	
			AWOL	Desertion
1965			Not available	Not available
1966			Not available	Not available
1967			46.8 per 1000	13.2 per 1000
1968		82	138.5 per 1000	15.7 per 1000
1969	239	117	46.9 per 1000	21.1 per 1000
1970	383	131	66.3 per 1000	25.8 per 1000
1971	333	Not provided	84.0 per 1000	33.9 per 1000
1972	58	Not provided	74.9 per 1000	27.5 per 1000
1973			77.0 per 1000	24.6 per 1000

In looking for reasons for desertion during the Vietnam War, the factors are no different than those in earlier wars.

Some of the frontline soldiers who deserted from Vietnam left for reasons similar to those cited by deserters over in America — disintegrating romantic relationships, family finances, etc. Others, though, departed as a direct result of their combat experiences. Antiwar critics subsequently contended that these desertions were acts of conscience triggered by prolonged exposure to a defoliated wasteland and an amoral war. Hawks, meanwhile, argued that the deserters were simply cowards whose instincts for self-preservation proved stronger than their sense of duty.[382]

The following are some typical reasons for desertion during the Vietnam War:

1. Disagreement with the cause of the war;
2. The horrors of war;
3. Resistance to military life;
4. Family and personal needs.

A closer look at each is instructive.

---

382. Hillstrom, p. 134.

DISAGREEMENT WITH THE CAUSE OF THE WAR

The US war in Vietnam was the most unpopular US war of the twentieth century. Much of America did not see a link between a civil war on the other side of the planet and a threat to the United States. Politicians orchestrating the war did not make a case sufficient to overcome these doubts.

Opposition to the war was not limited to any age group, geographical location or socio-economic standing. As the war intensified, so did opposition to it. "In 1965 demonstrations in New York City attracted 25,000 marchers; within two years similar demonstrations drew several hundred thousand participants in Washington, D.C., London, and other European capitals."[383]

Veterans themselves returned home and told how their experiences had motivated them to oppose the war. The veterans' movement gained momentum — along with publicity — in 1967 with the forming of the organization "Vietnam Veterans Against the War." At one peace demonstration, veterans who had received Congressional Medals of Honor and other awards marched on Washington and flung their medals over the fence surrounding the White House. In addition, prominent physicians, members of the clergy, actors and elected officials all spoke forcefully against continued aggression in Vietnam.

No

College students were at the forefront of the peace movement, not surprisingly since they were being drafted in huge numbers to fight the war. Their influence grew with the radicalization of the Students for a Democratic Society, founded in 1960, but growing in numbers by 1967 as opposition to the war soared.

The army was not ignorant of the problems among the soldiers. In 1971, Colonel Robert Heinl reported the following in an article titled "The Collapse of the Armed Forces." This article appeared in the June issue of the Armed Forces Journal.

✳ ✳
TELLS
ALL

> The morale, discipline and battleworthiness of the US Armed Forces are, with a few salient exceptions, lower and worse than at anytime in this century and possibly in the history of the United States.

> By every conceivable indicator, our army that now remains in Vietnam is in a state approaching collapse, with individual units avoiding or having _refused_ combat, murdering their officers and non commissioned officers, drug-ridden, and dispirited where not near mutinous.

TRUE
I SAW
IT IN RVN
1970-71

383. The Columbia Encyclopedia, 2004. Anti-Vietnam War Movement. Sixth Edition, p. 2307.

Elsewhere than Vietnam, the situation is nearly as serious.[384]

Among many other topics related to morale the article discusses desertion, US soldiers who joined the Vietcong, and the constant encouragement and help soldiers were receiving to desert.

With even the military recognizing these serious issues the fact that men were deserting is not surprising.

Disagreement with the cause of the war was a major cause of desertion. Political considerations colored the issue of desertion during this era more than at any time in history. They involved other countries — mainly Canada — and were often cited when the issue of desertion was analyzed. Even today the motivations of deserters are discussed and analyzed. The creation of the organization "Vietnam Veterans Against the War" and the outspoken protests of many veterans helped to validate the motivations of men who deserted due to their belief that the war was an immoral, imperialist exercise waged by an increasingly corrupt US government.

This belief was not without a sound foundation. The Principles of the Nuremberg Tribunal, established in 1950 following the Nuremberg trials of World War II criminals, established a defensible position for soldiers deserting due to disagreement with the war. The principles state, in part, the following:

> Principle VI
>
> The crimes hereinafter set out are punishable as crimes under international law:
>
> Crimes against peace:
>
> Planning, preparation, initiation or waging of a war of aggression or a war in violation of international treaties, agreements or assurances....[385]

US involvement in Vietnam, especially the escalation of hostilities after the Gulf of Tonkin Resolution, has never been adequately explained to show that this tenet was not violated. In combination with Principle VI is Principle IV:

> Principle IV
>
> The fact that a person acted pursuant to order of his Government or of a superior does not relieve him from responsibility under international law, provided a moral choice was in fact possible to him.[386]

This indicates the responsibility of individuals to refuse unjust orders.

---

384. Hillstrom, p. 228.
385. Brown, Bartram S. "Barely Borders: Issues of International Law." *Harvard International Review*, Vol. 26, 2004. Page 1.

These concepts are not alien to the United States. The concept of prosecuting high government officials and others who planned and waged aggressive wars evolved during the latter years of World War II. As a guiding principle it was first officially embraced in the Moscow Declaration of 1943, which was signed by Roosevelt, Churchill and Stalin.[387]

Against this background, desertion was not universally viewed as the government had for generations attempted to frame it, as a cowardly and traitorous act. Rather it was seen by many as at least a reasonable step, and at most an honorable and heroic action.

THE HORRORS OF WAR

This factor is closely intertwined with disagreement with the cause of the war. There were two sources of information that brought the horrors of war home to America. The first was the media. Never before had Americans in the comfort of their living rooms watched bombs dropping on screaming civilians, witnessed the graphic executions of Vietnamese prisoners or even considered — must less watched — Buddhist monks burning themselves to death in protest of the war. For the first time they saw anguished young Americans suffering from battle wounds, bleeding, writhing in the pain that is so much a part of any war. These were no longer statistics — nameless and faceless numbers — but were flesh and blood human beings. If the suffering Vietnamese could somehow be seen as less than human, suffering Americans could not.

Americans on the battlefield witnessed and participated in horrific scenes, although few soldiers were court-martialed for them. Between 1965 and 1973, 201 army personnel were convicted by court martial of serious offences against the Vietnamese. Between 1965 and 1971, seventy-seven marines were also convicted. These figures bear little relation to the extent of brutality in Vietnam of which the worst example was the My Lai massacre. On 16 March 1968, Charlie Company, a unit of the American Division, took part in a "search and destroy" operation directed against an enemy concentration supposedly centered upon

---

386. Falk, Richard A., Gabriel Kolko, Robert Jay Lifton.1971. *Crimes of War: A Legal, Political Documentary, and Psychological Inquiry into the Responsibility of Leaders, Citizens, and Soldiers for Criminal Acts in Wars.* Page 107.

387. Jackson, Robert Houghwout. 1949. *Report of Robert H. Jackson: United States Representative to the International Conference on Military Trials.* London: US Govt. Printing Office, p. 48.

the village of Son My in Quang Ngai province in northern South Vietnam. Although no enemy forces or hostile fire was encountered in the hamlet of My Lai, the unit butchered all the inhabitants, who were predominantly elderly people, women and children. In all, some 200 people in My Lai and a total of about 400 within the area of Son My lost their lives. Despite a year-long cover up, twelve men were charged following an enquiry into the case although only one, Lieutenant William Calley who led Charlie Company, was convicted and even he was released after serving a fraction of his sentence.

It is unlikely that other atrocities on the scale of My Lai actually occurred at the hands of US troops in Vietnam. However, cases involving a more limited number of victims almost certainly did and were never reported and brought to public attention.[388]

News of the My Lai massacre shocked the world, and people may have wondered how such a horrifying event could ever have happened. Although in no way a justification, it is instructive to note just what American soldiers encountered in Vietnam. "[M]any combat soldiers who saw buddies killed by booby traps laid by women and grenades thrown by children, came to direct their anger and frustration not upon enemy troops who could rarely be found but upon civilians whom they believed to be NLF[389] collaborators."[390]

Everyone was seen as an enemy; this concept was taught by the government. This, however, is no excuse. "[T]orture, rape and brutal murders are atrocities and crimes against humanity whether they are sanctioned by commanders or undertaken on the order of a superior officer. It is not an adequate excuse to blame the army for inculcating murderous intent and for producing brutalized automatons as a result of its training."[391]

Note that the quotation states that soldiers became "brutalized automatons," not "brutalizing automatons." That their own victimization found expression in victimizing others is part of a normal, albeit extremely unhealthy, vicious cycle. It is seen repeatedly in abused children who grow up to become abusive parents. Many men who experienced this training and became, on some level and for some time, "automatons" — implying a lack of decision-making rights and/or abilities, and only the obligation to "follow orders" — then felt the

---

388. Brown, T. Louise. 1991. *War and Aftermath in Vietnam*, p. 200.
389. National Liberation Front. A North Vietnamese guerilla movement established in 1961.
390. Brown, p. 200.
391. Brown, p. 201.

horror of their own actions, needed to escape in some way. This cannot seem unusual or unexpected.

The second method by which Americans at home learned of the horrors of war in a more graphic manner than any television news report or high school textbook could convey was from the returning soldiers themselves. Members of the Vietnam Veterans Against the War, mentioned above, testified before Congress and at other venues, discussing their own troubling experiences and even showing pictures they had taken, often as souvenirs. Now, far removed from the battlefield and the military's training, feelings of shame overwhelmed them, and they sought to use their experiences to prevent further suffering. The following is listed by the organization as number six of its nine objectives:

> To make clear that the United States of America has never undertaken an extensive open investigation of American war crimes in Indochina. We demand that the United States government, in its war in Indochina, affirm the principles of Nuremberg. As active-duty and former GIs we recognize the responsibility and guilt of the individual soldier to refrain from committing war crimes. We also recognize that the responsibility and guilt of war crimes committed in the name of America lies with our policy makers at all levels.[392]

Vietnam veterans themselves were now bringing to the attention of the world the horrors that were being inflicted on the people of Vietnam.

RESISTANCE TO MILITARY LIFE

The section above refers to soldiers being trained to become "brutalized automatons." As has been noted in previous chapters, the surrendering of will, individuality and deeply held beliefs is never done easily, and seldom done completely.

For an army to be effective, "there should be a modicum of independence for each member to the extent that personal pride can be attained and initiative recognized or rewarded."[393] This situation is sadly lacking in the US military.

As was also noted in previous chapters, actions performed by civilians that are completely legal may be serious crimes once a person is member of the US military. Additionally, basic rights afforded to American citizens under the US

---

392. Objectives of Vietnam Veterans Against the War. http://www.vvaw.org/veteran/ article/?id=317. Accessed August 15, 2005.

393. Shils, Edward. A Profile of the Military Deserter. *Armed Forces and Society*, Vol. 3, No. 3. May, 1977, p. 427.

Constitution are not granted to those in the service. Vietnam Veterans Against the War addressed this most serious issue in their third objective:

> To demand that all active-duty servicemen and women be afforded the same rights that are guaranteed by the United States Constitution and Bill of Rights that are presently denied by the Uniform Code of Military Justice. We are appalled that our active-duty GIs are treated as less than first class citizens. We endorse the efforts of our active-duty sisters and brothers to democratize the military.[394]

An example of this can be seen in the case of several young men in 1969, members of the Progressive Labor Party and the Young Socialists Alliance, who were drafted into the army. Before being inducted they told the board of their memberships in these organizations. There were inducted, and then later received less-than-honorable discharges due to their affiliation with "subversive" organizations.[395]

In this instance these men were taken by force (conscription) into the armed forces despite the fact that the military knew there were reasons that the military considered them unacceptable. They were then given the black mark of a less-than-honorable discharge. As US citizens they had every right to belong to the Progressive Labor Party, the Young Socialists Alliance, and any other organization of their choosing. As American soldiers, this right was denied them.

> It was not only the lowly private that suffered this deprivation of rights. In 1966, retired Admiral Arnold True was called in to a meeting with Rear Admiral John E. Clark, commandant of the Twelfth Navel District in San Francisco, California. True had had the audacity to speak publicly and forcefully against the US war in Vietnam. Arriving at Clark's office True noticed a poster on the wall with these words: "Let it be clear that this administration recognizes the value of daring and dissent — that we greet healthy controversy as the hallmark of healthy change." It was signed by President John F. Kennedy. True asked Clark about it and was told, "it doesn't apply to members of the naval service." Clark further told True that, ...even though he was retired, if he continued to criticize the Administration's Vietnam policies, "the next interview might not be pleasant." True took that to mean that he might be court-martialed. Only the intercession of Deputy Defense Secretary Cyrus R. Vance prevented the unpleasantness from occurring, for True refused to shut up.[396]

The methods the military uses to mete out its own brand of discipline in response to its own brand of justice has been uniform in only one way: its chronic unfairness. This was true during the Vietnam-era as it has been

---

394. Objectives of Vietnam Veterans Against the War. Accessed August 15, 2005.
395. Sherrill, p. 66.
396. Sherrill, p. 68.

throughout America's history. Methods condemned when used by enemy nations are acceptable when perpetrated by the US military. A telling example can be seen in behaviors at the Presidio military prison in San Francisco, California.

The details of the barbaric, overcrowded prison will only be outlined here. In February of 1968, Private Harmon Jones was placed in solitary confinement. Although he was troubled with kidney and prostrate problems,

> ...the guards had grown tired of releasing him from the barracks prison room to go to the toilet; so they put him in solitary and gave him a can and a roll of toilet paper. In his hysteria and anger, Jones threw the can and toilet paper outside, tore his clothes and urinated on the floor several times. Guards hosed out the cell, hosed Jones down as well, opened the windows (February can be very chilly on the San Francisco waterfront) and he was left for three days and nights without clothes or bedding. Later, "'[s]everal guards spit in my face,' Jones said. 'A guard got a rag off the floor, dipped it in urine and feces and rubbed it in my face and hair.'"[397]

Other inmates were beaten, slapped and deprived of medical attention needed due either to illness, wounds inflicted by guards, or suicide attempts, which were frequent at the Presidio.

When these inmates finally had their day in court, and these and related atrocities were enumerated, the military judge acted as might be expected.

The response of the military judge to these accounts was: "I have sat here now and listened to this, and from past experience I don't see how it is possible for you to make a statement that all these accused here are being mistreated in this fashion." When the attorneys continued to press their accusations of brutality, the judge responded coolly: "Well, gentlemen, I don't know what you want me to do. I can't go out there and personally supervise."[398]

Another comment made about conditions in Presidio highlights the hypocrisy of military justice as passed down from the most powerful offices in the country. Dr. Samuel Nelken of the University of California Medical Center testified at the Presidio trials.

> Referring to the treatment of GI prisoners at the "thought-reform universities" directed by the Chinese Communists during the Korean War, Nelken said: "We believed at that time, and properly, that the brainwashing methods used by the Chinese were cruel and unusual punishment. But we found in the [Presidio] stockade the same methods being used to break prisoners: isolation, confusion, threats of death and taunts about death of fellow prisoners."[399]

---

397. Sherrill, p. 10.
398. Sherrill, p. 11.
399. Sherrill, p. 69.

Men who grow up in the United States with a modicum of freedom, being able to find employment of their choosing; obtain higher education or not as their needs, desires and circumstances dictated; select their own living arrangements and romantic and/or sexual partners, and belong to whatever organizations interest them will not find it easy to surrender all they have ever known. To be suddenly thrust into a situation, not of their own choosing in the case of those who have been drafted, where their every move was scripted, their options removed, and deprived of all they ever held dear will never be an easy adjustment.

It must be noted that many who enlisted did so only hoping for a better deal, knowing that being drafted was inevitable. To make a distinction between deserters who were drafted and those who enlisted is unfair. Many enlistees did so only under the duress of a threatened draft. And most, if not all, who enter the military do so without a complete understanding of the life on which they are embarking.

A very difficult part of military life that is encountered by those who choose to desert pertains to military justice. In civilian life, a person accused of a crime is judged by a jury of his or her peers. A typical civilian jury, if there is such a thing among the diversity of people called to so serve, may include well-educated professionals along with laborers who never finished high school. There may be jurors with high-powered careers sitting beside people who work full-time tending home and family. It is this very diversity that serves as a protection for the accused who is, by law, innocent until proven guilty.

This is not the case in the military. Those who sit in judgment of the accused are all members of the military; while their backgrounds may be diverse, they are united in a common career, one that is outside the mainstream of life, one that makes its business that of war, destruction and killing. One man who deserted as a private during the Vietnam-era reported that at his court-martial the jury was comprised of military men all several ranks above him. He was quickly found guilty of the charge.[400] The rate of conviction during court martial trials is extremely high.

---

400. Conversation between the author and Gerry Condon, founder of "Soldier, Say No," on August 3, 2005.

FAMILY AND PERSONAL NEEDS

This factor is closely associated with "Resistance to Military Life." Once inducted into the US armed forces, family and personal needs are subjugated to the needs of the military. The fact that a man left behind a pregnant wife was and is no concern to the army, although it may be the soldier's first concern. A promising career, a desire for advanced education or simply a comfortable way of life all must be completely surrendered in order to fight a US government-defined enemy on the other side of the planet. For many men, this proved intolerable. The separation from a familiar and longed-for way of life to risk life for a cause that was at best nebulous was insufficient for many men. Desertion became the best option.

While a few men traveled to Sweden, and many more to Canada, one population of deserters remained for the most part in the US. African-Americans who deserted to Sweden faced the ugliness of racism there. For many, the best option was to return home and blend back into their own communities. This proved successful for most of them; the government made little or no effort to track them down. [401]

In some regards deserters and those who chose to serve out their assigned terms in the military faced a similar response from their families. The unpopularity of the war was somehow intertwined with an attitude of "my country right or wrong" that was often spoken by right-wing adherents during the Vietnam era. Veterans returned home having witnessed harrowing experiences. Often a major starting point to purging these troubling images from one is to discuss them. But many families did not seem interested in hearing about them.

Recalling discussions with veterans, Lifton remarked that "above all, the men had the impression that their parents did not want to hear or know about the extent of horror, absurdity, and corruption they had experienced in Vietnam. Many felt that their parents had been much more comfortable with them when they put on the uniform than when they threw it off.... Not that parents necessarily favored the war - a large number had apparently soured on it - but rather, as one of the men put it, 'They just didn't want me to do anything to rock the boat.' The 'boat' they didn't want rocked was the whole set of institutional arrangements and conventional cultural images and forms, within which one is expected to sit quietly over the course of a life's voyage."[402]

---

401. Ibid.

Some men who deserted had a parallel experience. One man who deserted during this era stated that, although his family opposed the war, they were uncomfortable with his actions. Had he remained within the mainstream, and risked his life or health in Vietnam, it would have been easier for them. They supported his decision, but were uncomfortable with it.[403] He too had rocked the boat of conformity, albeit in a different way.

A discussion of personal needs must by necessity mention self-preservation. Often a sense of duty can overcome self-preservation, the strongest and most basic urge in man. But with forced "service," either through conscription or its threat, in a war that in no way threatens the individual, his family or his country, the sense of duty is stronger to self and family.

As the war escalated, US servicemen looked for safe havens outside of American's borders. Remaining at home meant either imprisonment for desertion, or duty in Vietnam. For many, either option was unacceptable. Some had been welcomed in Canada, but the numbers fleeing to the north grew greatly after May of 1969.

> On the 22nd of May, the Canadian Minister of Immigration, Alan MacEachen, rose in the House of Commons to announce that henceforth American Vietnam draft and military resisters, that is, both "dodgers" and "deserters" would be admitted to Canada without regard to their draft or military status. MacEachen explained that this decision was the extension of a policy of "liberalization" in the treatment of "military applicants" that had been evolving for more than a year and that followed from a policy already in place allowing draft resisters the legal status of "landed immigrants" in Canada. "Our basic position," Minister MacEachen proclaimed, "is that the question of an individual's membership or potential membership in the armed services of his own country is a matter to be settled between the individual and his government, and is not a matter in which we should become involved."[404]

At least partly as a result of Mr. McEachen's statement, by August of 1969 the number of deserters and draft evaders going to Canada had tripled.

Young Americans who were subject to prosecution and penal sanctions under selective service and military law in the United States now could confidently seek and claim legal refuge as immigrants to Canada. This new policy was a turning point that resulted in more than 50,000 draft-age Americans migrating

---

402. Hillstrom, p. 274.

403. Gerry Condon, August 3, 2005.

404. Hagan, John. 2000. Narrowing the Gap by Wide the Conflict: Power Politics, Symbols of Sovereignty, and the American Vietnam War Resisters' Migration to Canada; *Law & Society Review, Vol. 34.* , p. 609.

to Canada in the largest northward exodus since the American Revolution. More than half of these now-middleaged American expatriates remain in Canada today.[405]

Certainly not all of these were deserters; many were draft evaders who faced conscription and opted to leave before needing to desert.

This Canadian policy caused some strains with the United States, but despite considerable posturing and disagreement within the Canadian government regarding how to deal with American draft evaders and deserters, the policy of accepting them never changed during the years America fought in Vietnam.

The response to the peace movement in the US was not nearly as benign. In response to the demonstration in Ann Arbor[406] and to similar protests that were beginning to occur throughout the United States, General Louis Hershey, Director of the Selective Service, made a portentous announcement. Students known to be involved in the antiwar movement would have their student deferments (S-1 status) revoked and would be subject to immediate induction into the military. The announcement went well beyond a simple change of policy. Rather, it was rife with far-reaching implications. Overtly, it was a formal declaration of war on the war resistors' movement, although the battle lines had already been drawn years earlier. This, of course, was tantamount to group retribution for the acts of a few — something that we all abhor today when it occurs in Africa, Southeast Asia, or the Middle East. It was also an indication that the draft, and thus the possibility of injury or death in combat, would be used as a means of punishing those young people who publicly took exception to America's Cold War military adventures. And it acted as a catalyst for what was then a small movement of military-age Americans who chose to go into exile, to leave their country rather than "serve their country," as the popular characterization puts it. Following the withdrawal of automatic S-1 status, the trickle of student war resistors deciding to move to Europe or, most frequently, to Canada became a steady flow.[407]

Circumstances throughout the 1970s could hardly have been more chaotic. In 1973 President Richard M. Nixon announced the signing of a ceasefire, which,

---

405. Hagan, p. 609.

406. In 1965 during an anti-war demonstration in Ann Arbor Michigan, the local Selective Service office was set afire.

407. Weinstein, Jay. 2002. 'Northern Passage: American Vietnam War Resistors in Canada. *Canadian Journal of sociology, Vol. 27.*

he said, brought "peace with honor" in Vietnam and Southeast Asia."[408] The signers were US Secretary of State Henry Kissinger and Le Duc Tho, who was the special advisor to the North Vietnamese delegation. That same year the draft was ended, and the last US troops exited Vietnam. Kissinger and Le Duc won the Noble Peace prize later that same year, but Le Duc refused his award, saying that true peace did not exist in Vietnam.

The following year saw the renewal of the war between the North and South. That same year President Nixon resigned in disgrace

In 1975 the war finally ended. The cities of Hue and the South's capital, Saigon, fell to the Communist North. President Gerald R. Ford announced that the war is "finished" and the last remaining Americans fled as Saigon fell.

The issue of deserters and draft evaders was not finished, however. Ford had inherited a country split apart by both the war and the Nixon resignation. In an effort to bring about some healing he pardoned Nixon for all his crimes,

> ...and then, a week later, began the process of reconciliation by announcing a program of "earned" amnesty for the fifty thousand draft evaders and deserters from the Vietnam War. As long as the deserters and draft dodgers were willing to engage in a brief stint of public service, Ford was willing to grant them immunity from prosecution. "All, in a sense, are casualties, still abroad and absent without leave from the real America," Ford told a veterans' convention. "I want them to come home if they want to work their way back."[409]

Ford's attempt at reconciliation was not well received. His pardon of Nixon angered Democrats, who saw the former president's actions as reprehensible, while his olive branch extended to draft evaders and deserters did not sit well with Republicans who felt the same way about men who they perceived had shirked their duty. Shortly after taking office, Ford's popularity plummeted.

Issues relating to draft evaders and deserters did not end there. In 1978 Ford was defeated by Georgia Governor Jimmy Carter. Keeping a campaign pledge Carter, on his first day in office, issued a presidential pardon to those who had avoided the draft during the Vietnam war by either not registering or traveling abroad.[410] The pardon meant the government was giving up forever the right to prosecute what the administration said were hundreds of thousands of draft-dodgers.

---

408. Chambers, p. 763.
409. Mann, Robert. 2001. *A Grand Delusion: America's Descent into Vietnam*, p. 719.
410. Rosenbaum, Herbert D. and Alexej Ugrinsky. *The Presidency and Domestic Policies of Jimmy Carter*, p. 134.

Still the controversy did not end. Some organizations faulted the new president saying that draft evaders should be prosecuted for the crime they committed.

> "We were very displeased with the pardon," (Tip) Marlow (of Veterans of Foreign Wars) said. "We feel that there is a better way for people who have broken laws to come back into the country, and that's though one of the pillars of the formation of our nation — and that is our present system of justice."[411]

The system of justice as interpreted and implemented by the military would give anyone sufficient reason to doubt this as a reasonable measure. Charges and punishments (the military had a 95% conviction rate in its court-martials) are arbitrary. Refusing to wear a uniform has resulted in sentences ranging from simple discharge to three years in prison. Refusing to obey an order has resulted in sentences ranging from a few weeks to sixteen years. Holding an antiwar bull session while in uniform on base has resulted in everything from an administrative discharge without punishment to ten years in prison and a dishonorable discharge.[412]

Carter's pardon did not include deserters or civilian protesters, and this brought criticism from amnesty groups. Others, however, praised it as a first step toward healing.

A comment made at that time by Louise Ransom, affiliate director of Americans for Amnesty, hits the mark regarding military service, especially compulsory service.

> "There seems to be a myth that because you once went into the army, there's some kind of esprit that you have accepted or believed in," Ransom said. "Well the truth of the matter is that so many of the draft-eligible young men legally avoided the draft that ... all the services took their people predominantly from poor and minority people in this country — took them right out of high school before they had the opportunity to even examine whether they were conscientious objectors."[413]

Although statistics about the poor seem to confirm Ransom's comments, the point of interest here is the apparent governmental/military belief that induction to the military automatically confers acceptance of the military's purposes, standards, measures, etc. Recruitment practices and especially the conscription methods of this era focused on young, impressionable men who, as

---

411. Carter's Pardon. http://www.pbs.org/newshour/bb/asia/vietnam/vietnam_1-21-77.html. Accessed August 15, 2005.

412. Sherrill, p. 65.

413. Carter's Pardon.

Ransom points out, had had little time to formulate opinions. The military apparently knows this, and strives to force its own opinions on these young men. The problems with desertion, AWOL, fragging and combat refusal strongly indicate the military's consistent inability to accomplish this disgraceful goal. Men may enter the military without well-formed, definite ideas about the military or a particular war, but they generally have well-formed ideals and principles. As men have done since America's difficult birth, they will naturally resist the military's efforts to strip these ideals and principles from them.

It's interesting to note that by 1977 the military itself had recognized the injustice of the Vietnam War. As reported in "Armed Forces and Society" that year, many people demanded amnesty because "the young men who deserted or who refused to be conscripted did so because they perceived the injustice of a war which the rest of the country and the government only later acknowledged to be unjust."[414]

Desertion from the US military during the time of Vietnam appears to indicate the recognition on the part of thousands of young men what it took the government tragic long years to realize. Of those who opted to leave, one can only wonder how many of them might not have survived a tour of duty in Vietnam.

---

414. Shills, Edward. 1977. A Profile of the Military Deserter. *Armed Forces and Society*, Vol. 3, No. 3. May, p. 427.

CHAPTER 10: THE GULF WAR

The hostilities that resulted in the Gulf War were based on oil rivalries between Iraq and Kuwait, two of the most oil-rich countries on the planet. On July 17, 1990, Saddam Hussein accused the Kuwaiti government of both over-producing oil beyond international agreements, and of stealing oil from Iraq's Rumailia oil field. Tensions escalated in the next several days.

However, the roots of disagreement between Iraq and Kuwait date back many years. Iraq never accepted Kuwait as an independent state. A more current problem stemmed from Iraq's belief that Kuwait was illegally exploiting the Rumailia oil field. Iraq felt that this area, partially straddling the international boundaries, belonged to Baghdad. Further, Baghdad believed that Kuwait and the United Arab Emirates (UAE) were overproducing oil beyond the quotas established by OPEC, thus drastically reducing Iraq's income.[415]

On July 22 1990, in consultation with April Glaspie, US Ambassador to Iraq, Hussein was advised that this dispute was between Iraq and Kuwait and lay outside of the interest of the United States.

Left with this impression, Iraq invaded Kuwait on August 2. Immediately the United Nations ordered Iraq to withdraw from Kuwait, and President George Bush froze all assets of both countries.

The political climate in the US was ripe for a war. In the mid-term elections the Democrats had made gains in Congress, and President Bush's popularity was low. "According to Elizabeth Drew, a writer for the New Yorker,

---

415. Hinchcliffe, Peter and Beverley Minton-Edwards. 2004. *Conflicts in the Middle East since 1945*, p. 94.

Bush's aid John Sununu 'was telling people that a short successful war would be pure political gold for the President.'"[416]

Between August and the end of the year the US, in conjunction with the United Nations, prepared to enforce the U.N.'s directive that Iraq leave Kuwait. A January 15, 1991 deadline for the withdrawal of Iraqi forces was set by the U.N. The deadline passed without Iraq's withdrawal. In the early morning hours of January 17, 1991, US warplanes began an attack on Iraq. By the end of the month, over 500,000 US troops were deployed in the Gulf.[417] America, once again, was at war.

Resistance to the war began almost immediately. There appear to have been four main reasons for desertion during the Gulf War

1. Cruelty towards the Iraqis;
2. Living conditions;
3. Disagreement with the war, and
4. The military's infamous "stop loss" policy.

Of these, the third and fourth reasons appear to stand out as the major causes of desertion.

As has been demonstrated in the earlier chapters, neither of these second two reasons is new. Starting with the American Revolution, soldiers left the ranks because of changing loyalties, or because they felt their enlistment time had expired. Many men and women in service during the Gulf War felt the same.

A look at each reason for desertion is helpful.

CRUELTY TOWARDS THE IRAQIS

While this has been noticed more during the Iraqi war than during the Gulf War, it was no less prevalent in the first. An attitude of racism — the belief that the 'enemy' is somehow less than human, or unworthy of basic human rights — pervaded the military. Erik Larson, an early deserter from the Marine Corps during the Gulf War, visited a high school class and repeated some chants he'd learned as a Marine:

---

416. Zinn, Howard. 2001. *A People's History of the United States;* (New York, 2001), p. 595.
417. Siddiqi, Moin A. "The Monetary Costs of a New Gulf War: The Global Economy will be Rocked by Soaring Fuel Prices, Severe Recession and Market Turmoil if the United States Iraqi Policy Backfires." *The Middle East*, April, 2003, p. 1.

Rape the town and kill the people;

That's the thing we love to do;

Rape the town and kill the people

That's the only thing to do;

Throw some napalm on the schoolhouse;

Watch the kiddies scream and shout;

Rape the town and kill the people;

That's the thing we love to do;

Napalm, napalm;

Sticks like glue;

Sticks to the mamas and the papas;

And the kiddies, too.[418]

Mr. Larson reported another chant: "Ready to fight, ready to kill, ready to die but never will."[419] In addition to indoctrinating impressionable youths with a killing mentality, the military tries to build on the adolescent feeling of invincibility. Too often these impressionable youths learn in the battlefield, as they witness and participate in unspeakable carnage, that they have been lied to. Then it is too late.

Another young recruit, Aimee Allison, enlisted to earn money to attend Stanford University. She reported the following about her military training:

> "I was standing there not being able to say anything and they yell 'what makes the grass grow?' And we are forced to yell, 'Blood. Blood makes the grass grow, Marines make the blood flow'. . .
>
> "And the woman next to me was just crying, holding her M-16, realizing what the words meant."[420]

The Marine Corp has a reputation as a 'killing machine.' In order to indoctrinate young recruits to kill they must be made to see killing as acceptable behavior. As indicated by the chants above, this acceptable killing is not restricted to self-defense, or even to the barbarity of hand-to-hand combat. Men, women and children are acceptable targets for the Marines and anyone in the US armed forces.

---

418. Syrop, Jeff. 1991. The New Order. http://www.zenhell.com/GetEnlightened/stories/neworder/neworder.htm. Accessed October 11, 2005.

419. Esch, Betty. 2001. The Greatest War Heroes: In Honor of our War Resisters. http://www.solidarity-us.org/atc/90Esch.html#R8. Accessed October 11, 2005.

420. Esch, 2001.

Not all soldiers who experienced these atrocities chose to desert. Some returned home and attempted to deal with what they had seen and done. Of those, some were unable to do so successfully. "Robert W. Haley, University of Texas Southwestern Medical Center, Dallas, reported...in an article published by the Associated Press that the Gulf War veteran also has a higher rate of depression and suicide."[421] For others, deserting from the military enabled them to obtain the peace of mind that appears to be so illusive for many Gulf War veterans. Many who served did so honorably, yet suffer mentally from the atrocities they witnessed, and physically from desert conditions; the so-called 'Gulf War Syndrome' has only been gradually and grudgingly acknowledged by the military as a real ailment. For the men and women suffering from Gulf War Syndrome, the nightmare of the war continues.

LIVING CONDITIONS

The abysmal living conditions under which the soldiers tasked with fighting wars usually must live were not experienced by all the Gulf War soldiers, but even those living in relatively clean environments were negatively impacted by them. Some soldiers were billeted in relatively new facilities, which were sometimes surrounded by 'tent cities' housing other soldiers. Both areas were extremely overcrowded.

> For the overwhelming majority of the force, there was no place to go — no place for people to physically escape from each other. The crowding — often considered a major source of stress — and the omnipresence of leaders gave soldiers and leaders both a sense of constant unbroken evaluation of each by the other to the discomfort of both.[422]

The military is not an environment in which a great deal of privacy is ever afforded. But during the Gulf War this enforced intimacy took a great toll. Soldiers needed to get away from each other.

> In interviews, a number of leaders and soldiers were adamant about the need to get away from each other and the emotional costs of this enforced togetherness. Over and over again each enunciated the sentiment: How the hell do I get away from them — my fellow soldiers, my leaders, my followers?[423]

---

421. Gulf War Syndrome. 2003. http://lef.org/protocols/prtcl-143.shtml. Accessed on October 18, 2005.
422. David H. Marlow. 2001. *Psychological and Psychosocial Consequences of Combat and Deployment: With Special Emphasis on the Gulf War*, p. 125.

One may also wonder how those in the tents felt, knowing their fellow-soldiers were housed in buildings. These living conditions could only negatively impact morale; their contribution to desertion cannot be underestimated.

During the Gulf War the air pollution experienced by the service personnel (not to mention the citizens of Iraq) reached extremely dangerous levels.

> Personnel have emphasized that air quality during the war was a major difficulty due not only to the high levels of dust generated from blowing desert sands, but also to the extensive oil field fires that contributed extensive hydrocarbon smoke plumes.[424]

A natural reaction to such pollution is constant coughing and irritation. While this may seem to be no more discomforting than a common cold, it must be remembered the those fighting this war were extremely close to the fires causing the smoke. Additionally, depleted uranium added to the extreme discomfort at the time, and is believed by many to be responsible for the long-term illness of many Gulf War veterans.

DISAGREEMENT WITH THE WAR

Unlike other wars, when the civilian population of the United States first opposed the war, it was soldiers who first began to speak out against the Gulf War. Marine Cpl. Jeff Paterson was another early deserter during this war. His reasons for desertion include all four of those mentioned above. On August 16, 1991, while stationed in Hawaii, Cpl. Paterson held a press conference in which he said:

> "I will not be a pawn in America's power plays for profits and oil in the Middle East...." Two weeks later...Jeff was ordered to board a military transport plane bound for Saudi Arabia.... As Jeff broke ranks, a struggle broke out, and he was physically forced back in line. When order was temporarily restored, Jeff sat down on the tarmac. After refusing all subsequent orders, he was arrested and taken to the Pearl Harbor Brig.[425]

---

423. Marlow, p. 126.

424. Scientists Study Depleted Uranium link to Gulf War Syndrome. 2003. http://www.lrri.org/cr/dustudy.html. Accessed October 11, 2005.

425. Jeff Paterson: First Military Resister to the Gulf War Available for Speaking and Other Anti-War Events; http://jeff.paterson.net/pdf/jp_resume.pdf. Accessed October 11, 2005.

Cpl. Paterson's desertion had nothing to do with cowardice or treachery, the usual reasons the military automatically ascribes to desertion. He'd served his country for four years as a US Marine. His desertion was not caused by inability to adapt to military life or family issues. In his own words, Cpl. Paterson was an 'ideological deserter,' one who grew in knowledge between his enlistment at the age of 22, and his aborted deployment to Saudi Arabia four years later.[426]

While in the Marines, Cpl. Paterson served in Korea, Japan and Okinawa, among other locations. He was in an 'NBC' artillery unit — Nuclear, Biological and Chemical weapons. During this time he was trained to build nuclear weapons, which he was told would only be used in the direst of circumstances, i.e. an actual invasion of enemy forces into the United States. In preparation for deployment in the Middle East early in the war, his commanding officer announced to his platoon: "If anything goes wrong, Cpl. Paterson will nuke all the ragheads until they glow."[427]

During this time, while stationed in Hawaii and with his enlistment period drawing to a close, Cpl. Paterson began attending lectures at the University of Hawaii. Information he'd learned by observation at the various sites where he'd served, and through his own study, confirmed that the US was not helping people around the world. His commanding officer's comment referenced above only further reinforced that belief. In the past he'd seen abject poverty around US military bases, along with prostitution rings facilitated by the military.

Additionally, Cpl. Paterson's four-year enlistment was drawing to a close. "stop loss" — a term that has become common since the start of the Iraq war — was first invoked during the Gulf War. "Stop Loss" is defined by the military as "a short-term policy that stabilizes Marines in their current assignment by preventing them from leaving the Corps at the end of their service."[428] Regardless of the sugar-coated wording, "stop loss" means that the Marine is required to exceed his or her commitment to the military, while the military is not required to adhere to its commitments to the Marine. This, to Cpl. Paterson, was also unacceptable.

---

426. This information is from a conversation between Mr. Jeff Paterson and the author on August 15, 2005.
427. Jeff Paterson, August 15, 2005.
428. The Marines: The Few, The Proud. http://www.usmc.mil/marinelink/mcn2000.nsf/ stoploss#WHATISSTOPLOSS. Accessed October 28, 2005.

Mr. Paterson's case demonstrates the military's customary mistreatment of deserters. After spending a month in the Pearl Harbor brig prior to his court martial, a Federal District Judge ruled that he was being held solely to stifle his freedom of speech. The military moved him to house arrest. A month later, the same judge ruled that house arrest had the same effect, and Cpl. Paterson was transferred to a rear unit.

During the trial, most of the witnesses — the soldiers who'd seen or been involved in the scuffle when Cpl. Paterson had refused to board the military transport plane — were in Saudi Arabia. The judge ordered them to travel 200 miles across the desert to testify via satellite. The military then tried to move the trial to Saudi Arabia. Cpl. Paterson's lawyer agreed to this change of venue, mentioning in passing that he expected to find new clients in the new location. The request for the change of venue was withdrawn.

Ultimately, Cpl. Paterson pleaded guilty to two charges of AWOL. The first was for a 24-hour period during the time he was giving his first press conference. The second was for a two-minute period when he was late returning to the compound, having been delayed answering reporters' questions. He was given a 'less than honorable' discharge.

The unfairness in Cpl. Paterson's case — singling him out due to his outspokenness — is blatant, but it is not unique. Consider the case of Clarence Davis, a young man in 1990 with a record of minor violations of the law. He was given a choice by a judge: jail or the military. He chose the Marines, although he eventually received both. He became one of the first soldiers sent to the Persian Gulf.

After arriving in Saudi Arabia, Davis decided he would not participate in the allied campaign against Iraq. In a letter, he wrote, "I can never support the same country or thought that killed millions of Native Americans, Vietnamese, Japanese, Africans, Iraqis, Panamanians etc. I can never support the same thought that does not include me in the Constitution that I supposedly enlisted to uphold and defend.... I am not a Muslim but another reason for my refusal to fight came from the immorality of killing a Muslim brother or sister."

After surrendering to his Commanding Officer, Mr. Davis was incarcerated until his court martial and subsequently "found guilty of refusing to obey a direct order. Though military law requires that a civilian lawyer be made available to soldiers charged with military crimes, Davis was denied this right on the grounds that it was too expensive to fly someone in for the trial."[429]

After the court martial, Mr. Davis wrote: "[I]magine a full bird Colonel and three officers all telling you that you are facing death or a life of long hard labor and ain't nothing you can do about it. It was basically an experience that will never leave me."

Capt. Yolanda Huet-Vaughn, a physician, was also court martialed as a result of actions she took during this war. Starting in January, 1990, Capt. Huet-Vaughn spoke out publicly against the war. She was the highest-ranking officer to refuse. Her defense was twofold: first, "that she had not just the legal right but the duty to refuse given that war crimes could be reasonably anticipated. This argument was built on evidence provided by former US Attorney General Ramsey Clark, who had visited Iraq in the midst of the bombing campaign and returned with footage documenting the systematic destruction of hospitals, schools and apartment buildings." Her second area of defense rested on the Nuremberg Code.

> ...the Nuremberg Code, which forbids experimentation on people without their consent. In the Gulf, thousands of GIs were inoculated without their consent with experimental vaccines for botulism and anthrax, allegedly to protect them from Iraqi weapons. As a physician Huet-Vaughn would have been expected to inject soldiers in violation of the principles established at Nuremberg.[430]

At her court martial, the prosecutor, Capt. David Harney, said this: "The accused's attitude is that she's a doctor first and a soldier up to the point where it conflicts with her conscience. Such an attitude is self-serving and totally incompatible with any concept of duty."[431] One would consider that any soldier has a duty to the Nuremberg Code and other international law.

Elenora Johnson was 18 when she joined the Army. Having grown up in poverty in Lynchburg, South Carolina, Ms. Johnson saw the Army as means of bringing her to a better future. After several years her religious convictions grew and she desired to leave the military. She summarized her situation:

> [I]n December 1990, I was ordered to the Persian Gulf. I was caught and torn between right and wrong. I couldn't see myself going over there to kill a human being or to assist in the killing. The Bible says, 'Thou shall not kill.'

> For refusing to go to the Persian Gulf, I was court martialed. The hearing took place on March 4th and 5th, 1991. I was not given a fair trial. The Judge was in a hurry to get the case over with because he 'had a plane to catch.' He refused to allow additional evidence favorable to my case. The jury panel convicted me on all counts.

---

429. Esch, 2001.
430. Esch, 2001.
431. Shapiro, Bruce. 1992. The High Price of Conscience; *The Nation, Vol. 254,*

I was given a Bad Conduct Discharge (BCD), reduced from E-4 to E-1 status, given three months of hard labor, and ordered to forfeit two-thirds of my pay for five months.[432]

Ms. Johnson's case is not unique: a soldier who has served well gradually changes her mind about military service and desires to separate from the military. Yet as has been stated before, choice is for citizens, not for soldiers. Those who insist on it pay a high price.

Keith Jones was sentenced to sixteen months for desertion. His defense was simple: "There are certain things I live my life by: equality, justice, fairness and honesty. I believe that it is impossible to uphold these values in war."[433]

The resistance of another young man, Doug DeBoer, began in boot camp. The chanting of racist, sexist and violent words convinced him that his involvement in the Gulf War would be morally wrong.

Often young men and women buy into the glitz of recruiting advertisements, which offer discipline and self-respect in addition to educational benefits. Or they enlist due to some event that they perceive threatens the security of the US in some way. Yet they sometimes grow to see things differently.

During a debate featuring Erik Larson at a high school, and a teacher who was in the Air Force Reserves, the following question was raised: If an 18-year-old man joined the German army at a time when Hitler was helping the economy and building new roads, and then, two years later, he found out that Hitler was using the military to round up Jews and kill them, should this young man continue to honor the contract he signed with the German army?[434]

The comparison, although possibly extreme, cannot be dismissed. If a man or woman today enlists with the best and purest of intentions, and then learns that rather than helping a downtrodden people, or defending American security, soldiers are merely risking their lives for corporate profits at the expense of the very people they hoped to assist, is he or she still morally responsible to maintain the contract?

And then, patriotism is not the only motivation for enlistment; perhaps it is not even the main one.

---

432. Paterson, Jeff. 1991. The Anti-Warrior. http://jeff.paterson.net/aw/awl_e_johnson.htm. Accessed October 28, 2005.
433. Paterson, Jeff. 1991. The Anti-Warrior. http://jeff.paterson.net/aw/aw2_nwo.htm. Accessed October 28, 2005.
434. Syrop, Jeff. 1991. The New Order. http://www.zenhell.com/GetEnlightened/stories/neworder/neworder.htm. Accessed October 11, 2005.

When the African American resisters talk about their experiences the similarities among them are undeniable. Though most were not antiwar when they signed up, neither do any of them tell a story in which patriotic idealism figured in their reasons for enlisting. "When I graduated high school I didn't want to work at MacDonalds," was the way Kweisi Ehoize said it. For Aimee Allison and Tahan Jones it was a way to school; for Clarence Davis a possible route to job training and out of jail.[435]

It is not only African-Americans who enlist for education benefits; other men and women often enlist for the same reasons.

In addition to disagreement with the war was uncertainty about the reason for the war.

> There were many questions about the US role: What was the United States going to do? How long would the deployment last? If we were not going to war, would they be there for weeks, months, or years? If this was to be a siege, when would they be rotated out? Three months? Six months? A year? Two years? Rumors were rife and answers were not forthcoming.[436]

One result of this uncertainty was that soldiers were given deployment orders, bade good-bye to tearful loved-ones and then had the orders temporarily rescinded. For some soldiers this happened repeatedly. The impact on morale that this would have cannot be questioned. This too may have been a contributing cause of desertion.

The rate of applications for Conscientious Objector status during the Gulf War was high; "[o]ver 2500 US soldiers filed for Conscientious Objector discharges during the Gulf War, the fastest rise in CO applications in US history."[437] "Over a thousand reservists declared themselves conscientious objectors."[438] However, the military, needing bodies for its war, used every means possible to delay processing these applications. Over one-hundred Conscientious Objector applicants were jailed during the war.

The regulations surrounding Conscientious Objector application and status are complex. The military's enlistment contracts preclude conscientious objectors from joining any branch of the military. It is recognized, at least in theory, that people change their minds and may come to object to war after they

---

435. Esch, 2001.
436. Marlow, David H. 1999. *Psychological and Psychosocial Consequences of Combat and Deployment: With Special Emphasis on the Gulf War*; p. 123.
437. Resisters to WarMaking: Past and Present. 2005. http://www.jonahhouse.org/McAlisterVetsForPeace1204.htm. Accessed October 28, 2005.
438. Zinn, p. 624.

are in the military. But the parameters are stringent; the objector must object to all war, in any and all circumstance. Recognizing the immorality and illegality of a particular war is not sufficient.

There is a chain of command that must be followed for CO applications. During the Gulf War, "[s]ome commands refused to accept applications, some have taken a year or longer to process applications, and some have denied CO applications without legal justification."[439]

Additionally, the military has the right to deploy the soldier while the application is being processed. The soldier can be sent into battle, but will not be required to carry a weapon. The absurdity of this is clear. The military may feel that the soldier will drop his or her CO application in order to have some means of defense while in the battlefield. However, for many soldiers this is not an option; desertion is.

The military cannot point to an illustrious record in dealing with soldiers applying for Conscientious Objector status. One incident that occurred in 1991 is particularly telling:

Pressed for troops and striking back at the resisters, on 28 December the Army handcuffed and forcibly deployed Specialist David Carson. David and at least seven other Army soldiers, all with pending CO discharge applications, were forcibly deployed from Germany to Saudi Arabia . Due to public pressure, charges were never filed against them.[440]

In any other setting, this would be kidnapping and would spark worldwide outrage. Fortunately there was sufficient negative response that Mr. Carson and the others were not charged with any crime. But that such actions are unfair is an extreme understatement; saying they are criminal is not an exaggeration.

THE "STOP LOSS" POLICY

This policy is another example of the military's lack of responsibility for keeping its commitments. When a person enlists in any branch of the military it is for a definite period of time. Jeff Paterson enlisted for four years. During that time soldiers are expected to perform a variety of duties, some of which may

---

439. Resisters to WarMaking.
440. Resisters to WarMaking. =

threaten their lives. Assuming that the soldier does not see conflicts between his/her conscience and the tasks he/she is required to perform, and is given the equipment necessary to perform those duties, it is completely reasonable to expect that the soldier will fulfill his/her contract, and at the end of the time for which he/she enlisted, he or she will be honorably discharged. They have fulfilled their part of the agreement and, as with any contract, they expect that the other party — in this case, the US military — will fulfill its part. However, unlike any other organization in the country, the US military is under no obligation to keep its part of the bargain. A contract violated by one party is null and void. However, the US military gives itself the right to violate its part of the contract with impunity. It does not grant that privilege to the other party in the contract — the soldier.

Extended or uncertain-length deployments were a major stress factor for Gulf War soldiers. The most salient stressor during this initial period was the high level of concern about a projected date of return to the United States. The question asked most often was, "When are we going home?" The deployment was perceived as open ended, which was very disturbing to most troops. Again, open-ended deployments had not been a part of Army culture since World War II. Even in combat such as Korea and Vietnam, the rotation system had bounded the time the soldier would spend away.[441]

The stop-loss policy caused this great uncertainty. Regardless of the length of time the man or woman enlisted for, the military could extend it at will.

Men and women who choose not to continue their military employment must not expect the same rights as non-military Americans. To do so would be tragically naïve. An example from Mr. Paterson's experience will illustrate the point.

After announcing his intention to miss deployment for the Gulf War, Mr. Paterson was physically forced into a line of soldiers waiting to board a plane to Saudi Arabia. His behavior — consisting of some statements against the war, his declaration that he wouldn't fight and his refusal to board the plane — was considered by the military to be so threatening to the morale of the unit that military officials demanded pretrial imprisonment. They said that Mr. Paterson's "'...serious criminal misconduct adversely impacts on the effectiveness, morale, discipline, readiness of command and the national security of the United States.' Mr. Paterson's commanding officer explained, 'his public defiance of orders and

---

441. Marlow, p. 124

statements of his intent to refuse deployment were causing open unrest within the unit.'"[442] It took a civilian judge to release Mr. Paterson from pretrial custody.

One must consider that if the actions of one soldier in refusing deployment jeopardize the national security of the United States then there must certainly be other, far more serious issues with which the military must cope. Additionally, the degree of unrest and dissatisfaction that Mr. Paterson's actions allegedly caused would seem to indicate a very weak commitment to the goals of the war among the other soldiers in his unit.

It appears that while the threat of dire consequences hangs over the head of every soldier who deserts the military, those who take a political stand are at greater risk. Of all the soldiers who deserted during the time of the Gulf War, those who gave press conferences, spoke at peace rallies and other events, were pursued, charged, tried, convicted and sentenced. One will look in vain for the trial of such a man or woman that ended in acquittal.

---

442. Jeff Paterson. 1991. http://jeff.paterson.net/pdf/jp_resume.pd. Accessed October 28, 2005.

CHAPTER 11: THE IRAQ WAR

Few wars have met with the level of opposition that has been seen regarding the war in Iraq. In the buildup to war millions of people the world over gathered and marched in protest. Some cities — notably Rome and London — saw more than a million of their people gather to protest the war.

In 2002, US President George Bush — inaugurated after losing the majority vote — began to proclaim that Iraq possessed chemical and biological weapons, was attempting to obtain the necessary materials for nuclear weapons and therefore represented an 'imminent threat' to the United States. Having labeled Iraq part of the 'axis of evil' a year earlier, the increased hostile rhetoric was not surprising.

President Bush told the U.N. the following, on September 12, 2002:

> Today, Iraq continues to withhold important information about its nuclear program — weapons design, procurement logs, experiment data, an accounting of nuclear materials and documentation of foreign assistance. Iraq employs capable nuclear scientists and technicians. It retains physical infrastructure needed to build a nuclear weapon. Iraq has made several attempts to buy high-strength aluminum tubes used to enrich uranium for a nuclear weapon. Should Iraq acquire fissile material, it would be able to build a nuclear weapon within a year. And Iraq's state-controlled media has reported numerous meetings between Saddam Hussein and his nuclear scientists, leaving little doubt about his continued appetite for these weapons.[443]

---

443. We Turn to the Urgent Duty of Protecting Other Lives. *The Washington Times*, September 13, 2002.

Secretary of State Colin Powell, addressing the U.N. on February 5, 2003, showed satellite photos that he said indicated the presence of 'active chemical munitions bunkers' disguised from inspectors.[444]

Further, Powell claimed that Iraq failed to account for its stockpile of between 100 and 500 tons of chemical weapons, including four tons of the nerve gas VX. He said a single drop of VX can kill a human being. "We have evidence these weapons existed," Powell said. "What we don't have is evidence from Iraq that they have been destroyed or where they are."[445]

Additionally, Mr. Bush and members of his administration — most notably Vice President Dick Cheney and Secretary of State Colin Powell — stated categorically that Iraq's leader, Saddam Hussein, had close ties with Osama bin Laden and was somehow responsible for the September 11, 2001 attack on the United States.

As recently as June 17, 2004, Mr. Cheney was proclaiming links between Al-Qaeda and Iraq. "Vice President Dick Cheney said Thursday the evidence is overwhelming that Al-Qaeda had long-standing ties with Saddam Hussein's regime in Iraq, and he said media reports suggesting that the 9/11 commission has reached a contradictory conclusion were 'irresponsible.'"[446]

Yet the same article contradicted this statement.

> Members of 9/11 commission found 'no credible evidence' that Iraq was involved in the September 11, 2001, terrorist attacks carried out by al Qaeda hijackers, and they concluded that there was 'no collaborative relationship' between Iraq and Osama bin Laden, the network's leader, according to details of its findings disclosed Wednesday at a public hearing.[447]

During the buildup to war, Congressional offices received tens of thousands of letters, email, telephone calls and faxes, encouraging members of the Senate and House to withhold authorization for war. However, on October 11, 2002, the Congress overwhelming authorized the use of force against Iraq. The stage was set for the next American war.

Throughout 2002 and 2003, Bush attempted to create an international coalition to support the US invasion. However, he was met with disappointment on

---

444. Threats and Responses: Powell's Address, Presenting Deeply Troubling Evidence on Iraq, *New York Times*, February 6, 2004.
445. Saddam Link to 9/11 Not Likely; No Credible Evidence found. *The Washington Times*, June 17, 2004.
446. Ibid.
447. Williams, Ian: *Coalition-Building a la Shakespeare.* Washington Report on Middle East Affairs, Vol. 22, May, 2003.

almost every side. Although a few countries — most notably Great Britain and Italy — supported his efforts, traditional long-time allies did not. France, Germany and Russia opposed the war and refused to assist in any way. The following is a list of the countries that agreed to participate:

Afghanistan, Albania, Australia, Azerbaijan, Britain and Bulgaria, Colombia, the Costa Rica, Czech Republic, Denmark, Denmark, Dominican El Salvador, Eritrea, Estonia, Ethiopia, Georgia, Honduras, Hungary, Iceland, Italy, Japan, Kuwait, Latvia, Lithuania, Macedonia, Marshall Islands, Micronesia, Mongolia, Netherlands, Nicaragua, Palau, Panama, Philippines, Poland, Portugal, Republic, Romania, Rwanda, Singapore, Slovakia, Solomon Islands, and South Korea, Spain, Turkey, Uganda, Uzbekistan.[448]

On March 20, 2003, so-called coalition forces invaded Iraq. The United States was once again at war.

It is not surprising that the most powerful military machine in the history of the world quickly vanquished the army of a nation suffering from a decade of U.N.-imposed sanctions. Thus, on May 1, less than two months after the invasion, President Bush declared an end to major combat operations, with Saddam Hussein overthrown and on the run, and most of the country occupied by US forces. But Mr. Bush and his administration were to be disappointed; Iraq's military had been defeated, but its citizens had not. As of this writing (August, 2005), the war drags on and over 1,800 Americans, and tens of thousands of Iraqis have been killed since Mr. Bush declared that the war was over.

As has been the case in many of America's wars, desertion existed from the start. But as the war dragged on those numbers have been spiraling upwards. Some estimates show that as many as 6,000 soldiers may have deserted, but as indicated by the following quotation, desertion has a vague definition.

> Fewer than two-thirds of the former soldiers being reactivated for duty in Iraq and elsewhere have reported on time, prompting the Army to threaten some with punishment for desertion. The former soldiers, part of what is known as the Individual Ready Reserve (IRR), are being recalled to fill shortages in skills needed for the conflicts in Iraq and Afghanistan. Of the 1,662 ready reservists ordered to report to Fort Jackson, S.C., by Sept. 22, only 1,038 had done so, the Army said Monday. About 500 of those who failed to report have requested exemptions on health or personal grounds.[449]

---

448. Ibid.
449. Squitieri, Tom. 2004. Former Soldiers Slow to Report. *USA Today*, September 27, 2004.

While many who are currently late in reporting may eventually report as ordered, some definitely will not. "According to the US military, there have been about 6,000 deserters from the Iraq war."[450] This report was issued in May of 2005; current indications are that there has been no reduction in the number of soldiers deserting since then.

Since no comprehensive studies of desertion during the Iraq war have as yet been completed, anecdotal evidence must be viewed to learn reasons for desertion.

Based on the evidence available at this time, there appear to be three main reasons for desertion:

1. Disagreement with the war;
2. The horror of war; and
3. The stop-loss program.

A look at each is instructive. As with the exploration of the other wars, these factors often overlap; it is seldom only one that causes desertion.

DISAGREEMENT WITH THE WAR

Based on the resistance and opposition to the war that began months before the invasion, the fact that many soldiers do not support the war effort cannot be surprising. The reasons that the Bush administration stated as causing the need for the infamous 'preemptive' strike against Iraq have all proved groundless. The fear of many of those who opposed the war from the start that an invasion and occupation would cause Iraq to become a training ground for terrorists has been realized. The US began its invasion by bombing population centers such as Baghdad; this is shocking under any circumstances, but even more so with the realization that over 50% of Iraq's population is under the age of fifteen.

The invasion of Iraq seems to clearly violate the Nuremberg principles, enacted after the Nuremberg trials of World War II war criminals. Principle VI lists crimes against peace:

> The crimes hereinafter set out are punishable as crimes under; international law:

---

450. Military Deserters Flee to Canada. 2005. http://www.wesh.com/news/4534806/detail.html. Accessed October 14, 2005.

Crimes against peace:

Planning, preparation, initiation or waging of a war of aggression or a war in violation of international treaties, agreements or assurances;

Participation in a common plan or conspiracy for the accomplishment of any of the acts mentioned under (i).[451]

That soldiers themselves recognize this is not surprising.

Sgt. Camilo Mejia was the first Iraq war veteran to publicly oppose the war. He felt deep conflicts between his early, private opposition to the war and his close association with other soldiers. After deploying to Iraq and coming home on leave, he denounced the war and deserted. He served nearly nine months of a one-year prison term, in addition to demotion to private, forfeiture of pay and a bad conduct discharge.[452]

For many soldiers, their experience in Iraq crystallized their opposition to the war. Sgt. Kevin Benderman filed for Conscientious Objector status after serving a tour of duty in Iraq. Although acquitted of desertion, he was convicted of 'missing deployment.' He is currently serving a fifteen-month sentence.[453]

Ordered for deployment to Iraq, Marine Corps Reservist Stephen Funk refused:

"I refuse to kill," said Funk, who had excelled as a rifleman during boot camp. "I object to war because I believe that it is impossible to achieve peace through violence. I am a conscientious objector because there is no way for me to remain a Marine without sacrificing my entire sense of self-respect."[454]

Mr. Funk, the first enlisted man to publicly refuse deployment to Iraq, also stated the following: "I will not obey an unjust war based on deception by our leaders."[455] He served a six-month prison term after conviction for being AWOL.

The words of another soldiers are instructive. Dan Felushko was a Marine who enlisted shortly after the September 11, 2001 terrorist attacks in the US. In

---

451. Boyle, Francis A. 2004. *Destroying World Order: US Imperialism in the Middle East before and after September, 11.* Page 131.

452. Conversation between Mr. Camilo Mejia and the author, August 17, 2005.

453. Kevin Benderman Defense Committee. 2005. http://www.bendermandefense.org/. Accessed October 28, 2005.

454. Freeman, Anita, Adam Holdorf and Jackie Renn. Brave Souls. http://www.realchangenews.org/pastissuesupgrade/2003_06_26/features/brave_souls.html.   Accessed October 28, 2005

455. Weller, Adrienne. 2003. Stephen Funk: Marine Refusenik Wins Backing. http://www.notinourname.net/funk/wins-backing-1sept03.htm. Accessed on October 28, 2005.

January 2003 he was ordered to Kuwait in preparation for President Bush's disgraceful 'pre-emptive' strike against Iraq. Said Mr. Felushko: "I didn't want 'Died deluded in Iraq' over my gravestone. I didn't see a connection between the attack on America and Saddam Hussein. If I died or killed somebody in Iraq, that would have been wrong. It is my right to choose between what I think is right and wrong."[456] With the military not allowing that basic right of choice, Mr. Felushko deserted.

Various non-military organizations with the purpose of aiding US soldiers report tremendous increases in the number of inquiries they receive daily. Not all questions come from the soldiers themselves: spouses, parents and other significant others call asking how their loved one can get out of the military.

While the reasons of three soldiers cannot be said to show conclusively that disagreement with the war is a major cause for desertion, their stories cannot be easily dismissed.

The rate of desertions has grown steadily since the start of the war. It is not unreasonable to expect this trend to continue. The stated reasons for the war have all proved false; it is likely that many more soldiers will refuse to risk their lives for a war based on lies. The only potential victors appear to be US oil companies, and few people believe they are worth dying for.

THE HORROR OF WAR

In no war has this not been an issue. As mentioned above, a large percentage of Iraq's population is under the age of fifteen. With the war brought into the cities and towns, the civilian death toll is horrifying. To date, estimates range from 10,000 to over 100,000 killed.

Mr. Mejia brings this horror into perspective by relating stories from his own experience.[457] Due to the abject poverty and extremely high rate of unemployment that have resulted from the invasion, gas is sold on the black market. Carried in metal 'gerry cans' people can be seen selling the gas on neighborhood street corners, near mosques and schools. Mr. Mejia's squad was ordered to shoot gerry cans whenever they were seen. A metal can full of gas, when shot,

---

456. 5500 Choose Desertion over Going to War in Iraq or Afghanistan. 2004. http://the-spark.net/newspaper/i741/8f01.html. Accessed on October 28, 2005.
457. From a conversation between Mr. Mejia and the author, August 17, 2005.

will explode. The horror that this causes to those carrying the cans — sometimes children — cannot adequately be described.

The suffering of the soldiers cannot be minimized. One soldier of Mr. Mejia's acquaintance was too close to an incendiary device (ID) when it exploded. Shrapnel remains in his head; removing it would be fatal. This man today has trouble speaking, difficulty with cognitive abilities, does not know when to laugh or be serious, and does not consistently recognize people of his acquaintance.

Mr. Mejia also saw what Americans are forbidden to see on their television screens: soldiers missing limbs, suffering from post traumatic stress disorder (PTSD) and other ailments. Not only does Mr. Mejia see the results of bombs, IDs and bullets, he saw them actually taking their toll.

During one mission of several days duration, Mr. Mejia reported that his squad killed dozens of Iraqis. Of those, he is aware that only two were armed.

Despite press censorship, the world was able to see the horrifying conditions at the Abu Gharib prison, and learn of the shocking abuse of prisoners at the hands of the Americans. Prior to these public revelations, Mr. Mejia had reported abuses. At one point he was assigned to guard prisoners at Al Asad, although he had never been trained on how to deal with detainees. Here the policy was that of sleep deprivation. Combatants and non-combatants were separated. Although Mr. Mejia was not responsible for determining who was a combatant and who a non-combatant, he knew the criteria: anyone caught with a rifle was a combatant. In Mr. Mejia's own words: "Everyone and his mother in Iraq has a rifle."[458]

The combatants were tied and hooded, seated on the floor on small rugs. Mr. Mejia's role and that of his fellow-soldiers was to assure that the prisoners remained sleep-deprived. This was done by yelling at them, forcing them to hold up their arms for long periods, to assure that they were moving, etc. If they were close to sleep, he was to slam the wall beside them with a sledge-hammer, which caused a sound like an explosion, or discharge a .9mm pistol by their heads, simulating an execution. After 48—72 hours, the prisoners were allowed to sleep for 15—20 seconds, further disorienting them. The goal, said Mr. Mejia, was to "screw up their heads."[459]

---

458. Ibid.
459. Ibid.

Not all the soldiers objected to the carnage, even when it jeopardized men and women under their command. One officer, so anxious to earn the coveted Combat Infantrymen Badge — an award only given after being engaged in direct combat with the enemy — violated the military's own teachings on safety and strategy in order to lure the enemy. Rather than making the movements of the soldiers unpredictable by varying their routines, this officer ordered them to sweep the same streets for IDs at the same time for several days. This predictability made them targets. Mr. Mejia discussed this:

> He accused his commanding officers of being more interested in seeing combat and "climbing up the military hierarchy than the safety of their troops" and he described being sent out on missions that were needlessly hazardous. "[Our commanding officers] were going for the glory even if it meant losing a few lives, our lives," he wrote.[460]

Poor leadership has been mentioned as a reason for desertion in many wars and future studies will identify if it was also a major issue during the war in Iraq. But the callousness of commanding officers as reported by Mr. Mejia leaves little doubt that loyalty towards those leading the soldiers into battle must be non-existent. A sense of loyalty is often a factor in keeping soldiers in the military; without it, desertion will certainly increase.

The events experienced by Sgt. Kevin Benderman while serving in Iraq also demonstrate the horror of this war. When Mr. Benderman applied for Conscientious Objector status prior to being ordered for redeployment in Iraq, he reported some of his observations; the memories continue to haunt him.

> Benderman told of bombed out homes and displaced Iraqis living in mud huts and drinking from mud puddles; mass graves in Khanaqin near the Iranian border where dogs fed off bodies of men, women and children. He recalled his convoy passing a girl, no older than 10, on the roadside clutching a badly injured arm. Benderman said his executive officer refused to help because troops had limited medical supplies. "Her arm was burned, third-degree burns, just black. And she was standing there with her mother begging for help," Benderman said. "That was an eye opener to seeing how insane it really is."[461]

For those who have not smelled burning human flesh, it is difficult to imagine. Those fortunate enough to have never witnessed dead, mutilated

---

460. Schaeffer-Duffy, Claire. 2004. Catholic Becomes First to Refuse Return to Iraq War. http://www.catholicpeacefellowship.org/nextpage.asp?m=2064. Accessed on October 28, 2005.

461. Bynum, Russ. 2004. Images Behind Soldiers Iraq Refusal. 2004. http://www.commondreams.org/headlines05/0117-08.htm. Accessed October 28, 2005

children lying by roadsides, or watched their anguished parents screaming in unrelieved grief cannot know what goes through the mind and heart of those who do witness it. For the large majority of the US population, to whom the war means placing an American flag decal on the window of their automobile, the wrenching suffering of a dying friend, his body bloodied from shrapnel from an IED or riddled with bullets, cannot be imagined. As he or she gasps a last few breaths, perhaps calling to a spouse, parent or child, those who witness it often wish it were they who were dying.

A third soldier was interviewed by author-journalist Amy Goodman in March of 2005. This man was currently AWOL, and was awaiting official designation as a deserter before turning himself in. He does not want to reveal his identity until that time. But his story is also illuminating.

This man enlisted while still a junior in high school and began basic training in June, 2002; he was 18 years old. He was deployed to Iraq and functioned as a military policeman from March, 2003 to March, 2004. His own words are chilling:

> We would drive around town and our sergeants, our officers, would get bored so they'd tell us to go raid this whole block of homes, you know. And so we'd go into every home, and if we found anything as small as a knife or a pistol in any home, which I think you could go in any home in America and find a knife or a pistol, but if we found anything like that, we'd arrest all the males in the house, ages eight to 80 and leave all the females behind crying their eyes out, and that was never very fun to watch. Then what we'd go do is throw these men who maybe didn't do anything in the same jails as the ones that we knew had set off I.E.D.s and had set off — and had tried to kill soldiers. So, you're just throwing them all in with each other, and eventually it is going to change their minds. You know, you are going to make the distant relatives bitter, and you are going to — you are starting a whole new war with people who really don't deserve it.[462]

Scheduled to return to Iraq with his unit in January of 2005 this man "did the thing I never wanted to do, and I went AWOL."[463]

For a once-idealistic young man to witness such flagrant abuse of authority and power is in itself heart-wrenching. That this same young man would decide to oppose the power of the US military machine is inspiring.

462. Three US Soldiers Refusing to Fight Speak Out Against the Iraq War. 2005. http://www.democracynow.org/article.pl?sid=05/03/15/1454208&mode=thread&tid=25. Accessed October 28, 2005.
463. Ibid.

The destruction of the country of Iraq means the killing of men, women and children. These events are often too horrifying; soldiers will risk whatever necessary in order to prevent further participation in the carnage.

The difficulties that some soldiers have in applying for Conscientious Objector status have been noted. But it appears that this difficulty, rather than encouraging active military involvement, has the opposite effect.

Although the option to apply for conscientious objector status for active-duty soldiers has not been withdrawn, the military is making the process so onerous that some of the hundreds applying have simply given up — and gone AWOL.[464]

At present the military is seldom punishing deserters, preferring, as in the nation's early wars, to return them to the battlefield since there is such a shortage of soldiers. Those who wish to leave the military cannot, however, depend on leniency, being ignored or being returned to battle. The military can, at any time, arbitrarily change its treatment and handling of soldiers who desert. Soldiers who take a public stand against the war seem far more likely to be pursued by the government and charged with criminal activity.

THE STOP-LOSS PROGRAM

As mentioned previously, stop loss is defined as a short-term policy that stabilizes Marines in their current assignment by preventing them from leaving the Corps at the end of their service. Currently it is not restricted to the Marines.

Ironically, the implementation of stop-loss, the goal of which is to force soldiers to remain in uniform long after their enlistment period ends, seems in itself to contribute to desertions. Men and woman making plans for their lives following their military commitment often resent this action on the part of the military to the point that they chose to ignore it. Mr. Mejia's experience with stop loss is telling.

In January of 2003, approximately five months prior to completing his eight-year enlistment, the infamous "stop loss" program was invoked, and Mr. Mejia was advised that his enlistment was being extended. He was activated for an additional two years, but would remain on call for several more. Like many

---

464. Reeves, Tom. 2005. Exposing the Coming Draft. http://www.counterpunch.org/ reeves03192005.html Accessed on October 28, 2005.

service personnel reaching the end of their enlistment period, Mr. Mejia had made plans for his future. Extending his time in the military was not among them. Shortly after this forced extension he was sent to Iraq.

Some soldiers have reported being in line to get on a plane in Iraq to head home when they were pulled out of line and told that their deployment was extended. They had to tearfully, by long-distance telephone, tell anxious and hopeful spouses, parents and children that the long-awaited reunion was being postponed at the last minute. At the point where they were on the threshold of safety, when they were one plane ride away from the horror of war, they and their loved ones were told to wait once again. This meant enduring the agony of war for the soldier, and the agony of constant worry and anticipation for his or her loved ones. The effect of such actions on morale can only be imagined.

With the implementation of stop-loss, the government has less interest in tracking down deserters. Those who publicly criticize the war are still targets, but men and women who quietly slip away are not sought. In early wars rewards were offered for deserters, often as a means of replenishing the ranks; if deserters could be found, they could be forced back into the trenches. With stop-loss preventing soldiers from being able to leave when their enlistment period expires, 6,000 deserters can easily be replaced.

For the deserters who are pursued and charged, the infamous military justice system — a serious misnomer — is activated. Once again, Mr. Mejia's story explicates the complete disregard for justice under which the military operates.[465]

After making the decision not to return to Iraq, Mr. Mejia went through all the proper legal channels. In his case, stop loss was illegal for several reasons: he'd served his 8 years; he wasn't a US citizen; his Green Card was to expire before the end of his deployment. A representative from the National Guard acknowledged that the extension was an error. Yet his Commanding Officer advised that with his leave ending, he had to return to Iraq. The fact that his deployment had been illegal from the start apparently made no difference; soldiers were needed, so they would be obtained however possible.

As his court martial approached he retained a civilian lawyer, a graduate of West Point and himself a conscientious objector. He worked on his defense against charges of AWOL and desertion for five months. Mr. Mejia continued to

---

465. This information was given to the author during his August 17, 2005 conversation with Mr. Mejia.

speak out publicly against the war. He was the first combat veteran of the Iraq war to do so and he did not mince words.

> In press interviews, Mejia gave several political reasons for his refusal to fight in Iraq. He called the "oil-driven" war illegal, unjustified and based on "lies about weapons of mass destruction, and the connection between Saddam Hussein and Al Qaeda."[466]

Comments like these set Mr. Mejia apart from soldiers who quietly leave the military. They are not generally pursued; he was.

The ensuing court martial can only be considered a farce when judged by any but military standards. Entrance to the base where the trial was to be held was restricted, and his supports were given wrong directions to get there. Mr. Mejia reported the following:

> [A]ccess to the base was restricted to military personnel, my attorneys, and a few family members. Everyone else was directed to gate number three, but the signs leading to that gate were taken down during the three days of my trial. The entire block of the courthouse was barricaded, and there were civilian and military police offers patrolling the area.... Reporters were contained in a media center about a mile away from the courthouse, and everyone's computers, cameras, recording devices, and cell phones were confiscated prior to entering the courtroom.[467]

Additionally, soldiers were brought in to the courtroom to reduce the amount of seats for his supporters. This manipulation of the physical environment set the stage for the travesty that would take place inside.

> All of our pretrial motions were struck down, and many key witnesses and crucial pieces of evidence were not allowed in the case. Violations of army regulations by my unit, and violations on international law and the supreme law of the land by the military, were readily ignored, and the prosecution was allowed to bring the entire case down to the question of whether I got on a plane or not, thus receiving an easy, undeserved victory.[468]

Mr. Mejia's lawyers, who included former Attorney General Ramsey Clark, subpoenaed a wide range of witnesses, including the National Guard representative who had said the extension was illegal. The military judge would not admit their testimony. A treaty between Costa Rica and the US (Mr. Mejia holds

---

466. Schaeffer-Duffy, Claire. 2004. Catholic Becomes First to Refuse Return to Iraq War. http://www.catholicpeacefellowship.org/nextpage.asp?m=2064. Accessed on October 28, 2005.

467. Camilo Mejia. GI Resister, Conscientious Objector and Iraq War Veteran. 2005. http://www.freecamilo.org/words.htm. Accessed on October 28, 2005.

468. Ibid.

dual citizenship in Nicaragua and Costa Rica) that states that neither country will force citizens of the other into its military, was not allowed to be introduced as evidence.

The jury consisted of several officers; the lowest ranking one was a First Sergeant. A decision to convict was quickly reached, and a sentence of a year in prison, demotion, forfeiture of all pay and a bad conduct discharge was issued.

Immediately after Mr. Mejia's sentencing his mother went to his barracks to get his things. The lock to his personal possessions had been cut and they were all gone. Apparently there had been no question about what the verdict would be. There was no point in waiting to collect his belongings. His shocked mother called a press conference, and Mr. Mejia's possessions were immediately returned.

The decision to leave the military prior to the end of the enlistment period is never done easily. Mr. Benderman, like Mr. Mejia, reported internal conflicts:

> As I went through the process which led to my decision to refuse deployment to Iraq for the second time, I was torn between thoughts of abandoning the soldiers that I serve with, or following my conscience, which tells me: war is the ultimate in destruction and waste of humanity.[469]

Yet what he had experienced in the front lines — he entered Baghdad a week behind the initial assault — convinced him of the fact that war is wrong. With ten years experience as an army mechanic, Mr. Benderman asked himself this question: "Do I really want to stay in an organization where the sole purpose is to kill?"[470]

The response to his decision from the military was what might be expected: his commanding officer called him a coward. It is difficult to understand how a man could be branded a coward after having served valiantly in some of the most horrific battles of the war. Even his chaplain, from whom one might reasonably expect tolerance, if not compassion and understanding, said he was ashamed of him. The knee-jerk reaction — if a soldier deserts he is either a coward or a traitor — so long ingrained in the American psyche, immediately was activated.

Mrs. Monica Benderman expressed her frustration at some of the reaction to her husband's decision:

---

469. Kevin Benderman: A Matter of Conscience. http://www.bruderhof.com/articles/benderman-k.htm. Accessed on October 28, 2005.
470. Bynum, Russ. 2004. Images Behind Soldier's Iraq Refusal. 2004. http://www.commondreams.org/headlines05/0117-08.htm. Accessed October 28, 2005.

What's gone wrong when a man and his wife receive phone calls and emails from all over the country asking them to explain themselves, calling them cowards, wondering if they have ever read the Bible or studied the scripture, all because that man has chosen to speak out against war and violence, and his wife has chosen to stand with him? What's gone wrong when a man's mental stability is doubted and his morality is brought into question by a chaplain (a supposed man of God), all because he has decided he cannot use a weapon to kill another person for any reason?[471]

Mr. Benderman's efforts to obtain Conscientious Objector status were rebuffed not only by his commanding officer, as might be expected, but also by his chaplain.[472] The chaplain initially criticized his decision, telling him directly that he was wrong, and indicated a willingness to debate him on the issue, rather than in guiding him spiritually through this difficult time. His military attorney worked hard to obtain the Conscientious Objector status, recognizing that soldiers, like anyone else, have the right to change their minds. This is especially true for anyone as they obtain more knowledge about a topic, as Mr. Benderman certainly did about war.

Despite their confidence in their military attorney, the Bendermans decided to retain the services of a civilian lawyer. The military attorney was forbidden to speak to the press; such a restriction is not applied to a civilian attorney.

From the start, Mr. Benderman utilized the military channels as required. When his chaplain continually refused to provide him with the necessary forms to apply for Conscientious Objector status, he finally obtained them from the GI Rights Hotline. After completing the forms he emailed them to the chaplain, since the chaplain was unwilling to meet with him to accept paper copies from him. On the same day, Mr. Benderman filed a formal request with his commander to file for Conscientious Objector status. This should have triggered the process for review of his application. However, the commander returned the form to Mr. Benderman, marked 'recommend disapproval.'

Eventually Mr. Benderman met with another chaplain, who worked with him over a period of time. This chaplain ultimately supported Mr. Benderman's Conscientious Objector application, and wrote a letter indicating his belief in

---

471. Kevin Benderman: A Matter of Conscience. http://www.bruderhof.com/articles/benderman-k.htm. Accessed on October 28, 2005.

472. This information was obtained during a conversation between Mrs. Monica Benderman, Kevin Benderman's wife, and the author.

the sincerity of Mr. Benderman's convictions. Once this letter became public, the first chaplain publicly criticized Mr. Benderman, saying he was ashamed of him.

As was the case with Mr. Mejia's court martial, the inconsistencies and inaccuracies in Mr. Benderman's trial would never have been tolerated in any civilian court in the country. One officer gave five different versions of a meeting with Mr. Benderman; each version is a sworn statement and each exists and is available for review. The same officer, when testifying in court, gave yet another version. For example, in the first sworn statement about the initial meeting with Mr. Benderman about his conscientious-objector application, he stated that he read Mr. Benderman his rights as soon as he entered the room. In his sworn testimony in court, the same officer said that Mr. Benderman badgered him for several minutes before the officer had an opportunity to read Mr. Benderman his rights. When questioned about his five previous, all differing versions of the same incident, the officer claimed he was not clear on the facts then, but had since remembered them. This spurious testimony was accepted.

Mr. and Mrs. Benderman have found a supportive atmosphere among enlisted men and their families, although there have been some exceptions. It seems apparent that some soldiers — younger than the Bendermans, perhaps right out of high school with little or no adult life experience — do not know of any alternatives. They enlisted to satisfy basic human needs: food, shelter and clothing. Some of these go AWOL not knowing what to do.

A story of one young soldier focuses a harsh but truthful light on how the military operates to provide soldiers for the Iraqi war machine. This 24-year-old man attempted suicide just prior to deployment, preferring to die near his wife than in a far off country. His wife found him in time to get help and rushed him to a local civilian hospital where he was treated sufficiently to be out of danger. The military, upon hearing about this, forced his removal to a military hospital despite the assertions of the civilian hospital personnel that he should not yet be moved. Once at the military hospital his wife was denied access to him; she was given no information about his condition except that he was malingering.

Through the efforts of Mrs. Benderman the young man's wife was able to visit her husband. Two doctors treated him, one of whom denied he was at risk of suicide, and one who felt he definitely was. Since this was a military hospital, the military removed the second doctor from his case, leaving the soldier in the care of the doctor who denied his suicidal tendencies.

Once he was well enough to leave the hospital, the soldier was told that his deployment to Iraq was scheduled and he went AWOL. He tried in vain to obtain assistance from a chaplain. At last report he was in Iraq, with a one-year supply of tranquilizers and other medications.

This is not the only case of the military sending injured men back into the field of battle. One man, nearly deafened in a battle, has been redeployed. Another with a rotator cuff injury drives a Humvee while on painkillers. The combination of the injury and the medications numbs his hand, rendering him unable to pull the trigger of a gun.[473]

US soldiers who desert in the current environment do so at great personal risk. With the risk of arrest, trial and imprisonment facing them in a country that appears to have an increasing appetite for war, many soldiers seek refuge in Canada. Jeremy Hinzman, who served in Afghanistan and was scheduled for deployment in Iraq, said that "I was told in basic training that if I'm given an illegal or immoral order, it is my duty to disobey it. I feel that invading and occupying Iraq is an illegal and immoral thing to do."[474]

The obligation of a soldier to refuse such an order has been discussed. While this is a regulation that is taught to soldiers, it is one that is not followed, as indicated by the responses to the many dedicated men and women who have invoked it over the years.

How many soldiers will eventually desert from the military during the Iraq war and occupation will only be known in future years; if current trends continue, the number will be significant. Desertion will continue as a severe problem for the military as long as the US government ignores the basic needs of military personnel, and continues to wage imperial wars.

---

473. From a conversation between Mrs. Monica Benderman and the author.
474. Thousands of US Soldiers Desert 'Illegal' and 'Immoral' War. 2005. http://www.theinsider.org/news/article.asp?id=0782. Accessed on October 28, 2005.

CHAPTER 12: OTHER CONFLICTS; PEACETIME DESERTION

While the major wars that America has waged or participated in are discussed in earlier chapters, there were several other conflicts over the years. Additionally, the issue of desertion was not limited to times of war; soldiers chose to depart during peacetime for a variety of reasons. At different times throughout history there was a great deal of interest in identifying the causes of desertion. Yet little was done to address them.

A constant theme in the country's early history is the lack of pay, or greatly delayed pay, for soldiers. This was no less an issue in peacetime than it was during times of war. Part of the reason was the difficulty in getting the money to the soldiers. "In mid-October 1795, Captain Pike at Fort Massac dispatched a lieutenant with an escort of a sergeant and twelve soldiers to pick up the pay at Greenville, some 300 miles away. It was January 2, 1796 before Lieutenant Thomas Underwood returned and paid the command six months wages. "Lack of pay, combined with ragged clothing, inadequate housing and food dependent to a great extent on local hunting and fishing conditions..."[475] often led soldiers to desert.

In the new century, conditions remained unchanged and soldiers continued to desert. The rate of desertion was sufficient that the government offered blanket pardons in 1807 and 1810.[476]

---

475. Coffman, Edward M. *The Old Army: A Portrait of the American Army in Peacetime, 1784 – 1898*, p. 21.
476. Coffman, p. 21.

Following the War of 1812, desertion continued to be a problem for the peacetime army. "In 1823, the total number of enlisted men was 5,424, and 668 (12%) deserted."[477] The following year, "Secretary of War James Barbour termed it 'a serious evil,' and his successors would continue to find it so throughout most of the nineteenth century."[478] By 1830, the percentage of soldiers who deserted doubled from the 1823 rate, to 24%.

The reasons for desertion during peacetime in the first half of the nineteenth century were mainly consistent with those in wartime, with the exception, of course, of the horror of battle. Money remained an issue: "[a]vailable statistics indicate that military base pay was generally less than that of civilians."[479] Soldiers often deserted for more lucrative employment. Inadequate military pay has been an issue soldiers have been forced to endure from the nation's birth to the present time. Throughout the nineteenth century a man could make more working on a farm than in the military. With families to support there was little incentive to keep a man in the army.

Perhaps one of the most significant reasons for desertion at this time was the injustice inherent in the military system, a problem that persists to this day (See Chapter 13, Summary and Analysis). This resulted in extreme abuses, manifested in brutal corporal punishments and the almost complete failure of the military to bring to justice those who perpetrated it. The lessons from over two hundred years experience have not been learned.

> Many soldiers deserted because they suffered from inconsistent or illegal trial proceedings and sentences, which violated the expectations of men recruited from a free society.[480]

The military justice system then did not appear to work any better than it does today. In the early nineteenth century officers functioned in military courts as prosecutors and judges, despite not having had any training to do so. As a result soldiers received far different sentences for the same crime.

Following one trial in which no trace of fairness or impartiality could be found, an aide to General Henry Atkinson who overturned the convictions wrote to Zachary Taylor, expressing the General's "sincere regret that proceedings so

---

477. Vargas, Mark A. 1991. The Military Justice System and the Use of Illegal Punishments as Causes of Desertion in the US Army, 1821 - 1835. *The Journal of Military History, Vol. 55, No. 1*, p. 1.

478. Coffman, p. 193

479. Coffman, p. 153

480. Vargas, p. 2.

loose, and evincing so little regard for the soldier's rights, are to be placed on file in the Adj. General's Office...."[481] The overturning of a conviction was the exception, not the rule, although the lack of anything resembling justice was the norm.

The punishments that were part or all of the sentence for those convicted of or even only charged with any of a variety of alleged crimes were often physical; floggings and beatings — though illegal at this time — were common, and were often inflicted without a charge, trial or sentence. Even President Andrew Jackson, whose own reputation for cruelty to soldiers under his command is legend, protested against this kind of mistreatment. Said he: "[e]ven by a Court Martial, stripes and lashes cannot be inflicted, because the law prohibits them...."[482]

The reasons for these injustices were many and varied. Military law pertaining to justice was sufficiently vague as to allow a wide interpretation. Many soldiers were stationed at remote outposts that were infrequently visited by authorized military judges. Often in these circumstances the officers at the outpost assumed this duty. Without training, and often being able to use this as an excuse to vent their anger at soldiers accused of some crime, the officer could sentence the soldier and carry out the sentence.

In most courts martial, the officers — those who usually administered the beatings — were protected. They seldom accused each other and were rarely accused by their victims; enlisted men were perhaps hesitant to accuse an officer, fearing reprisal when the almost inevitable "not guilty" verdict was read. "Between 1821 and 1835, general courts-martial tried only thirteen officers for beating their men."[483] Only three were found guilty.

There are few records of enlisted men attempting to bring officers to justice. Two examples are illustrative.

One man, Private Archibald Allison, brought charges against Surgeon John Gale, accusing him of having flogged him. Testimony in the trial included that of another surgeon who said he'd handed Gale the whip, and another witness who testified that he "saw Gale inflict at least one hundred lashes on Allison's bare back."[484] With these accounts one can only wonder how a verdict of not guilty was reached.

---

481. Vargas, p. 8.
482. Vargas, p. 3.
483. Vargas, p. 12.
484. Vargas, pp. 13 – 14.

Another case involved Major George Talcott, who whipped Private Daniel Thompson in full view of the post garrison. In the court-martial, two officers claimed they saw nothing, and no other witnesses were called. The prosecutor presented the court with a copy of a letter Talcott sent to Brigadier General Gaines, in which the major admitted to the whipping. Talcott objected to the evidence because it was not the original letter, and because it forced Talcott to testify against himself. The court sustained Talcott's objection and ended the proceedings, and a second trial ended with similar results.[485]

The fact that only a few officers were charged with inflicting illegal corporal punishment on the men in their command, and even fewer were convicted, must not be construed to mean that physical punishments were rare. It must be remembered that the situation was sufficiently severe that Andrew Jackson — no proponent of kindness and humanity to soldiers — felt the need to address it as a problem.

> In summary, the failure of the army's justice system led to widespread cruelty, which in turn, forced many men to desert.[486]

The Seminole Wars, when the US forcibly removed the Seminole Indians from the territory of Florida, raged for years in the middle of the nineteenth century. While information on desertion during these wars is limited, the punishments inflicted for desertion were the same as earlier. During the second Seminole War (1835 — 1842), "[o]ne deserter was sentenced to pay the government back for time lost and to receive fifty lashes with cowhide on his bare back. Other deserters suffered the same, in addition to six months hard labor with a ball and chain attached."[487]

Following the Civil War, the size of the US army declined, moving from approximately 57,000 in 1866 to 25,000 in 1874. Maintaining the army was expensive, and the country attempted to economize by limiting this expense. "Each year the Army Appropriation Act was passed only after bitter debate."[488]

In addition, the citizens were not sympathetic to having a large standing army. The difficulty in funding the army reflected the hostility of the citizenry that existed toward the Army in the postwar years. Soldiers were used for purposes beyond that of defense, including southern reconstruction, unpopular

---

485. Vargas, p. 13.
486. Vargas, p. 19.
487. Mahon, John K. 1985. *History of the Second Seminole War, 1835 – 1842*, (Gainesville, 1985), p. 288.
488. Foner, Jack D. *The United States Soldier Between Two Wars*, (New York, 1970), p. 1.

wars against Indians, and during the railroad strikes of 1877 and 1894. And the perception of the military as a 'lower class' occupation had not yet begun to fade.

The rates and issues of desertion during the Civil War have been detailed in Chapter 4. Following the conclusion of that war in 1865, the issue for the peacetime army did not fade. "It was reported in August, 1866 that the number of desertions was increasing daily."[489] Within a year, the desertion rate exceeded 25%. The number of enlisted men in 1867 was 54,138; 14,068 deserted that year. By 1871 desertions reached their highest rate during the entire period of time between the end of the Civil War and the beginning of the Spanish-American War, with nearly one-third of soldiers deserting.

Between 1880 and 1889 the number of desertions was approximately 40% of the number of enlistments. The following table details this information.[490]

Table 12.1: Desertions between 1880 and 1889

Fiscal Year	Enlistments	Desertions	Percent
1880	5,006	2,043	40.81
1881	5,637	2,361	41.88
1882	7,734	3,741	48.37
1883	7,931	3,578	45.11
1884	8,775	3,672	41.84
1885	7,164	2,927	40.87
1886	5,327	2,090	39.23
1887	6,168	2,240	36.31
1888	6,693	2,244	36.39
1889	8,133	2,835	34.89

Officers deserted at a far less rate than did enlisted men, mainly because officers had the option of resigning their commission. However, "between 1870 and 1891, twenty-one officers deserted. Among them were some distinguished veterans; twelve had served on the Union side during the Civil War, and all had been promoted for gallant or meritorious service.[491]

The reasons for desertion during this time period tended to mirror those during wartime:

---

489. Foner, p. 6.
490. Foner, p. 224.
491. McDermott, John D. 1997. Were They Really Rogues? Desertion in the Nineteenth-Century US Army. *Nebraska History. Vol. 78, No. 4*, p. 167

1. Poor pay;
2. Disgraceful conditions;
3. Inability to adjust to military life; and
4. Poor leadership.

POOR PAY

During wartime, one expects that although the government will do every-thing in its power to provide for the needs of the soldiers,[492] conditions on the battlefield are such that this may not always be possible. There may be problems getting food, ammunition, clothing, etc. to the soldiers, along with difficulties in providing them with other needs such as blankets and tents. But in peacetime there can be no excuse for the failure to provide the soldiers with their needs. Yet this shameful practice continued throughout the nineteenth century.

In 1864, the monthly pay of the enlisted man was increased from thirteen dollars to sixteen dollars. This was to be a temporary increase, although no date was stipulated for the reduction back to the lower amount. On July 15, 1870, Congress voted to lower the amount back to thirteen dollars a month effective June 30, 1871.

The announcement of a prospective pay cut had a serious effect upon Army morale. 'Half of this Army will desert if the pay is reduced,' one soldier warned. This prediction, while exaggerated, was basically accurate, since the desertion figures for the year following the enactment of the law reached what Paymaster-General Benjamin Alvord called 'the extraordinary figure' of 8,000. This trend continued for the following year after the pay reduction was actually put into effect, when the desertion figure was 8,313.[493]

Soldiers felt that their contract with the American military had been vio-lated by the government, thus releasing them from any further obligation. As a natural result, they deserted in large numbers.

It wasn't only the decrease in wages that irritated the soldiers; their pay often continued to be several months in arrears. One soldier vented his frus-tration with the situation by comparing his surprise at seeing a paymaster to the same as if he had seen an angel: "when they (paymasters) did arrive, soldiers

---

492. See Chapter 13: Summary and Analysis, for information on how the government still falls short of this goal in 2005.
493. Foner, p. 15.

were as much surprised to see them as they would be 'were the airy visitants of the blue ethereal suddenly to flap their heavenly wings and alight among us.'"[494] The somewhat humorous view this soldier was able to put on the problem did not mask his frustration with it.

By 1866, while the problems of receiving pay had not been resolved in the least, a new benefit for the soldiers was instituted. Those assigned for more than ten consecutive days in certain departments — quartermaster, commissary, etc. — were eligible for additional pay. However, it was not long before those making the assignments learned how to abuse their position: men were often assigned to these tasks for less than ten days, thus making them ineligible for the extra pay. In 1890, Adjutant-General J. C. Kelton reported that the abuse continued to persist, although to a lesser degree, but still caused "irritation and discontent."[495]

CONDITIONS

The conditions in which the men lived also contributed to desertion. Up to a hundred men lived in crowded squad rooms with little in the way of comforts besides the bare necessities of bed, chair and a very few candles. "One officer wrote that if the General of the army wanted to understand the reasons for discontent among enlisted men, 'he has only to look into our dungeon barracks with the men huddled around the flickering flame of one or two candles. How many evenings would he or any officer spend in such a hole?'"[496]

In these crowded rooms two men shared a narrow uncomfortable bed. When single, iron bedsteads replaced the crowded double bunk beds in 1875 they were packed in so closely due to the overcrowding as to not offer much improvement. Additionally, the infestation of roaches and bedbugs that plagued most squad rooms made sleeping in the beds almost impossible. If the weather was warm, the men often opted to sleep outdoors.

Regulations stated that all soldiers must bathe at least weekly, but for many men there were no facilities to do so. Bathroom and kitchen hygiene was almost non-existent. Kitchen slops were emptied into crude sewers close to the barracks, which soon became clogged with grease, scraps and other garbage,

---

494. Foner, p. 16.
495. Foner, p. 17.
496. Foner, p. 18.

producing foul odors and attracting flies in swarms. The privies were erected over sinks dug in the earth, and were moved from time to time until the back-yards "became literally honey-combed with deposits of filth." For soldiers who were married, provision was made for housing them and their families. "Their only uniformity lay in the fact that they were all equally unfit for occupancy."[497]

After the Civil War, uniforms that were issued to the soldiers were often leftover from that war. There appeared to be no consideration to size when issuing a uniform to a man, and each soldier was responsible for paying for the tailoring of his uniform.

Perhaps the most serious problem facing soldiers was that of food. Meals consisted almost exclusively of beef, salt pork, bread, coffee and beans. Gardens were cultivated in locations that were suitable for the growing of vegetables, but this was by no means possible at most of them.

Preparation of meals was assigned on a rotating basis. This was done to prepare the soldiers to be self-sufficient should they need to be during time of battle. However, the meals produced reflected the inexperience of the cooks. Many soldiers commented that the Army cooks were responsible for killing more soldiers than the Indians were.

A major issue relating to foods occurred with the creation of post, regimental and company funds. These funds were to provide recreational or educational facilities not provided by the government. The money that went into these funds was found by selling a portion of the soldiers' already meager rations. Funding these additional services assumed that the soldiers already had more than enough food and that the benefits to be gained by educational or recreational activities justified the diversion of some food expenditures.

> Both of these assumptions were widely and seriously questioned. Not only did the critics maintain that the ration was too meager to allow for any reduction, but they also insisted that it was the responsibility of the government to provide the facilities and services for which these funds were being used. Music and books were worthwhile, these critics said, but a soldier ought not to be forced to improve his mind at the expense of his stomach.[498]

This new policy paved the way for a variety of abuses. Some company commanders built up large funds in order to demonstrate their efficiency to their superior officers. Others were accused of diverting funds from food for their own

---

497. Foner, p. 19.
498. Foner, pp. 21 – 22.

use, purchasing books for themselves or decorating their offices with funds that were allotted for food for the enlisted men.

An 1872 study of deserters imprisoned at Alcatraz Island revealed "that the primary cause for their desertion was the want of sufficient food."[499]

The benefits to the soldiers supposedly to be gained by diverting these funds were not frivolous. Stationed in remote outposts, many men felt a great isolation, rarely receiving mail from home and with little but monotony for companionship. "One soldier, writing from Fort Townsend, Washington, in 1884, said that no one could imagine what a lonesome and monotonous place it was."[500] The additions that the post, regiment and company funds were to provide would have helped alleviate some of this discomfort. The opportunity for recreation, reading and enhancement of education would have greatly assisted in passing the time that was not spent in hard, monotonous labor.

During this time, medical services were barbaric. In 1899 the hospital at West Point was examined by the Board of Visitors. They said "that no humane person would permit a horse to live in such a room, and that to place a sick man in this alleged hospital 'would appear like an attempt to insure his death.'"[501] The lessons of the Civil War, where the need for a trained medical corps was first identified, had not been learned.

INABILITY TO ADJUST TO MILITARY LIFE

Conditions in the military have never been easy. During the second Seminole Indian War many soldiers were accompanied by their families. Conditions were extremely harsh for them, and one Lieutenant Colonel Green requested that they be carried on the rolls at half rations. Many of the children had lost one parent, further complicating their lives.[502] Soldiers had to deal with caring for their families, with inadequate supplies, while preparing for battle.

Whatever men of this time period expected when they enlisted appears to have been far from the reality of what they received. In 1867, "[o]ne ex-soldier described the enlisted man's life as a 'hang-dog, demoralizing life, unfitting a

---

499. McDermott, p. 170.
500. Foner, p. 24.
501. Foner, p. 23.
502. Mahon, p. 288.

man for any respectable civil position, destroying all self-respect, sinking all that makes a man a man."[503]

Another soldier's viewpoint in 1879 is also instructive: "The regular soldier on the frontiers is no more nor less than a beast of burden, and what is still worse, he is treated as such."[504]

POOR LEADERSHIP

Poor leadership during peacetime differs from the same issue in time of war. A poor leader on the battlefield risks the lives of those he is charged with leading. In peacetime, poor leadership has more of an impact on the personal dignity of the enlisted man.

> In an 1867 letter to the Army and Navy Journal a deserter from the Corps of Engineers blamed ignorant, low-bred, and degraded noncommissioned officers for abusive and degrading treatment of privates. One correspondent, calling himself "Old Soldier," surmised that half of all desertions were the result of the petty tyranny of sergeants. Most of the one hundred prisoners interviewed at Alcatraz in 1872 claimed cruelty at the hands of their overseers.[505]

In addition, soldiers assigned to areas where their commanding officers may have been abusing their food rations for their own personal gain were surely aware of this fact. Soldiers who do not feel that their sacrifices and contributions are respected, and who experience abuse in such blatant ways, cannot be condemned for taking the necessary steps to improve their situations. This often means desertion.

Punishments for desertion during this time continued the tradition of cruelty and barbarism that had been common since the Revolution. Flogging, which sometimes resulted in death, was not outlawed until August 5, 1861. It had previously been outlawed on May 16 of 1812, but was reinstated on March 22, 1833.[506]

Other common punishments during this time included being tied to a tree, sometimes for as long as a day, wearing a ball and chain and the infamous picketing (described in Chapter 1, Revolutionary War).

---

503. McDermott, p. 169.
504. McDermott, p. 169.
505. McDermott, p. 170.
506. McDermott, p. 165.

A more benign punishment was being "drummed or bugled out of the service, which according to one observer, 'amounts to gratifying his desire to leave, and he is tendered in addition the gratuitous ovation of a parting serenade."[507] This involved bringing the prisoner in front of the entire command, removing his buttons and insignia, followed by the playing of the 'Rogue's March.' The following are the words to the march:

> Poor old soldier, poor old soldier,
> Tarred and feathered and sent to hell,
> Because he would not soldier well.[508]

Following this ceremony, the deserting soldier was escorted to the edge of the military installation where he was free to leave.

It is interesting to note that some soldiers who deserted underwent the most draconian of punishments, sometimes resulting in death and more often resulting in permanent scarring. Branding was not outlawed until 1872, prior to which time branding with the letter 'D', two inches in height, was permitted on the forehead, cheek or hip. There does not appear to be any reason why some soldiers were thus tortured and disfigured, while others were simply dishonorably discharged in the ceremony detailed above, and then allowed to depart. This blatant unfairness and inconsistency remains in 2005, although the punishments are less barbaric.

In 1887, a young man who didn't reveal his name — he signed this letter 'An Ex-Soldier — described his experience in the army. "In 1887 I was in the prime of youth and vigorous manhood. Being a young man I determined to spend five years in the regular army." With this optimism, he and several other new recruits were sent to the notorious Jefferson Barracks in Missouri, where they were "met by uniformed ruffians, and assigned to quarters with as much severity as though we had been prisoners guilty of some atrocious crime."

The abuse by officers continued, as one "persistently cursed the recruits and frequently drew his sword threatening to drive it down our throats."

Food at Jefferson Barracks was also an issue, as it has frequently been in the US military. "The food was the vilest I ever saw. It consisted of decayed salt pork and a soup called 'slum gullion,' that would have nauseated a hungry dog."

---

507. McDermott, p. 166.
508. Ibid.

This man further notes the discrepancy between what the officers ate and what the privates had. During meals, it was "noticeable that [the officers'] table was supplied with milk, sugar, and butter."

The result of this mistreatment is not surprising: "After four weeks at Jefferson Barracks, I had fallen from strong young manhood to a mere shadow. From 150 pounds, sickness had, in four weeks, reduced me to 130 pounds." He became increasing ill, finally so desperate for medical attention that he sought help at the base hospital, known to him and the other soldiers as the "Human Slaughterhouse." Here he received one dose of useless medicine, not surprising since "the army doctor paid no more attention to the sick soldiers than to so many flies to be got rid of." Finally, he became so weak that one morning he was unable to dress in the time allotted, and as a result was incarcerated. Said he: "No murderer was ever treated with greater brutality."

This soldier further discussed sleeping on a hard, damp floor, working at hard labor despite his illness, and the stench of his cell. Based on the tales of heroism and bravery that are part of American military folklore, it may be hard to believe that the conditions under which this man was forced to live were part of the American military system. But truth is often sacrificed for political expediency.

This young man, who entered the military wanting to serve his country and feeling confident in being able to do so in the capacity of a soldier, experienced a very rude awakening. "I notice by the papers that thousands of young men are deserting from the army, and people wonder why they do so. Some look upon these deserters as if they were criminals. But every time I hear of these poor fellows leaving the army, I feel like going to them and congratulating them for their splendid courage."[509]

The period of 1880—1890 was one in which the US was not at war. During this time the death rate for American soldiers was as follows:[510]

509. Bergey, Ellwood. 1903 *Why Soldiers Desert from the United States Army*, Philadelphia, pp. 27-33.
510. Bergey, p. 89.

Table 12.2: Death Rate for American Soldiers from 1880 to 1890.

Year	Death Rate per Thousand
1880	10.21
1881	11.41
1882	9.98
1883	11.60
1884	10.94
1885	7.54
1886	8.82
1887	8.12
1888	8.15
1889	6.33
1890	8.69
Average	9.25

During this same time period the death rate for British soldiers averaged 4.32 per thousand, and for Canadian soldiers the average was 3.5 per thousand.[511] This in itself indicates the atrocious conditions under which US soldiers were forced to live.

As the century drew to a close the US targeted other areas for expansion. This resulted in the three-month Spanish-American War, which then continued into the Philippine-American War (see Chapter 6, Philippine-American War).

Like most wars, the reasons for the Spanish-American War were complex. America had begun to invest heavily in Cuba, which was straining against its Spanish colonization. The American press supported Cuban independence initiatives, often reporting the horrors of Spanish rule and highlighting those stories with gross exaggerations or outright fabrications.

Additionally, the last major American war, the Civil War, had become a long-ago memory, with recollections of its horrors fading as heroic stories of courage and glamour grew. War was being seen once more as a grand opportunity to assert individual and collective manhood. This fallacy rears its ugly head repeatedly, most recently in 2003 (See Chapter 13, Summary and Analysis).

Another reason was a long-standing American belief in its own mission, "that it was on the righteous golden path."[512] From the War for Independence

---

511. Bergey, pp. 89 — 90.
512. McSherry, Patrick. The Spanish-American War — One American's View. http://www.spanamwar.com/Americanview.htm. Accessed October 31, 2005.

America has often believed that it was somehow a chosen land, destined, whenever possible, to spread its democratic ways to other nations, whether they wanted them or not. Many Americans felt it to be a right and a duty to expand its reach further into the world.

In 1894, the Wilson-Gorman tariff removed the privileged trade status that Cuba had in exporting sugar to the United States. "Since about 80 per cent of the Cuban economy was in sugar production, the result was a catastrophic depression in Cuba. Mass poverty and suffering sparked widespread discontent that in February, 1895, flared into a rebellion against Spanish rule."[513]

Although America took great interest in this situation, President Grover Cleveland would not be dragged into it in any way. He issued a proclamation of neutrality and refused to give the rebels any legitimacy.

In 1897 William McKinley became president and he appears to have taken more interest in the Cuban crisis than did his predecessor. He ordered the battleship Maine to Havana harbor, ostensibly as a goodwill visit. However, "in reality it was intended to emphasize US concerns over the crisis on the island and to urge the granting of Cuban independence."[514]

On February 15, 1898, the Maine exploded, killing 260 American sailors. Although the reason for the explosion was never determined, America readily believed it had been caused by a mine planted by the Spanish.[515] The outrage was overwhelming. "Fanned by the flames of a jingoistic press, the national sense of pride and honor would settle for nothing less than military satisfaction."[516] On April 21, following a US investigation into the Maine catastrophe, the US and Spain were at war.

Although the war was short, desertion was an issue, although the rate of desertion was very low. However, this war can be viewed as part of the Philippine-American war since the US purchased the Philippines (under duress; Spain had little choice but to sell), as a result of the Spanish-American War. The

---

513. Morris, Richard B., William Greenleaf and Robert H. Ferrell. 1971. *America: A History of the People, Vol 2,* (Chicago), p. 477.
514. Keenan, Jerry. 2001. *Encyclopedia of the Spanish-American and Philippine-American Wars,* p. 218.
515. The US investigation into the explosion at the time it occurred was apparently poorly handled. For a detailed explanation, see Edward J. Jarolda's *Theodore Roosevelt, the US Navy, and the Spanish-American War.*
516. Keenan, p. 219.

total number of soldiers involved, including both officers and enlisted men, was 223,235.[517] Of those, 5,285 were known to have deserted.[518]

The abominable conditions, which certainly contributed to the high desertion rate, were chronicled in a diary kept by a young soldier. Harry Carpenter was a twenty-one-year-old drugstore clerk when the war broke out. Filled with feelings of patriotism he enlisted in the army. On May 13, two weeks after enlisting, he described the food he and the other enlisted men were served and the conditions they were living in, while on the boat, the Seneca:

> The officers have every comfort on board, good quarters and good food, but the men are fed upon stale hardtack and canned corned beef, filled with chunks of fat, strips of entrails, and other refuse parts. Our quarters are vile and filthy, such as would disgrace even the lowest dens of filth in New York. [519]

Less than a month later, on June 8, Mr. Carpenter was on board the Vigilancia, and he once again described conditions. "We have been stored away in the hold, and it is a veritable pig-pen. We have no facilities, not even for washing our faces. The place is so filthy it is unfit for animals to stay in, to say nothing of human beings."

Mr. Carpenter further reported that men were put in the guard house if they attempted to purchase food from the ship's cook or drank ice water from the officers' quarters. It was not a lack of food that was the problem, since the officers had plenty. But mismanagement also played a role in this travesty. "We had hardtack and very poor canned beef all the way, while lots of potatoes on board were allowed to rot, and at last were thrown overboard. The boys would have given anything for these potatoes."

As Mr. Carpenter grew ill from bad food and filthy, cold conditions, he languished in a hospital and begged for assistance. Finally he wrote to his grandmother to send some sandwiches, desperate as he was for food. On August 21 they arrived, "but they would not let me have them. They said they were not good for me. I am sure anything would be better than what they give me to eat."

On August 30 he was furloughed, and wrote the final entry in his diary. In addition to criticizing specific officers he'd known, he commented on the effect of his treatment on future generations. "I was as patriotic as anybody, but I am afraid that patriotism will be killed for a generation by the treatment the boys

517. Military Service #5, http://www.ibiblio.org/pub/academic/history/marshall/military/ mil_hist_ inst/m/milsrv5.asc. Accessed October 15, 2005.
518. Chambers, p. 212.
519. Bergey, p. 12.

have received at the hands of the low politicians who have control of things." [520]
Five days later Mr. Carpenter arrived at the home of his uncle, where he died.

Mr. Carpenter's death from disease is not surprising, considering that the death rate in some camps during this war reached a staggering rate of 44.7 per thousand. The conditions referenced above, coupled with the disdain with which army doctors treated suffering soldiers, obviously brought about this shocking death rate.

During the opening years of the twentieth century the desertion rate fluc-tuated, starting at 4.00 and steadily increasing until 1906, and then decreasing until 1923. The lowest rates during that time were during the Great War (See Chapter 6). In 1920, the desertion rate was only 1.57. This was due to a number of reasons, including the military's intensive pursuit and punishment of deserters. Starting in 1907, the government began a "campaign for the pursuit and appre-hension of deserters by broadcasting finger prints, photographs, descriptive lists, etc...."[521] Other measures were implemented to catch deserters and prevent desertion. The maximum punishment for desertion was increased to three years' imprisonment and dishonorable discharge, and courts were encouraged to sen-tence soldiers found guilty of desertion to the maximum penalty, and clemency was almost always denied.

Table 12.3: Desertion Rates 1900—1919.[522]

Year	Percent		Year	Percent
1900	4.00		1910	3.66
1901	4.12		1911	2.28
1902	5.00		1912	3.00
1903	7.10		1913	4.15
1904	6.61		1914	3.10
1905	6.79		1915	3.23
1906	7.43		1916	3.10
1907	5.62		1917	1.86
1908	4.59		1918	N/A
1909	4.97		1919	N/A

---

520. Bergey, pp. 11 - 13.
521. Porter, Lieutenant Colonel Ralph S. 1926. Peace Time Desertion in the Regular Army. *The Military Surgeon*, Vol. 59. No. 5, p. 528.
522. Course at the Army War College, 1926–1927, p. 3. The Army War College, Wash-ington Barracks, D.C. US Army Heritage & Education Ctr., US Army Military History Institute.

A variety of reasons were suggested by the government for this fluctuation. During the period of 1898 to 1906, during which desertion rose significantly, the following conditions were thought to exacerbate the problem: prohibition of the sale of intoxicants at Post Exchanges, restoring to duty deserters whose 'crime' appeared to be caused by youth or inexperience, and the end of post-war conditions.

From 1906 to 1917, when desertion rates dropped dramatically, it was thought that several factors influenced this. They included the initiation of an intensive campaign to apprehend deserters — described above — the reestablishment of the Military Prison, an increase in pay and a severe economic turndown in 1907.

As desertion rates rose again from 1917 to 1926, the military again sought for the reasons. End of war conditions, deteriorating housing facilities and poor leadership were among the suggested causes.

Another interesting factor that was suggested was the "[u]tilization of war stock uniforms."[523] "A man cannot feel proud of being a soldier when he finds himself dressed in a shoddy ill-fitting uniform which while suitable for the rough service of war is not a creditable peace-time garment."[524] Inadequate clothing was often cited as a reason for desertion in the nation's early wars, but never was 'a shoddy, ill-fitting uniform' mentioned.

Other factors seem to have reduced the number of desertions during the early part of the twentieth century. The pay for enlisted men was increased at a time that the US economy was deteriorating. Economic considerations often influenced desertion, either encouraging or discouraging it. When economic conditions are poor, men are more likely to enlist in the Army; conversely, during times of prosperity, when jobs and opportunities are plentiful, men are more likely to leave the military to find better employment. As early as the American Revolution men enlisted to provide extra funds for their families, and deserted when those funds were not forthcoming, or when planting or harvest season required them at home. In the twentieth century during times when employment opportunities were scarce, men often saw the military as a means of providing food, shelter and clothing for themselves. When the economic shifts

---

523. Porter, pp. 528 - 529.
524. Loughry, Major H. K., et. Al. 1926. Present Desertion Rates. Course at the Army War College, 1926 - 1927. The Army War College, Washington Barracks, D.C. US Army Heritage & Education Ctr., USArmy Military History Institute, p. 3.

turned in more positive directions, industry beckoned some of them out of the army and into corporate life.

In addition to these factors, the government identified several overriding reasons for desertion during this time period that included the following:

- Public indifference to the seriousness of the offense;
- Leniency;
- Military environment: housing, ration, recreation and clothing, and
- Poor leadership.[525]

It should be noted that the fourth and fifth are conditions over which the government has complete control, yet by the early twentieth century they had not be rectified, although they had been identified as far back as the War for Independence, and in every war since.

As noted in Chapter 6, World War I, the desertion rate was very low during that war. This trend did not continue after the war. The time period between the two world wars marked a steady increase in desertions. The following table shows the rate of desertions for the period from 1920 to 1926.

Table 12.4: Desertion rates from 1920 to 1926.

Year	Rate
1920	1.57
1921	4.57
1922	5.27
1923	6.40
1924	7.03
1925	7.39
1926	8.13

The government again looked for reasons for this trend. Among the conditions said to contribute to this increase were the following:

- Reduction in funds for military welfare and recreation;
- Increasing dilapidation of utilities and housing facilities;
- Leniency, and
- Poor leadership.

Poor leadership again is shown to cause desertions. One can only wonder why the military, with vast sums of money at its disposal and access to the best minds in the world, has been unable to resolve this basic problem. It continually identifies it as a cause of desertion, and then attempts to prevent desertion by

---

525. Porter, pp. 528 — 529.

addressing other issues or increasing the punitive actions taken against soldiers who desert. Why not, instead, look at the military institutions that train tomorrow's military leaders and use the vast resources available to study and implement better methodologies? Why not explore the successes of other nations and implement policies that work there? Perhaps it is simply easier to promote to leadership positions men and women who maintain the reputation of tough, unyielding leaders that are the topics of myth and legend, and brand men and women who leave the service illegally as traitors or cowards.

The Korean War (see Chapter 8, Korean War) followed quickly on the heels of World War II. Shortly after its conclusion America first began intervention in Vietnam (see Chapter 9, Vietnam War). This war was, of course, a disaster for humanity and, most dangerously for the world, for US foreign policy. The Vietnam War is considered by many as the only war the US ever lost. This belief indicates a lack of knowledge of the War of 1812 and the Korean War, neither of which can realistically be considered a victory for the US. Nevertheless, the stigma of the Vietnam defeat haunts politicians to this day. President Ronald Reagan appears to have been the first president to try to rid the nation of that particular blemish, by invading the Caribbean island of Grenada (Operation Urgent Fury) in October of 1983. Ostensibly this was to protect American medical students in Grenada following the overthrow of the government. In the New York Times on October 29, 1983, the myth of that danger was exposed by correspondent Bernard Gwertzman.

> The formal request that the US and other friendly countries provide military help was made by the Organization of Eastern Caribbean States last Sunday at the request of the United States.... The wording of the formal request...was drafted in Washington and conveyed to the Caribbean leaders by special American emissaries.[526]

Why would the US want to invade Grenada, if neither America nor Americans were in any way threatened? "[O]ne high American official told Gwertzman...that the United States should show (determined to overcome the sense of defeat in Vietnam) that it was truly a powerful nation...."[527]

Six years later, Panama was targeted for partially the same reasons. In addition, Panama's president Manuel Noriega had been indicted in Florida as a

---

526. Zinn, p. 588.
527. Zinn, p. 589.

drug trafficker. This quick victory cost the lives of thousands of Panamanians and left at least 14,000 homeless.

This need to prove the military superiority of the US is not new. As America prepared for war with England in 1812, David R. Williams, a member of Congress, said this: "We ought not to calculate on peace; it has become more than ever necessary to prove that we will not only declare war, but can prosecute it with energy and courageous enterprise."[528] George M. Troup concurred: "The next campaign must be opened with vigor, and prosecuted to success."[529]

Neither Williams nor Troup mentioned the reasons for the war, beyond the need to prove successful in an aggressive military, imperialistic venture.

As the twentieth century drew to a close, America found itself in a relatively peaceful environment. This was not to last as the infamous phrase 'pre-emptive strike' entered the country's vocabulary, but for a brief time the nation was at relative peace. While this may have impacted the rate of desertion, it certainly did not eliminate it.

The following table shows desertion rates for the four branches of the military from 1997 to 2004 (where available).[530]

Table 12.5: Desertion rates from 1997 through 2004 (N/A = not available).

Year	Deserters							
	Army	Per Thousand	Air Force	Per Thousand	Navy	Per Thousand	Marines	Per Thousand
1997	2,218	4.58	26	0.07	1,858	4.86	1,375	7.94
1998	2,520	5.20	27	0.07	2,038	5.33	1,460	8.43
1999	2,966	6.13	45	0.12	2,485	6.50	1,689	9.75
2000	3,949	8.16	46	0.12	3,255	8.51	2,019	11.66
2001	4,597	9.50	62	0.17	1,619	4.23	1,310	6.56
2002	4,483	8.26	88	0.24	N/A		1,136	7.14
2003	3,678	7.60	56	0.15	N/A		1,236	7.49
2004	2,376	4.91	50	0.14	N/A		N/A	

Even in peacetime the desertion rate is often high. This seems to indicate that the usually-identified reasons for this "crime" - cowardice, treachery, 'low moral character" - are not valid. The US military must look inward for the reasons if it ever expects to reduce these numbers.

528. Hickey, Donald R. 1989. *The War of 1812: A Forgotten Conflict.* (Chicago), p. 111.
529. Hickey, p. 111.
530. US Military Desertion Rates, http://usmilitary.about.com/od/justicelawlegislation / a/desertionrates.htm, Accessed October 15, 2005

Peace was shattered on September 11, 2001, when terrorists flew jets into New York's World Trade Center, the Pentagon and a field in Pennsylvania. Shortly thereafter, under the guise of searching for the mastermind, Osama bin Laden, President George W. Bush ordered the invasion of Afghanistan. This was ostensibly because the Taliban, in control in Afghanistan, were apparently shielding bin Laden. However, there may have been another reason. The invasion may simply have been "a pretext for replacing the Taliban with a relatively stable government that would allow Union Oil of California to lay its pipeline for the profit of, among others, the Cheney-Bush junta."[531] This pipeline, to go from Turkmenistan through Afghanistan and Pakistan and then onto Karachi, India had been forbidden by the Taliban.

While the war in Afghanistan has been overshadowed by the war in Iraq, some results of it are being seen in the United States. "As many as one out of four veterans of Afghanistan and Iraq treated at Veterans Affairs hospitals in the past 16 months were diagnosed with mental disorders, a number that has been steadily rising...." Following the Vietnam War, veterans did not immediately seek assistance, and it is believed that veterans of the Afghanistan and Iraqi wars will also delay. However, "if they come in the numbers predicted, the numbers the VA's own studies predict, we could be overwhelmed...."[532] said a VA spokesman.

This sobering fact denotes the serious consequences that war has on military personnel. The US government and its military arm do not appear to take this very real, very human cost into account when considering its wars. This is yet another lesson that must be learned if the government is serious about reducing the desertion rate.

---

531. Vidal, Gore. 2002. *Dreaming War: Blood for Oil and the Cheney-Bush Junta;* New York, p. 40.
532. Elias, Marilyn. 2005. Mental disorders are on the rise among Afghanistan, Iraq veterans. www.usatoday.com/news/ nation/2005-03-30-veterans-disorders_x.htm. Accessed October 10, 2005.

CHAPTER 13: SUMMARY AND ANALYSIS

For many, the word "deserter" is an insult; it conjures up thoughts of cowardice and treason and is considered a despicable label. Even the peace movement seems to prefer "war resister" to "deserter," and while that is most probably a more apt description of the men and women herein described, it is not a term that is likely to catch on with the general public. "Deserter" is too strongly embedded from centuries of government propaganda.

As has been shown, there are several legitimate reasons for soldiers to desert the US military, and many of them have been part of all the nation's wars. The US military gives names to its various operations such as "Operation Iraqi Freedom," or "Operation Enduring Freedom," yet it denies basic freedoms to the men and women under its jurisdiction. This has been demonstrated in earlier chapters and will be detailed herein.

Hypocrisy seems to play a major role in US government policy, and this frequently involves military interventions. Some examples from the latter part of the twentieth century and the beginning of the twenty-first demonstrate this clearly.

In September of 1963, the US Ambassador to Vietnam, Henry Cabot Lodge, made a fact-finding trip to that country. The purpose of that trip "was to 'make [an] effective case with Congress for continued prosecution of the war effort' and [President John F.] Kennedy had cabled Lodge that he needed 'ammunition I will get from an on-the-spot and authoritative military appraisal' to mislead the people's representatives."[533]

---

533. McMaster, H.R. 1997. *Dereliction of Duty*, p. 57.

This does not appear to have been an unusual circumstance. "To support Kennedy's Vietnam policy, [Maxwell Davenport Taylor, Chairman of the Joint Chiefs of Staff, and Defense Secretary Robert McNamara] had a long background of suppressing bad news."[534] The suppression of the 'bad news' constantly occurring in Vietnam "took the lives of fifty-eight thousand Americans and well over one million Vietnamese. It left Vietnam in ruins and consumed billions of American dollars, nearly wrecking the American economy."[535]

Hiding the truth from the American public about Vietnam was not unique to the Kennedy Administration. His successor, Lyndon Johnson, also utilized the services to Mr. McNamara "to conceal from the American public and Congress the costs of deepening American involvement in Vietnam...."[536] Although the names changed during the Nixon Administration, the result did not.

When Americans cannot trust their elected, representative leaders to tell them the truth about matters no less serious than life and death, those leaders cannot realistically expect unwavering loyalty from the populace.

President George W. Bush's misinformation campaign designed to obtain approval for an invasion of Iraq is detailed in Chapter 11, Iraq War. It is little wonder that many American's are referring to Iraq as Bush's Vietnam, and are using the same words — such as quagmire — to describe the Iraq war, that were used a generation ago to describe the Vietnam war.

The October, 2003 issue of "Soldiers Magazine" commented that 3,800 soldiers deserted in 2002.[537] These were the ones who were AWOL for more than thirty days. This number does not include those who were AWOL for less than thirty days; many of them will, in all likelihood, become deserters.

The article states that most soldiers who go AWOL are between the ages of 18 and 25. The writer of the article concedes that "Going AWOL isn't necessarily an act of cowardice, but an action taken to correct what appears to be a mistake, that being that joining the Army wasn't the right thing for the individual to do...."[538]

Yet the advice given is hardly helpful, in view of the facts as outlined in previous chapters. "Soldiers should also speak to chaplains, post counselors and

---

534. McMaster, p. 57.
535. McMaster, p. xiii.
536. McMaster, p. 54.
537. Boyne, Heather. Don't Bolt! — Why Military Personnel Desert Their Posts. *Soldiers Magazine*, October, 2003.
538. Ibid.

psychologists from post mental-health clinics and family support groups before making the choice to run away from a problem."[539]

In Chapter 12: Iraq War, an interview with a young soldier who wished to remain anonymous is quoted. He spoke with his chaplain before his desertion. His words describe his experience:

> I've been yelled at by chaplains many times, including basic training. Chaplains are not what they pretend to be, men of God in the army. They're army all the way through. They are soldiers. They would bleed green before they would ever consider God, at least in — at least in my experience.[540]

Kevin Benderman also met with his chaplain, but the chaplain only wanted to debate him, and withheld Conscientious Objector application forms from him. It seems little wonder that the military would encourage a potential deserter to speak to his chaplain if the chaplains in Mr. Benderman's and the anonymous soldier's experiences are typical.[541]

It appears that this is not an anomaly. During the Spanish-American War, soldiers en route by ship to Cuba purchased and/or traded for additional food and water. While still on board the order from headquarters was received banning the practice. This ban did not stop the practice, but merely made it surreptitious. Said one soldier: "I don't know of an officer but who turned his back if in the dining salon, or if outside hurried by the thwartship companionway so as to save embarrassment and see nothing illegal. Except the chaplain!"[542]

This chaplain witnessed two enlisted men purchasing a leftover plate from the meal of an officer; it had hardly been touched. One was also buying water from a steward. The chaplain ordered their arrest. The men were charged and convicted, but given "a nominal sentence, for sympathy was with them."[543]

The soldier also reports that the same chaplain ordered the arrest of two soldiers lying on the deck in a space reserved for officers, although no officers were present. This was not all. "Unfortunately, the chaplain added other

---

539. Ibid.

540. Three US Soldiers Refusing to Fight Speak Out Against the War in Iraq. 2005. http://www.democracynow.org/article.pl?sid=05/03/15/1454208&mode=thread&tid=25. Accessed November 1, 2005.

541. It should be noted that when Mr. Benderman was eventually allowed to see a second chaplain, that clergyman was extremely supportive of him. See Chapter 12: Iraq War for details.

542. Post, Charles Johnson. 1999. *The Little War of Private Post*. Boston. p. 104.

543. Post, p. 104.

blunders in his career and in Cuba and in his devotion to the 'pride, pomp and circumstance of glorious war.'"[544]

Capt. George Imorde, commander of the 82nd Airborne Division Replacement Detachment, who advised in the article in "Soldiers Magazine" that potential deserters seek out their chaplain, also said this: "There will be someone who understands your problem. Going AWOL has never solved any problems; it has just added to them."[545]

Certainly going AWOL and then deserting brings problems to the soldier who makes this decision. But Capt. Imorde appears to have made three significant misstatements in those two brief sentences. Most soldiers who have problems and concerns sufficiently severe to leave the military do not find that illusive, understanding commander or chaplain. Rather, they meet with abuse and degradation.

Mr. Daniel Gillis of Baltimore was convicted of disobeying an order and missing a movement during the Gulf War. His words betray Capt. Imorde's assurance of finding an understanding ear in the military.

> My Battalion Commander told me that my C.O. status was denied, and he ordered several white officers to jump on me... They held me down and beat me while others put cuffs on me and they tried to forcibly make me board a bus bound for the airport to Saudi Arabia.[546]

Mr. Marques Leacock, age 22, had a similar experience. Convicted of desertion and missing a movement during the Gulf War, his words are enlightening. "[We were] the only ones who had eight platoon sergeants to take care of fourteen of us.... We were called 'communist pigs', 'traitors' and [derogatory] references to our race and cultures."

Mr. Sam (Maung M.) Lwin, 21, was convicted of missing movement during the Gulf War. His commanding officer did not offer the understanding that Cpt. Imorde promised. "My commanding officer, Captain Gesper, said, 'I hope the sergeants... beat the shit out of you... One day when you're walking down a street, I hope a mugger stabs you... I hope the general beats the shit out of you.'"[547]

---

544. Post, p. 105.

545. Boyne, Heather. Don't Bolt! — Why Military Personnel Desert Their Posts. *Soldiers Magazine*, October, 2003.

546. The Anti-Warrior. 1991. http://jeff.paterson.net/aw/aw2_nwo.htm. Accessed November 1, 2005.

547. Joyner, James. 2005. Marine Recruit Jason Robert Tharp Drowns. http://www.outsidethebeltway.com/archives/9311. Accessed November 1, 2005.

Erik Larson, who also deserted during the Gulf War, applied for Conscientious Objector status. His application was rejected by five levels of command. Said Mr. Larson: "Each recommendation reflected the same opinion that I was too political." "The government agencies that are investigating my activities seem to think a person who acts politically must not be a conscientious objector."[548]

The fact that Mr. Larson spoke publicly against the war seems to have somehow tarnished his integrity as a Conscientious Objector in the eyes of the military.

This denying of CO status was not new during the Gulf War. Another man, who was remanded to the federal prison in Ashland, Kentucky, during World War II, reported that

> ...more and more of the Ashland population consisted of Selective Service violators. A few, like me, had refused to register. Most were there because their draft boards had not recognized their sincerity as pacifists. Since these men had followed the law and should have been classified as conscientious objectors, it was the boards that had violated the regulations — but it was the objector who landed in prison. The regular parole available to federal prisoners was almost always denied to resisters....[549]

Early in 2005, marine recruit Jason Tharp wrote home the following: "I told him [the drill instructor] I couldn't cut it.... I still don't think I belong here, and I think I should go home and get a grant."[550] Mr. Tharp had enlisted after his high school graduation in order to earn money for college. He did not appear, however, to get the understanding attitude from his drill instructor that Capt. Imorde promised.

> On February 7, News 10 was shooting a story at Parris Island about potential base closures. WIS [TV- South Carolina] happened to shoot video of a young recruit having a tense interaction with his drill instructor. That recruit was Jason Robert Tharp. Jason died at that pool 24 hours almost to the minute after the tape was shot.[551]

> "Tense interaction with his drill instructor" does not, however, adequately describe the situation. "[V]ideo footage taken February 7 by a local television sta-

---

548. The Anti-Warrior. 1991. http://jeff.paterson.net/aw/aw2_nwo.htm. Accessed November 1, 2005.

549. Gara, Larry and Lenna Mae. 1999,p. 86.

550. Hurley, Clare. 2005. Recruit's Death Highlights Brutality of Marine Training. http://www.guerrillanews.com/H01247. Accessed November 1, 2005.

551. Joyner, James. 2005. Marine Recruit Jason Robert Tharp Drowns. http://www.outsidethebeltway.com/archives/9311. Accessed November 1, 2005.

tion turned up documenting physical abuse of the young recruit by his drill instructor."[552]

Physical abuse by the military is not new; it has been documented herein repeatedly. In 1903, a writer who studied desertion determined the following:

> No class of human being receives so little public attention and solicitude as those comprising the enlisted men in the United States Army; consequently it is not generally known that 'under the free flag of the United States' hundreds of the nation's youths are languishing to-day within the walls of American military prisons, victims of extreme cruelty and injustice, such as would have shed disgrace upon the brute deeds of primitive man.
>
> The widely prevalent notion that all Christendom had long since ceased, officially, to countenance torture is belied by the excruciating forms of punishment systematically inflicted on our private solider by commissioned officers and apparently sanctioned by the highest civil functionaries of our Government.[553]

It appears that little had changed by the end of the century or the start of the new millennium. One might think that soldiers would receive understanding when approaching commanding officers about problems and doubts they had if not for the fact that so many soldiers experienced the opposite.

Cpt. Imorde further states that 'going AWOL has never solved any problems.' For the soldiers described in this book going AWOL has indeed solved a wide variety of problems. For some it enabled them to return to the farm to support their families after money promised by the US government was not paid. Men who left the battlefield during the American Revolution returned to the wheat and cornfields to tend crops. After enlisting to earn 'bounties,' money they expected to send to their families, they needed to return home when that money was not paid.

For others it enabled them to return home to obtain much needed medical attention, without which they may have died. For some it enabled them to live with themselves, knowing that, even if they once participated in horrifying carnage they would never do it again. Consider Mr. Mejia's experiences, watching death close at hand for months at a time. Or Mr. Benderman's experiences, seeing suffering children and unable to assist them. Both men made the decision not to return to battle. For others, desertion kept them from ever witnessing those indescribably awful experiences.

---

552. Hurley, Clare. 2005. Recruit's Death Highlights Brutality of Marine Training. http://www.guerrillanews.com/H01247. Accessed November 1, 2005.
553. Bergey, p. 3.

During the War of 1812 men deserted due to lack of food, other supplies, ammunition and pay. Going AWOL and deserting resolved life-threatening problems for them, problems that had little or nothing to do with combat.

Some men in the Mexican–American war deserted and joined the Mexicans after maltreatment stemming from religious persecution caused them to grow sympathetic to the Mexican cause. They sacrificed their lives but were able to die knowing they were true to their consciences.

And so it is throughout America's history. Men and women, for a variety of reasons, see going AWOL and deserting as a means to resolve a significant problem in their lives.

The third misstatement that Cpt. Imorde made was that desertion only adds to the soldier's problems. Yet desertion eliminates more severe problems while bringing a new set of problems that the soldiers consider less serious. Ms. Elenora Johnson's words reflect the opinions of many soldiers who deserted.

> "Now that the war is over, I have been asked if I regret not going to the Persian Gulf. My answer is, 'No!' I am still committed to my religious beliefs. I am glad the fighting and the killing have come to an end (for now). I thank God for giving me the strength to go through my ordeal."[554]

Ms. Johnson was given a Bad Conduct Discharge, in addition to being demoted from E-4 to E-1 status. Her sentence also included three months of hard labor and forfeiture of two-thirds of her pay for five months. Yet despite these problems, she has no regrets. She was apparently willing to exchange the problems caused by being in the military with those that would be caused by her departure.

The article in Soldiers Magazine quotes SSG Sean M. Benge. Said he: "What soldiers don't realize is that they are better off serving out their terms, receiving college benefits and starting off fresh in the civilian world."[555] It seems that for the soldiers who chose to desert, Mr. Benge's words do not ring true. Mr. Mejia, who refused redeployment after one tour of duty in Iraq, had already learned that the promised college benefits paid for only one year of his university education. He and others also learned that many soldiers were unable to "start off fresh in the civilian world," because they did not survive their military terms.

---

554. The Anti-Warrior. 1991. http://jeff.paterson.net/aw/awl_e_johnson.htm. Accessed November 1, 2005.
555. Boyne, Heather. 2003. Soldiers Magazine Don't Bolt! — Why Military Personnel Desert Their Posts.

Anyone enlisting in the military must recognize this risk, although SSG. Benge does not appear to consider this possibility.

Many soldiers who desert mentioned their opposition to the war they were mandated to fight. This concept garnered much attention during the Vietnam War and every war since, although it was an issue in many of the country's earlier wars. The reasons the US has entered these wars are many and varied and, in the case of the Iraq war, ever-changing. From the need for 'regime change,' to the threat of chemical, biological and nuclear weapons of mass destruction — weapons that Iraq did not have — to the current reason as explained by Mr. Bush: "'We owe them (soldiers who have died in the war) something,'" Mr. Bush said. 'We will finish the task that they gave their lives for.'"[556]

The president's latest rational for the war did not sit well with many of those who have lost loved ones in Iraq. The mother of a National Guardsman who died in Iraq said this:

> [It is] an argument that 'makes no sense. No one wants young men and women to die just because others have already made the ultimate sacrifice. The families of the dead do not want that, any more than they want to see more soldiers die because politicians cannot bear to admit that they sent American forces to war by mistake.'[557]

A common euphemism that is often used when referring to soldiers who died in war is 'fallen soldiers.' Somehow it seems to either glamorize or minimize the fact that the man or woman is dead. There seems to be a hesitancy to say the word 'dead,' as if avoiding it somehow elevates the tragic loss to some higher plain. Indeed, in America in 2005, pictures of flagged-draped coffins returning from Iraq are not allowed to be shown on national television, making the much-praised American 'freedom of the press' nothing more than a hypocritical farce. The fact remains, however, that the soldier thus referred to as 'fallen' has lost all of life's opportunities, and left a gaping hole in the lives and hearts of loved ones.

One reason for the Iraq war that has not changed is possibly the most troubling one. With that as a basis, desertion cannot be questioned.

> During a trip to the Middle East to attempt to implement the Road Map to Peace, Bush met with the new Palestinian Prime Minister Mahmoud Abbas, also known as Abu Mazen, and Israeli Prime Minister Ariel Sharon. Later, when Abbas gathered with other Palestinian factions to detail the Road Map, and his meeting with the American and Israeli leaders, Abbas told the group that President Bush

---

556. President Bush's Loss of Faith, *The New York Times*, August 24, 2005.
557. Ibid.

had claimed to have been spoken to by God. According to the minutes of the meeting, Bush said: "God told me to strike at Al Qaeda, and I struck at them, and then he instructed me to strike at Saddam, which I did, and now I am determined to solve the problem in the Middle East. If you help me, I will act, and if not, the elections will come and I will have to focus on them."

The text of the president's words came from the Israeli newspaper Ha'aretz, and the Moscow Times, which published excerpts from minutes of the meeting between Abbas and other Palestinian organizations.[558]

There is no question that Mr. Bush projects the notion that he feels he and he alone is on God's side. "I believe that God wants me to be president" Mr. Bush said at a Southern Baptist Convention.[559] He is also said to have made the statement that God speaks through him. Whether or not he actually made such a statement, he does not hesitate to frame his politics in very rigid 'us vs. them' terms. "We are in a conflict between good and evil. And America will call evil by its name."[560]

The arrogance with which the US embarks on its imperial adventures is legendary. Less than two months after Mr. Bush announced the end of major combat operations, he said: "There are some who feel like that the conditions are such that they can attack us there. My answer is bring them on...."[561] The words of General Jay Garner also demonstrate this militaristic view of the innate superiority of the U.S: "We ought to look in a mirror and get proud and stick out our chests and suck in our bellies and say: 'Damn, we're Americans.'...."[562] Since Mr. Bush's callous and shocking invitation, Iraqi freedom fighters have indeed 'brought it on,' resulting in the deaths of nearly 2,000 Americans. Since General Garner has encouraged feelings of conceited and misplaced pride, tens of thousands of Iraqis, many of them children, have been slaughtered by American-led invaders.

When soldiers initially are led to believe that they are fighting to save America from the 'imminent danger' that the Bush Administration claimed existed, and then learn that there never was any such danger and the Commander-in-Chief is sacrificing their lives on a misguided crusade, a quick

558. Moore, James. 2004. *Bush's War for Reelection: Iraq, the White House and the People*, p. 44.

559. Stanley, Alessandra. *Television Review: The President and his God*, New York Times, April 29, 2004.

560. Swomley. John M. Parlaying Tragedy into Empire. *The Humanist*, Vol.62, September-October, 2002.

561. Sharpton Calls Bush L.A. Gang Leader; "Bring Them On" Remark Seen Provocative. The Washington Times, July 7, 2003.

562. What Occupation Looks Like. *The Progressive*, Vol. 67, June, 2003.

departure by whatever door they can open must look appealing — and legitimate.

Mr. Bush is not the first US president to be so 'divinely' instructed. President William McKinley also claimed that his invasion of the Philippines was directed by God. "McKinley claimed that he found the Philippines on a world map, went down on his knees, talked to God, and that by divine inspiration he felt compelled to civilize and Christianize his 'little brown brothers' by offering them benevolent assimilation.'"[563] This benevolent assimilation was one of the most unspeakably cruel and savage activities every embarked on by the US (See Chapter 5, Philippine-American War). The horrors witnessed by many soldiers and apathy toward the cause of that war were major factors in desertions.

Hypocritical words seem to be believed when they strike at what is closest to the hearts of those hearing them. Coupled with this is the sad ability to twist words and actions from their obvious, pure meaning to make the hearer understand something quite different.

In the 2002 mid-term elections, Georgia Senator Max Cleland's opponent suggested that Sen. Cleland lacked the commitment to defend the country.[564] Mr. Cleland, a triple-amputee as a result of his military service in Vietnam, had offended the Bush administration once too often.

> [I]n the race's closing weeks, Bush and (Representative Saxby) Chambliss hammered at the fact that Cleland was voting with Senate Democrats against Bush's proposed Homeland Security Department because of its infamous provision limiting union rights. The message was that Cleland was kowtowing to big labor at the cost of protecting America. Most famously, Chambliss ran a vicious ad on Cleland's homeland security votes featuring images of Osama Bin Laden and Saddam Hussein.[565]

The smear campaign was successful. By inferring that a decorated war hero — one who sustained permanent, devastating injuries in the war — was unpatriotic, Bush was able to add to Republican strength in the Senate. It should be remembered the Bush's own military record during the Vietnam era is questionable at best, and Vice President Dick Cheney has said he didn't serve because

---

563. Sison, Ramon. "War for Independence: The View From a Small Town" in Hector Santos, ed., *Philippine Centennial Series*; at http://www.bibingka.com/phg/cabugao/. US, 14 November 1996.

564. Nichols, John. Will the Senate Tip? *The Nation*, Vol. 279, July 12, 2004.

565. Crowley, Michael. 2004. Former Senator Max Cleland. How the Disabled Senator became the Democrats' Mascot. http://slate.msn.com/id/2098171/. Accessed November 1, 2005.

he had 'other priorities.' (One must wonder if the 58,000 Americans who died in Vietnam might also have had 'other priorities' besides dying in a political war.). With this background, Bush was able to paint Cleland as unpatriotic, and defeat him.

Similarly, in the 2004 election, Massachusetts Senator John Kerry, another decorated Vietnam War veteran, was smeared as his performance and Congressional awards were called into question. Even the support and testimony of those who served with him in those dark days in Southeast Asia could not overcome the tarnishing of his reputation by organizations financed by the opposing campaign.

If soldiers feel that following the glitz and public relations of military recruiting ads will bring them some level of status, certainly the treatment of Senators Cleland and Kerry would dissipate any such thoughts. Those who have already bought in, and now want to exercise the non-existent option of leaving legally, are left with no choice but desertion.

American soldiers who go to war do so after being told that the war is necessary to protect the cherished freedoms held so dear, at least in principle, by many citizens. Yet when hearing about citizens detained without access to lawyers or family, or the shocking abuses of political prisoners in occupied countries, the security in American institutions is shaken.

These actions had their roots in the earliest days of the nation's history. During the American Revolution, "Anyone arrested on suspicion of disloyal activity had the privilege of posting bail." However, this was not always the case. "Persons were held incommunicado in order to deter them from giving aid to the enemy."[566] That some were allowed to post bail and others were confined only serves to show that military justice was inequitable then as now.

Examples of military injustice are replete within these chapters. They can be categorized roughly into two major areas:

1. Contracts, and

2. Judicial.

---

566. Harry M. 2000. *The War for Independence and the Transformation of American Society.* New York. p. 50.

CONTRACT INJUSTICES

The military is under no obligation to honor its commitments. Young men and women may be promised "stateside" deployment, only to find themselves in far off battlefields. Monies may be promised in return for enlistments — bounties in the nation's early history and college tuition today — but the recruit often learns after enlistment that such bonuses are either not forthcoming or are very limited. A term of enlistment is meaningless; while the concept of "stop loss" may be mentioned in the lengthy and complex enlistment contract, few 18-year-olds are sufficiently savvy to understand it. Certainly it is not explained by recruiters. Many organizations today assure that contracts, if in "legalese," are also available to be understood by layman. The US military makes no such concession, resulting in unhappy soldiers, some of whom complete the term they committed to and then depart.

JUDICIAL INJUSTICES

It is here, possibly, that the military's behavior and ethics are most shocking. While it may seem difficult to separate military contracts interpreted and/or enforced by the military judiciary from that judiciary itself, for the purposes of analysis it will be done so. But the dependency of the first on the second cannot be ignored.

Military courts operate in an environment all their own; they govern themselves. Soldiers charged with military offenses such as going AWOL, missing movement (not arriving for deployment) and desertion are prosecuted by military prosecutors, defended by military lawyers and judged by military judges and juries. Being judged by one's peers simply means by other members of the military. That they may all be career officers sitting in judgment of a private is considered completely fair.

In civilian cases in the United States, in order to pass the death penalty a jury with twelve members must agree unanimously.

> A fundamental principle of death penalty law in the United States is that no person may be convicted of a capital crime except by the unanimous verdict of a 12-member jury. That is the law in all of the 38 states that have the death penalty, as well as in federal cases. There is, however, one exception. A jury of five is all that is required to sentence a member of the armed services to death in a court-martial.[567]

One may well wonder why a member of the military, who has chosen to spend a certain part of his or her life working in the defense of the American way of life, is deprived of the very rights he/she is called to defend. In the British Literary Magazine, Peter A. French asserts the following:

> American constitutionalism is premised on the belief that its fundamental principles should extend to all citizens. The independence of the military legal system, however, under conditions of both war and peace, typically places military personnel beyond the reach of the most important constitutional provisions, to their detriment.[568]

French further suggests that military crimes, including desertion, be handled by military courts, while all other crimes for which a soldier may be accused — murder, manslaughter, rape, larceny, robbery, forgery, arson, extortion, assault, burglary, etc. — would be tried in federal or other civilian courts.

A civilian trial is judged by a man or woman with vast experience in a wide variety of cases; before being elevated to the bench judges gain this experience in courtrooms as prosecutors, defense lawyers, or both. A civilian judge has generally seen cases ranging from petty larceny, juvenile delinquency and family issues to corporate crimes, grant theft and murder. The environments in which those alleged crimes were committed are extremely varied: from back-alley ghettos to luxurious corporate boardrooms. Some alleged perpetrators are uneducated and already have criminal records. On the other end of the spectrum are those with advanced degrees, responsible jobs in powerful corporations and who have never had the smallest hint of illicit activity in their background. This wide experience enables a judge to look broadly at context, situation, background and other factors of the alleged crime and the alleged perpetrator.

A military judge's experience is generally limited to military situations. The trials over which he/she presides concern crimes allegedly committed in a military environment, an environment which is the main focus of the judge's perspective. The judge him/herself has made a career of the military and is extremely familiar with its workings, but perhaps not with the fact that the accused is a human being first and a soldier only second (or possibly third). The charge is

---

567. Push is on for Larger Jury in Military Capital Cases. 2001. http://www.deathpenalty-info.org/article.php?scid=17&did=337. Accessed November 1, 2005.

568. French, Peter A. Constitutionalism and Military Justice: Making Justice from Military Justice. *British Literary Magazine*, Vo. 3. 1983.

seen as a violation of military law by a possession of the military, a possession with no rights as a civilian.

A general Court Martial, the level that is able to pass a death sentence, is comprised of a military judge and five jurors (note that in the military they are not called jurors, but "members"). The accused can request to be judged by only the judge, or can request additional members. However, the accused cannot request to be tried by a civilian court.

In a civilian jury trial, all parties need to agree on either a guilty or not-guilty verdict. If that does not occur it is a "hung jury" and a mistrial is declared. The prosecution has the option of retrying the case.

> In a military trial, only two-thirds of the members (jurors) must agree. After this comes a separate sentencing stage with the same members. For a sentence of death, all members must agree. For a life sentence, three quarters must agree and for any other sentence there must be agreement of two-thirds of the members.[569]

For a civilian convicted of a crime there are a variety of appeals that can be made, all the way to the Supreme Court. This provides the defendant with the opportunity of having his/her case heard by other judges with other experiences and viewpoints. This process is built in to the American justice system to help insure that anyone accused of a crime has every opportunity to prove his/her innocence.

The same is not true within the military justice system. The appeals that are available are only available through other military courts, the judges and members of which will all have the same narrow scope of experience related only to the military environment. It is possible that a military case could reach the US Supreme Court, but that is the only civilian court that could hear a military case.

The civilian court process does not ensure that justice will always prevail any more than the military system ensures that it never will. However, the built-in protections that are part of the civilian justice system do not exist within the military. Those rights enjoyed by civilians accused of even the most heinous of crimes are not granted to soldiers.

"From the beginning of our country, the Bill of Rights has had little or no relevance to the code of justice governing the military."[570]

One can only wonder why such a situation exists in a nation that prides itself on rights and freedom. Those who surrender two or more years of their

---

569. Powers, Rod. 2004. http://forums.about.com/n/pfx/forum.aspx?nav=messages&-tsn=15&tid=62525&webtag=ab-usmilitary. Accessed November 1, 2005.
570. Sherrill, Robert, p. 1.

lives, putting on hold normal educational and career pursuits in order to strengthen and maintain the freedoms that America claims to hold sacred, are denied those very freedoms.

Soldiers who speak out publicly against a war may be advised that they are "too political" to be conscientious objectors. Or they may be warned that continued public speaking will result in "unpleasant" consequences. A civilian employed by any company in American cannot be penalized for taking an outspoken political stand.

Any civilian employee can, at any time and for any reason, terminate his/her employment. The employer may offer incentives for the employee to remain: increased salary, more prestigious position, better benefits, etc. There may be penalties for departure within a certain timeframe: repayment to the company of relocation or training expenses; forfeiture of promised bonuses, etc. Yet the decision is entirely that of the employee. He or she can leave at will.

If that same civilian then puts on the uniform of any branch of the US military, and subsequently decides he or she no longer wants to be a member of the military, no such option exists. He/she can proceed through the onerous and often unsuccessful process of becoming a Conscientious Objector, but it is very possible that that is not the reason the soldier wants to leave. Perhaps with the start of a family, the soldier wants to return to the flexibility of civilian life. Perhaps a lucrative job offer has been made available to him or her, something in which a successful career can be established. The reasons for wanting to make a change from military to civilian life are as many and varied as there are for wanting to make any job change. But only in the military is such an action forbidden.

One of the attractions that enlistment in the military has for many young people is the appealing benefits package. Service for a period of eight years entitles the soldier to some benefits during that period of time, but most benefits, including medical, cease once the soldier is discharged. The exception is for career military personnel who spend twenty or more years in the military, or Veterans Administration medical care, which is generally provided if the physical illness or injury was caused or aggravated by the soldier's military service.

However, the military is not always generous in its dealing with soldiers, even if they have served valiantly. On October 14, 2004, ABC News reported this: "Following inquiries by ABC News, the Pentagon has dropped plans to force a severely wounded US soldier to repay his enlistment bonus after injuries had forced him out of the service."[571]

The soldier in questions was Army Spc. Tyson Johnson III of Mobile, Al. While on duty in Iraq, Mr. Johnson lost a kidney in a mortar attack. During his recovery at the Walter Reed Army Medical Center, he received notice from the Pentagon's collection agency demanding that he repay more than $2,700 because he would not fulfill his full 36-month tour of duty. This "bill" was shown on his credit report as an unpaid loan from the government. Because of it, he was prevented from renting an apartment or getting a credit card. "'When you're in the military, they take good care of you,' said the 23-year-old Johnson. 'But now that I'm a vet, and, you know, I'm out of the military — not so good. Not so good.'"[572]

At the time this was reported, Mr. Johnson was recuperating from his injuries while living in his car.

Mr. Johnson's case is shocking, but not unique. While deployed in Iraq, Staff Sgt. Ryan Kelly was riding in an unarmored Humvee when the vehicle was blown up. He lost his right leg below the knee.

> Kelly attests to receiving excellent medical care at Ward 57, the amputee section of Walter Reed, but said he quickly realized that the military had no real plan for the injured soldiers. Many had to borrow money or depend on charities just to have relatives visit at Walter Reed, Kelly said.
>
> A third soldier who lost both arms when a helicopter he was repairing exploded in Iraq considers himself fortunate because he will probably get full disability. Although the military provides no lump sum for such injuries it does provide monthly disability payments. However, the army had not, as of October 14, 2004, advised him of what those payments would be. In fact they told him that the paperwork concerning his case had been lost.[573]

Not unexpectedly, it is not only injured war veterans who suffer economic deprivations. While the army purports to provide a living for its soldiers, "[t]he most recent Department of Defense report, from 1999, found that 40% of lower rank soldiers face 'substantial financial difficulties.'"[574]

Loretta Schwartz-Nobel, author of the book *Growing Up Empty*, includes information about military families in her book.

---

571. Ross, Brian, David Scott and Maddy Sauer. 2004. Injured Soldiers Returning from Iraq Struggle for Medical Benefits, Financial Survival. Accessed November 1, 2005. http://abcnews.go.com/Primetime/IraqCoverage/story?id=163109&page=2

572. Ross, Brian, David Scott and Maddy Sauer. 2004. Injured Soldiers Returning from Iraq Struggle for Medical Benefits, Financial Survival. Accessed November 1, 2005. http://abcnews.go.com/Primetime/IraqCoverage/story?id=163109&page=2

573. Ibid.

> To my astonishment, I found that hunger exists among enlisted personnel in every branch of the United States military. I learned that not only do our soldiers stand on our front lines, they and their wives and their children also stand on our food stamp lines and our free bread lines'[575]

> The situation is not well-known, and there is a reason for that. Hunger in the military has been kept even more of a secret than hunger in the rest of America. The old message that the military takes care of its own is so deeply ingrained in the American belief system that it is extremely hard for people to absorb anything else. It's even hard for me to believe and I see it every day.[576]

Growing Up Empty was published in November of 2002, and things in the military have not improved much since. In October of 2004, CBS News reported the following:

> It has been reported that families of American soldiers working abroad, mostly in Iraq, have been left in poverty. According to American news channel CBS News, the majority of families are living below the poverty line, living off welfare benefits and charity.[577]

Many families report the need for both spouses, even the one in the military, to work multiple jobs. One can only question the logic of a system that mandates tremendous sacrifice — including, for many, the loss of life — yet leaves them and their families in poverty.

The much-heralded educational benefit is only available if the soldier participates in the program by having $100.00 per month deducted from their first year's pay. Any promised benefits are withdrawn if the soldier is other than honorably discharged.

Throughout the military history of the US, the foot soldier has been the most neglected "tool" in the American military machine. This had not changed by 2003, when the US invaded the sovereign nation of Iraq.

On October 16, 2004, the San Francisco Chronicle reported on an Army Reserve unit from the Jackson, Mississippi area that refused direct orders in Iraq. The soldiers considered it a suicide mission.

---

574. Mann, Brian. 2003. Thousands of Military Families Live in Poverty. http://www.globalpolicy.org/socecon/inequal/2003/0115military.htm. Accessed November 1, 2005.

575. Schwartz-Nobel, Lorett. 2002. *Growing Up Empty: The Hunger Epidemic in America*, p. 29

576. Schwartz-Nobel, p. 109.

577. CBS News. Families of Soldiers Working Abroad Suffer Badly. 2004. http://www.zaman.com/?bl=hotnews&alt=&trh=20041020&hn=13176. Accessed November 1, 2005.

> The group refused, citing the poor condition of their vehicles and the lack of an armed escort.... American convoys, which are usually accompanied by armored cars and sometimes also by aircraft, are often attacked by insurgents. "Yesterday, we refused to go on a convoy to Taji," Spc. Amber McClenny, 21, said in a message she left on the answering machine of her mother, Teresa Hill.... "We had broken-down trucks, non-armored vehicles. We were carrying contaminated fuel."[578]

The report further stated that the 19 soldiers were held at gunpoint for almost two days for disobeying orders. A statement by an unidentified officer reveals the twisted logic that is so much a part of military justice. After saying that the soldiers had voiced "valid concerns," he said: "Unfortunately it appears that a small number of the soldiers involved chose to express their concerns in an inappropriate manner."[579]

One can only wonder what manner would have been more acceptable to the military, beyond perhaps expressing an opinion and then risking their lives on a suicide mission. Refusal to obey the order, a serious offense in wartime, was the only option open to them to preserve their lives.

Rep. Bennie Thompson, D-Mississippi, took notice of the situation after being contacted by some constituents.

> I would not want any member of the military to be put in a dangerous situation ill-equipped. I have had similar complaints from military families about vehicles that weren't armor-plated, or bullet-proof vests that are outdated. It concerns me because we made over $150 billion in funds available to equip our forces in Iraq.
>
> President Bush takes the position that the troops are well-armed, but if this situation is true, it calls into question how honest he has been with the country....[580]

Rep. Thompson identifies two significant questions: 1) where has that vast sum of money gone, if not to protecting the soldiers in the field, and 2) how candid has the president been with the country?

The problem of inadequate supplies continued throughout the year. On December 9, 2004, less than two months after this incident, a soldier questioned Defense Secretary Donald Rumsfeld about military vehicles that were inadequately constructed to protect the soldiers riding in them. "Why do we soldiers have to dig through local landfills for pieces of scrap metal and compromised ballistic glass to up-armor our vehicles?" asked Army Spc. Thomas Wilson. Mr. Rumsfeld's response that "you have to go to war with the army you have, not the

---

578. Banerjee, Neela and Ariel Hart. 2004. Soldiers refuse convoy orders. Reservists Called Unprotected Duty 'Suicide Mission.' *New York Times*, October 16, 2004.
579. Ibid.
580. Hudson, Jeremy. 2004. Platoon Defies Orders in Iraq. http://www.truthout.org/docs_04/101604X.shtml. Accessed October 8, 2005.

army you want" is disingenuous. The Iraqi war was not and is not a war of necessity; the current US administration decided to invade Iraq using as justification dubious reports from questionable sources, after disdaining the work of the United Nations in inspecting possible weapons sites in Iraq. Had the US been threatened in some way there may have been some credibility in Mr. Rumsfeld's statement. However, as one of the architects of the war, nearly frantic to flex America's military muscle in a lustful quest for Iraq's precious natural resources, he must certainly know that his invasion could have been delayed while the soldiers were equipped with the facilities needed to protect their lives. Instead, their poorly-protected Humvees explode as they ride over mines, or are blasted with gunnery, killing the young men and women who are trying their best to serve their country's misguided and dishonest goals. Mr. Rumsfeld continued: "You can have all the armor in the world on a tank, and it can still be blown up."[581]

The soldiers in Iraq are not asking for all the armor in the world; they are simply asking for the basic equipment, available from a variety of manufacturers, that can be installed on the vehicles they are assigned to drive that will provide them with optimum protection. As in many of America's earlier wars, once again the military does not provide the troops with the basic equipment they need.

The same meeting in December brought questions about the infamous "stop-loss" policy, which has long caused problems for the military. Men and women who agree to a period of service are denied the right to leave the military when that term ends; they must remain until the military determines that they can leave. Following the War of 1812 (see Chapter 2), soldiers were executed because they misunderstood their commitment, believing that they had enlisted for three months when the military then ordered them to remain longer.

In addition, many soldiers serving in Iraq and Afghanistan, and their families, had to purchase body armor and other gear out of their own funds. As a result, Sen. Christopher Dodd of Connecticut introduced legislation that was signed into law by President Bush that required "the Pentagon to set rules by February 25, 2005 for reimbursing US troops, their families and charities up to $1,100 for the purchase of protective, health and safety gear to use in [Afghanistan and Iraq]."[582] As of October 3, 2005, these rules had not been devised. It

---

581. Schmitt, Eric. The Conflict in Iraq: The Military; Troops' Queries leave Rumsfeld on the Defensive. *New York Times*, December 9, 2004.

582. Gonsalves, Sean. 2003. Wilsonian Idealism or PR Gimmick? http://www.commondreams.org/views03/0506-11.htm. Accessed November 1, 2005.

appears that the lives of the men and women charged with fighting Bush's war are given little priority or importance in the planning or execution of that war.

While the country often supports a war, at least initially, long, bloody wars fought for less than honorable causes soon lose their popularity. At the time of the US invasion of Iraq, polls indicated that an overwhelming majority of Americans supported that action. Three years later, with nearly 2,000 Americans and tens of thousands of Iraqis dead, and no end in sight, the poll numbers are the reverse. This phenomenon is nothing new; even leaders who bring the nation to war eventually become disillusioned. As World War I drew to a close, "Woodrow Wilson, the president who had demanded US participation in 'A War to Make the World Safe for Democracy,' reached a point of utter disillusionment when he said 'Is there any man, woman or child in America – let me say, is there any child here – who does not know that this was an industrial and commercial war?'"[583]

What are the solutions? What can occur that will cause soldiers to remain in the military to complete their terms? It must be recognized that any organization — including multinational corporations, corner stores and military organizations — is a place of employment that people select for a variety of reasons. Reducing turnover in these organizations usually ensures for the employee some level of health benefits, opportunity for career advancement, and a general sense of security. It also enables the organization to benefit from the experience of long-term employees. The following list of military reforms was suggested in 1903: over one hundred years later most of them are yet to be implemented, yet they would certainly contribute to a more stable military force.

1. Private soldiers to receive a substantial increase in pay.
2. The employment of trained cooks.
3. Recognition of the right of all soldiers of whatever position to engage in criticism and in free speech at all times and under all circumstances.
4. All the food a soldier wishes to eat, instead of being limited as at present, to an inadequate "ration."
5. Absolute amnesty to all deserters from the army and navy.
6. The erection of modern sanitary buildings at all places where troops are quartered.
7. Service in the army to be limited to two years.
8. Abolition of military salutes and all other imbecile and servile practices.

---

583. Crocker, George N. *Roosevelt's Road to Russia*, p. 135.

9. Thorough practice in mobility, rapid field movements, quick concentration, with special attention to supplying the troops promptly and regularly with abundant, wholesome nourishing food.

10. All soldiers and officers, whatsoever, to eat exactly the same food, and to be houses or quartered alike at all times and in all places.

11. Prohibition of all forms of torture and violence.[584]

One cannot realistically see any of these suggestions as radical or revolutionary. Item 3 is free speech, a Constitutionally-guaranteed right to all Americans. Soldiers serving in the US military, ready to protect these rights should not themselves be deprived of them.

The implementation of Items 8 and 10 would remove perhaps the last vestige of a caste system still operable in America. That one group of men and women is relegated to a class that must actually salute another in a nation that prides itself on equality is yet another blatant example of military hypocrisy that should be eliminated. The provision of inferior foods to enlisted personnel while officers are provided with food of both better quality and quantity is a barefaced injustice.

That Item 11 is still an unresolved issue in the US military should shock and horrify every thinking citizen of the nation. Young Jason Thorpe's video-taped abuse by a 'superior' officer just twenty-four hours before his death should have raised a clamor for a full investigation and immediate reforms. Why this did not occur is a stunning indictment of the citizenry as much as the actual crime is of the military.

The US government will continue to struggle with desertion from all branches of the armed forces as long as the American military doggedly persists in practices that the same government condemns when practiced by other nations. Only when the military reflects the democratic principles it purports to uphold will men and women consistently remain in it to serve for their enlistment period.

---

584. Bergey, pp. 154 – 155.

BIBLIOGRAPHY

Alcohol, Alcoholism, and the Air Force. 2005. http://
www.jimmydoolittlemuseumpromotions.com/chapter7.htm. Accessed October 28,
2005.

Alotta, Robert I. 1978. *Stop the Evil*. London, Presidio Press.

Armstrong, Hamilton Fish, and Allen W. Dulles. 1939. *Can America Stay Neutral?* New York,
Harper and Brothers Publishers.

Banerjee, Neela and Ariel Hart. 2004. ""Soldiers refuse convoy orders. Reservists Called
Unprotected Duty 'suicide Mission." *New York Times*, October 16.

Brown, Bartram S. 2004. "Barely Borders: Issues of International Law." *Harvard
International Review*, Vol. 26.

Bautista, Veltisezar. 1998. *The Filipino Americans: From 1763 to the Present*. Farmington Hills:
Bookhaus Publishers.

Bemak, Fred, and Lawrence R. Epp. 2002. "Transcending the Mind-Body Dichotomy:
Schizophrenia Reexamined." *Journal of Humanistic Counseling, Education and Development*,
Vol. 41.

Benn, Carl. 2002. *Essential Histories: The War of 1812*. Oxford: Osprey Publishing.

Bergey, Ellwood. 1903. *Why Soldiers Desert from the United States Army*. Philadelphia: Wm. F.
Fell & Company.

Bloom, Alexander, ed.: *Long Time Gone: Sixties America Then and Now*.2001. New York: Oxford
University Press.

Boyle, Francis A. 2004. *Destroying World Order: US Imperialism in the Middle East before and after
September, 11*. Atlanta: Clarity Press.

Boyne, Heather. 2003. "Don't Bolt! – Why Military Personnel Desert Their Posts." *Soldiers Magazine*. October.

Bray, Robert M., John A. Fairbank and Mary Ellen Marsden. 1999. "Stress and Substance Abuse among Military Women and Men." *American Journal of Drug and Alcohol Abuse*, *Vol. 25*.

Brown, T. Louise. 1991. *War and Aftermath in Vietnam*, New York: Routledge.

Bynum, Russ. 2004. Images Behind Soldier's Iraq Refusal. http://www.commondreams.org/headlines05/0117-08.htm. Accessed October 28, 2005.

Camilo Mejia. GI Resister, Conscientious Objector and Iraq War Veteran. http://www.freecamilo.org/words.htm. Accessed on October 28, 2005.

Carey, Neil and Merrill B. Twining. 1996. *No Bended Knee: The Battle for Guadalcanal. The Memoir of Gen. Merrill B. Twining, USMC (Ret.)*. Novato: Presidio Press.

Cashin, Joan E., Editor. 2002. *The War was You and Me: Civilians in the American Civil War.* Princeton: Princeton University Press.

CBS News. Families of Soldiers Working Abroad Suffer Badly. 2004. http://www.zaman.com/?bl=hotnews&alt=&trh=20041020&hn=13176. Accessed November 1, 2005.

Chambers, John Whiteclay, ed. 1999. *The Oxford Companion to American Military History*. New York: Oxford University Press.

Chiasson Lloyd Jr. 1995. *The Press in Time of Crisis*. Westport: Greenwood Publishing Group.

Christensen, Carol and Thomas Christensen. 1998. *The US – Mexican War*. San Francisco: Bay Books.

Coffman, Edward M. 1986. *The Old Army: A Portrait of the American Army in Peacetime, 1784 – 1898*. New York: Oxford University Press.

Cooper, John Milton. 1990. *Pivotal Decades: The United States, 1900 – 1920*. New York: W.W. Norton & Company.

Copes, Jan M. and Timothy J. Runyan. 1994. *To Die Gallantly: The Battle of the Atlantic*. Boulder: Westview Press.

Cramer, Marc. 1996. "The Fighting Irish of Mexico." *America*, March – April. Vol. 48.

Crowley, Michael. 2004. Former Senator Max Cleland. How the Disabled Senator became the Democrats' Mascot. http://slate.msn.com/id/2098171/. Accessed November 1, 2005.

Douthat, James L. 1982, *The 1814 Court Martial of Tennessee Militiamen*. Signal Mountain: Mountain Press.

Dvorchak, Robert J. 1993. *Battle for Korea: A History of the Korean Conflict*. New York: Da Capo Press.

Dye, Captain Dale. GI Joe: US Soldiers of World War Two. Wars and Conflict: World War II. http://www.bbc.co.uk/history/war/wwtwo/us_soldiers_01.shtml. Accessed October 28, 2005.

Dzwonkowski, Ron. 2001. Ron Dzwonkowski: It's time to pardon Pvt. Eddie Slovik;' http://www.freep.com/voices/columnists/erdz27_20010527.htm. Accessed October 28, 2005.

Edmondson, James Howard. 1971. *Desertion in the American Army during the Revolutionary War.* Lafayette: Louisiana State University.

Eisenhower, John. 2002. *Yanks: The Epic Story of the American Army in World War I.* New York: Free Press.

Elias, Marilyn. 2005. 'Mental disorders are on the rise among Afghanistan, Iraq veterans.' www.usatoday.com/news/ nation/2005-03-30-veterans-disorders_x.htm. Accessed October 10, 2005.

Esch, Betty. 2001. 'The Greatest War Heroes: In Honor of our War Resisters.' http://www.solidarity-us.org/atc/90Esch.html#R8. Accessed October 11, 2005.

Falk, Richard A., Gabriel Kolko, Robert Jay Lifton.1971. *Crimes of War: A Legal, Political Documentary, and Psychological Inquiry into the Responsibility of Leaders, Citizens, and Soldiers for Criminal Acts in Wars.* New York: Random House.

Foner, Jack D. 1970. *The United States Soldier Between Two Wars.* New York: Humanities Press.

Foos, Paul. 2002. *A Short, Offhand, Killing Affair.* Chapel Hill: University of North Carolina Press.

Fragging and Combat Refusals in Vietnam. http://home.mweb.co.za/re/redcap/vietcrim.htm. Accessed on August 1, 2005.

Francisco, Luzyiminda. 1973. "The First Vietnam: The US –Philippine War of 1899;" *Bulletin of Concerned Asian Scholars, Vol. 5., Page 15.*

Freeman, Anitra, Adam Holdorf and Jackie Renn. Brave Souls. http://www.realchangenews.org/pastissuesupgrade/2003_06_26/features/brave_souls.html. Accessed October 28, 2005

French, Peter A. 1983. "Constitutionalism and Military Justice: Making Justice from Military Justice." *British Literary Magazine,* Vo. 3.

Gambone, Michael D. 2002. *Documents of American Diplomacy: From the American Revolution to the Present.* Westport: Greenwood Press.

Gara, Larry and Lenna Mae Gara. 1999. *A Few Small Candles: War Resisters of World War II Tell their Stories.* Kent: The Kent State University Press.

Gatewood, Willard B., Jr. 1975. *Black Americans and the White Man's Burden, 1898-1903.* Urbana: University of Illinois Press.

Gilbert, Martin. 1989. *The Second World War.* New York: Henry Holt and Company.

Gilbert, Martin. 1994. *The First World War.* New York: Henry Holt and Company.

Gonsalves, Sean. 2003. Wilsonian Idealism or PR Gimmick? http://www.commondreams.org/views03/0506-11.htm. Accessed November 1, 2005.

Gulf War Syndrome. 2003. http://lef.org/protocols/prtcl-143.shtml. Accessed on October 18, 2005.

Hagan, John. 2000. "Narrowing the Gap by Wide the Conflict: Power Politics, Symbols of Sovereignty, and the American Vietnam War Resisters' Migration to Canada;" *Law & Society Review,* Vol. 34.

Harrington, Fred Harvey, ed. 1971. *America: A History of the People; Vol. 2.* Chicago: Rand McNally & Company.

Heitman, Francis B. 1903. *Historical Register and Dictionary of the United States Army.* Washington, DC: GPO.

Hickey, Donald R. 1989. *The War of 1812: A Forgotten Conflict.* Chicago: University of Illinois Press.

Hickey, Donald R. 1995. *The War of 1812: A Short History.* Urbana and Chicago: University of Illinois Press.

Hill, Henry Wayland, Ed. 2002. *Municipality of Buffalo, New York, A History. 1720-1923.* New York: Lewis Historical Publishing Company, Inc.

Hillstrom, Kevin and Laurie Collier Hillstrom. 1998. *The Vietnam Experience: A concise Encyclopedia of American Literature, Songs, and Films.* Westport: Greenwood Press.

Hogan, Michael. 1997. *The Irish Soldiers of Mexico.* Guadalajara: Fondo Editorial Universitario.

Homesickness. 2004. University of Missouri – Rolla. http://campus.umr.edu/counsel/selfhelp/vpl/homesickness.html. Accessed October 29, 2005.

http://www.bibingka.com/phg/cabugao/default.htm. Accessed November 1, 2005.

http://www.commondreams.org/headlines05/0117-08.htm. Accessed October 28, 2005.

Hudson, Audrey. 2003. "Sharpton Calls Bush L.A. Gang Leader; 'Bring Them On' Remark Seen Provocative." *The Washington Times,* July 7.

Hudson, Jeremy. 2004. Platoon Defies Orders in Iraq. www.truthout.org/docs_or/101604s.shtml. Accessed October 8, 2005.

Huie, William Bradford. 2004. *The Execution of Private Slovik.* Yardley: Westholme Publishing, LLC.

Humber, Robert C. 1942. *Absences and Desertions during First World War.* Carlisle: US Army Heritage and Education Center, US Army Military History Institute.

Hurley, Clare. 2005. Recruit's Death Highlights Brutality of Marine Training. http://www.guerrillanews.com/H01247. Accessed November 1, 2005.

Adaptability as a Court-Martial Offense? 2005. The New American, Vol. 21, January 10.

Jenkins; 2004. http://www.ipetitions.com/boards/viewtopic.php?topic=2460&forum=6. Accessed on July 7, 2005.

Joyner, James. 2005. Marine Recruit Jason Robert Tharp Drowns. http://www.outsidethebeltway.com/archives/9311. Accessed October 11, 2005.

Keenan, Jerry. 2001. *Encyclopedia of the Spanish-American and Philippine-American Wars*. Santa Barbara: ABC-Clio, Inc.

Keene, Jennifer Diane. 1994. "Intelligence and Moral in the Army of a Democracy: The Genesis of Military Psychology during the First World War." *Military Psychology*, Vol. 6.

Kevin Benderman Defense Committee. 2005. http://www.bendermandefense.org/. Accessed October 28, 2005.

Kevin Benderman: 2005. A Matter of Conscience. http://www.bruderhof.com/articles/benderman-k.htm. Accessed on October 28, 2005.

Kihl, Young Whan. 1984. *Politics and Policies in Divided Korea: Regimes in Contest*. Boulder: Westview Press.

King, Rosemary. 2000. "Border Crossings in the Mexican American War." *Bilingual Review*. Vol. 25.

Korean War Educator. 2005. Desertions. http://www.koreanwar-educator.org/topics/brief/p_desertions.htm. Accessed October 28, 2005.

Kotlowitz, Robert. 1997. *Before Their Time*. New York: Alfred A. Knopf.

Leonard, Ron. 2000. 'Vietnam War Statistics and Facts.' http://25thaviation.org/id275.htm. Accessed October 11, 2005.

Liggett, Hunter. 1925. *Commanding an American Army*. Boston: Houghton Mifflin Company.

Lonn, Ella. 1998. *Desertion During the Civil War*. Lincoln: University of Nebraska Press.

Loughry, Major H. K., et. Al. 1926. Present Desertion Rates. Course at the Army War College, 1926 – 1927. The Army War College, Washington Barracks, D.C. US Army Heritage & Education Ctr., US Army Military History Institute.

Lynd, Staughton. 2005. We Won't Go: Narratives of Resistance to World War II, the Korean War, the Vietnam War, the 1990 – 91 US- Iraq War, and the 2003 – US-Iraq War; http://www.unitedforpeace.org/downloads/wontgo5-24.doc. Accessed July 12, 2005.

Mahon, John K. 1985. *History of the Second Seminole War, 1835 – 1842*. Gainesville: University of Florida Press.

Mann, Robert. 2001. *A Grand Delusion: America's Descent into Vietnam*. New York: Basic Books.

Mann, Brian. 2003. Thousands of Military Families Live in Poverty. http://www.globalpolicy.org/socecon/inequal/2003/0115military.htm. Accessed October 11, 2005.

Marlow, David H. 2001. *Psychological and Psychosocial Consequences of Combat and Deployment: With Special Emphasis on the Gulf War*. Santa Monica: Rand.

Martel, Gordon. 1999. *The Origins of the Second World War Reconsidered: A.J.P. Taylor and the Historians*. New York, Routledge.

Matloff, Maurice, ed. 1996. *American Military History, Vol. 1: 1775 – 1902*. Conshohocken: Combined Books.

McDermott, John D. 1997. "Were They Really Rogues: Desertion in the Nineteenth-Century US Army." *Nebraska History*. Winter.

McMaster, H.R. 1997. *Dereliction of Duty*. New York: Harper Collins Publisher.

McSherry, Patrick. The Spanish-American War – One American's View. http://www.spanamwar.com/Americanview.htm. Accessed October 31, 2005.

Mead, Gary. 2000. *The Doughboys: America and the First World War*. New York: The Overlook Press.

Military Deserters Flee to Canada. 2005. http://www.wesh.com/news/4534806/detail.html. Accessed October 14, 2005.

Military Service #5,' http://www.ibiblio.org/pub/academic/history/marshall/military/mil_hist_inst/m/milsrv5.asc. Accessed October 15, 2005.

Miller, Robert Ryal. 1989. *Shamrock and Sword: The Saint Patrick's Battalion in the US – Mexican War*. Norman: University of Oklahoma Press.

Moore, William. 1975. *The Thin Yellow Line*. New York: St. Martin's Press.

Morris, Richard B., William Greenleaf and Robert H. Ferrell. 1971. *America: A History of the People, Volume 2 – From 1865*. Chicago: Rand McNally and Company.

Mowat, R. B. 1925. *The Diplomatic Relations of Great Britain and the United States*. New York: Longmans, Green and Co.

Nichols, John. 2004. "Will the Senate Tip?" *The Nation*, Vol. 279, July 12.

Objectives of Vietnam Veterans Against the War.' http://www.vvaw.org/veteran/article/?id=317. Accessed August 15, 2005.

Osburn, Hobart G., Charles Brown, Janice Chreitzberg, Wayne Heild, Edward Seidel, Donald Watson. 1954. "A Preliminary Investigation of Delinquency in the Army." *US Army Military History Institute*, George Washington University Human Resources Research Office operating under contract with the Department of the Army.

Paterson, Jeff. 1991. The Anti-Warrior. http://jeff.paterson.net/aw/awl_e_johnson.htm. Accessed October 28, 2005.

Paterson, Jeff . 1991. http://jeff.paterson.net/pdf/jp_resume.pdf. Accessed October 28, 2005.

Paterson, Jeff : First Military Resister to the Gulf War Available for Speaking and Other Anti-War Events; http://jeff.paterson.net/pdf/jp_resume.pdf. Accessed October 11, 2005.

Peter, Laurence J. and Raymond Hull. 1969. *The Peter Principle*. Cutchogue: Buccaneer Books.

Philippine History Group of Los Angeles. War for Independence: The View from a Small Town. http://www.bibingka.com/phg/cabugao/default.htm.

Philippine History Group of Los Angeles.' The Balaniga Massacre: Getting Even. http://en.wikipedia.org/wiki/Balangiga_Massacre.

Pierre, Andrew J. 1985. *Third World Instability: Central America as a European-American Issue*. New York: Council on Foreign Relations Press.

Post, Charles Johnson. 1999. *The Little War of Private Post*. Boston: First Bison Books.

Powel, Anthony L. The Philippine Revolution and the Philippine-American War.' Through my Grandfather's Eyes: Ties that Bind: African American Soldiers in the Filipino War for Liberation. Anthony L. Powell. http://www.boondocksnet.com/centennial/sctexts/powell98a_d.html.

Powers, Rod. 2004. http://forums.about.com/n/pfx/forum.aspx?nav=messages&tsn=15&tid=62525&webtag=ab-usmilitary. Accessed November 1, 2005.

New York Times. President Bush's Loss of Faith. August 24, 2005.

Push is on for Larger Jury in Military Capital Cases. 2001. http://www.deathpenaltyinfo.org/article.php?scid=17&did=337. Accessed November 1, 2005.

Quimby, Robert S. 1997. *The US Army in the War of 1812: An Operational and Command Study*. East Lansing: Michigan State University Press.

Reeves, Tom. 2005. Exposing the Coming Draft. http://www.counterpunch.org/reeves03192005.html Accessed on October 28, 2005.

Resisters to WarMaking: Past and Present. http://www.jonahhouse.org/McAlisterVetsForPeace1204.htm. Accessed October 28, 2005.

Rinfred, Peter. 2001. The 104th Infantry Regiment of the 26th Infantry Division;' http://www.rinfret.com/ww2.html#anchor45432. Accessed August 6, 2005.

Rising-Moore, Carl and Becky Oberg. 2004. *Freedom Underground*. New York: Chamberlain Brothers.

Rosenbaum, Herbert D. and Alexej Ugrinsky. 1994. *The Presidency and Domestic Policies of Jimmy Carter*. Westport, Greenwood Press.

Ross, Brian, David Scott and Maddy Sauer. 2004. Injured Soldiers Returning from Iraq Struggle for Medical Benefits, Financial Survival. http://abcnews.go.com/Primetime/IraqCoverage/story?id=163109&page=2. Accessed November 1, 2005.

Rothbard, Murray N. 1978. *For a New Liberty: The Libertarian Manifesto.* New York: MacMillan Publishing Company.

Royster, Charles 1979. *A Revolutionary People at War: The Continental Army and American Character, 1775 – 1783.* Chapel Hill: The University of North Carolina Press.

Schaeffer-Duffy, Claire. 2004. Catholic Becomes First to Refuse Return to Iraq War. http://www.catholicpeacefellowship.org/nextpage.asp?m=2064. Accessed on October 28, 2005.

Schirmer, Daniel B. and Stephen Rosskamm Shalom. 1987. *The Philippines Reader: A History of Colonialism, Neocolonialism, Dictatorship, and Resistance.* Boston: South End Press.

Schmitt, Eric. 2004. "The Conflict in Iraq: The Military; Troops' Queries leave Rumsfeld on the Defensive." *New York Times,* December 9.

Schwartz-Nobel, Lorett. 2002. *Growing Up Empty: The Hunger Epidemic in America.* New York: Harper Collins.

Scientists Study Depleted Uranium link to Gulf War Syndrome. http://www.lrri.org/cr/dustudy.html. Accessed October 11, 2005.

Scott, John. 2005. Justifications for War. http://www.v7n.com/forums/showthread.php?t=18431&page=1 Accessed October 21, 2005.

Selig, Robert A. The Revolution's Black Soldiers; http://americanrevolution.org. Accessed October 21, 2005

Seper, Jerry. 2004. "Saddam Link to 9/11 Not Likely; 'No Credible Evidence' Found." *The Washington Times,* June 17.

Shapiro, Bruce. 1992. "The High Price of Conscience;" *The Nation,* Vol. 254, January.

Shaw, Lt. R.C. 1919. Analysis of the Causes of 200 Desertion Cases. *Army Chief of Staff, Entry 8, # 1050, Records of the War Department General and Special Staffs (Record Group 165).*

Sherrill, Robert. 1970. *Military Justice is to Justice as Military Music is to Music,* New York: Harper Colophon Books.

Shills, Edward. 1977. "A Profile of the Military Deserter." *Armed Forces and Society,* Vol. 3, No. 3.

Singer, Margaret Thaler, PH. D., Richard Ofshe, Ph.D. 2005. Thought Reform Programs and the Production of Psychiatric Casualties. http://www.refocus.org/mental.html. Accessed October 29, 2005.

Sison, Ramon. 1996. "War for Independence: The View From a Small Town." *Philippine Centennial Series;* at http://www.bibingka.com/phg/cabugao/. US, 14 November 1996.

Skeken, C. Edward. 1999. *Citizen Soldiers in the War of 1812.* Lexington: The University Press of Kentucky.

Smith, Robert Aura, 1958. *Philippine Freedom, 1946 – 1958.* New York, Columbia University Press.

Squitieri, Tom. 2004. "Former Soldiers Slow to Report." *USA Today*, September 27.

Stanley, Alessandra. 2004. *Television Review: The President and his God.* New York Times, April 29.

Stanley Sandler. 1999. *The Korean War: No Victors, No Vanquished.*London, University Press of Kentucky.

Statistics on Decline in Military Status and Discipline during Vietnam Era. http://www.drake.edu/artsci/PolSci/pols124s02/statistics.html. Accessed October 11, 2005.

Strachan, Hew. 1998. *The Oxford Illustrated History of the First World War.* Oxford: Oxford University Press.

Swomley. John M. 2002. "Parlaying Tragedy into Empire." *The Humanist*, Vol.62, September-October.

Syrop, Jeff. 1991. 'The New Order.' http://www.zenhell.com/GetEnlightened/stories/neworder/neworder.htm. Accessed October 11, 2005.

Taylor, Maureen. Rhode Islanders and Pancho Villa. http://www.newenglandancestors.org/education/articles/research/localities/rhode_island/across_border.asp. Accessed October 28, 2005.

The Anti-Warrior. 1991. http://jeff.paterson.net/aw/aw2_nwo.htm. Accessed November 1, 2005

The Columbia Encyclopedia, 2004. *Anti-Vietnam War Movement.* Sixth Edition. 2004. New York: Columbia University Press

The Marines: The Few, The Proud. http://www.usmc.mil/marinelink/mcn2000.nsf/stoploss#WHATISSTOPLOSS. Accessed October 28, 2005.

The Philippine-American War. http://www.historyguy/PhilippineAmericanwar.html. Accessed July 20, 2005.

The William C. Cook Collection: *The War of 1812 in the South.* The Williams Research Center, The Historic New Orleans Collection.

Thousands of US Soldiers Desert 'Illegal' and 'Immoral' War. 2005. http://www.theinsider.org/news/article.asp?id=0782. Accessed on October 28, 2005.

New York Times. 2004. "Threats and Responses: Powell's Address, Presenting 'Deeply Troubling' Evidence on Iraq." February 6.

Three US Soldiers Refusing to Fight Speak Out Against the Iraq War. http://www.democracynow.org/article.pl?sid=05/03/15/1454208&mode=thread&tid=25. Accessed October 28, 2005.

US Military Desertion Rates, http://usmilitary.about.com/od/justicelawlegislation /a/desertionrates.htm, Accessed October 15, 2005

Uncle Sam says POW Deserted. http://www.orwelltoday.com/manchuriankoreapow.shtml. Accessed August 15, 2005.

Vance, Laurence M. 2005. The Execution of Eddie Slovik; http://www.lewrockwell.com/vance/vance34.html. Accessed on October 10, 2005.

Vargas, Mark A. 1991. "The Military Justice System and the Use of Illegal Punishments as Causes of Desertion in the US Army, 1821 – 1835." *The Journal of Military History*,' Vol. 55, No. 1.

Walker, George K. "Information Warfare and Neutrality." *Vanderbilt Journal of Transnational Law*, Vol. 33, 2000.

War of 1812: People and Stories. http://www.galafilm.com/1812/e/people/hanks_memoirs4.html. Accessed October 6, 2005

Ward, Harry M. 2000. *The War for Independence and the Transformation of American Society*. New York: UCL Press.

The Washington Times, 2002. "We Turn to the Urgent Duty of Protecting Other Lives." September13.

Vidal, Gore. 2002. *Dreaming War: Blood for Oil and the Cheney-Bush Junta*. New York: Nation Book.

Weinstein, Jay. 2002. 'Northern Passage: American Vietnam War Resistors in Canada. *Canadian Journal of Sociology*, Vol. 27.

Welch, Richard E. Jr. 1987. *Response to Imperialism: The United States and the Philippine-American War. 1899 – 1902.* Chapel Hill: University of North Carolina.

Weller, Adrienne. 2003. Stephen Funk: Marine Refusenik Wins Backing. http://www.notinourname.net/funk/wins-backing-1sept03.htm. Accessed on October 28

Werner, Jayne. 1985. "A Short History of the War in Vietnam." *Monthly Review*, Vol. 37, June.

Westerfield, Donald L. 1996. *War Powers: The President, the Congress and the Question of War*. Westport, Praeger.

"What Occupation Looks Like." 2003. *The Progressive*, Vol. 67, June,

Zinn, Howard. 2001. *A People's History of the United States*, New York, 2001: Harper Collins Publishers.

Zweiback, Adam J. 1998. The 21 'Turncoat GIs': Nonrepatriations and the Political Culture of the Korean War. *The Historian, Vol. 60*.

INDEX

257

Printed in the United States
63854LVS00004B/9